PENGUIN BOOKS

MY SISTER'S KEEPER

Margaret Moorman is a contributing editor of ART-News Magazine who has also written for The New York Times, New York Newsday, and other publications. A former painter, she is currently working on Light the Lights!, an illustrated book for children. She lives in New York City with her husband and daughter.

MY
SISTER'S
KEEPER

Learning to Cope with a Sibling's
Mental Illness

MARGARET MOORMAN

PENGUIN BOOKS

PENGUIN BOOKS
Published by the Penguin Group
Penguin Books USA Inc., 375 Hudson Street, New York, New York 10014, U.S.A.
Penguin Books Ltd, 27 Wrights Lane, London W8 5TZ, England
Penguin Books Australia Ltd, Ringwood, Victoria, Australia
Penguin Books Canada Ltd, 10 Alcorn Avenue, Toronto, Ontario, Canada M4V 3B2
Penguin Books (N.Z.) Ltd, 182–190 Wairau Road, Auckland 10, New Zealand

Penguin Books Ltd, Registered Offices: Harmondsworth, Middlesex, England

First published in the United States of America by
W. W. Norton & Company, Inc., 1992
Published in Penguin Books 1993

1 3 5 7 9 10 8 6 4 2

For legal reasons, some of the names in this book have been changed.

THE LIBRARY OF CONGRESS HAS CATALOGUED THE HARDCOVER AS FOLLOWS:
Moorman, Margaret.
My sister's keeper: learning to cope with a sibling's mental illness/
by Margaret Moorman.
p.   cm.
ISBN 0-393-02987-5 (hc.)
ISBN 0 14 02.3121 8 (pbk.)
1. Moorman, Sally—Mental health.   2. Schizophrenics—United States—Biography.
3. Schizophrenics—United States—Family relationships.
4. Moorman, Margaret—Family.   5. Sisters—United States.   I. Title.
RC514.M58M66   1992
616.89′82′0092—dc20   {B}   91–26667

Printed in the United States of America
Set in Goudy Old Style and Corvinus Medium
Designed by Chris Welch

"*Am I my brother's keeper? No,
I'm my brother's brother.*"
William Sloane Coffin

To Fiona Graham and Gene Marie Sinclair

THIS BOOK IS ALSO DEDICATED TO:

• My sister, Sally Moorman, for allowing me to write about both of us from my point of view. She never tried to influence my perspective or asked me to soften the details of what is often a painful story.

• The memory of my beloved parents, Robert and Sara Moorman.

• The members of my local chapter of the Sibling and Adult Children's Network (a committee of the National Alliance for the Mentally Ill), for their sympathy, humor, and insight.

• Jill Bialosky, my editor at W. W. Norton & Co., for her faith in the value of this project, and much, much more.

• Rhonda Buckner, director of the Personal Support Network in Falls Church, Virginia, who was my mainstay as well as Sally's during the most difficult year of my life.

• Everyone at the Personal Support Network and the Association for Retarded Citizens, for their good sense and equanimity.

• My mother's friends and neighbors, for their many, many acts of kindness and their enduring care.

• My own friends, especially Deborah Pond, Mary Joan Waid, and Andrea Woodner, for their loving presence after my mother died; Elizabeth Mitchell, Sherry Markovitz, Isabel Hamilton, and Fay Jones, for a much-needed vacation; Fran Black, for legal help; Paul Gardner, Vajra Kilgour, and Nancy Traver, for encouragement to write this book; and April

Kinser, Elizabeth Stille, and Rick Woodward, for reading the manuscript and making helpful suggestions.

• Silvia Marquez Yarema, whose expert care kept my daughter, Emma, busy and content as I worked nearby on the word processor.

• Harvey Quaytman, my husband, who among other excellent things is a happy man and a great cook.

CONTENTS

....

MY
SISTER'S
KEEPER

PART ONE

MY PRIVATE ICEBERG

....

F or a long time after my mother died, I would talk to her at
night as I lay sleepless. I missed her so much, missed discussing politics with her, missed her southern accent on my
answering machine, missed her envelopes of newspaper clippings with exclamation points penciled in next to notable bits
of information. Every morning, on my way to work, I held
back my tears only with the greatest effort. I would look
around me at the others on the subway reading the *Times*,
yawning over a cup of coffee, or just staring into space. They
looked as if the world were the same as it had always been. I
was astonished—didn't they know my mother was dead?

If anyone had told me in my twenties that I would grieve
like this, or if they had predicted I would come to love and
admire my mother as much as I did, I would not have believed
them. As a friend, she was the best—sensitive, loyal, and generous—but as a mother, she was difficult—anxious, quick
tempered, and honest to the point of tactlessness. She could
be devastating if she found fault. But she was also smart and
brave: After my father died of a heart attack at age fifty-four in
1963, she went back to work for the first time in thirty years,
as a librarian. She was fifty-one years old.

Always frugal—she had come of age during the Great Depression—she became utterly self-sacrificing, always buying

on sale, never taking vacations. She was saving her money for the sake of her two daughters, building up a legacy, and nothing anyone said to her could persuade her to relax her tight fists. Her persistence enabled her to leave a substantial trust fund for my sister, Sally, who has been mentally ill most of her life, and indirectly for me, so that I would not be financially burdened by Sally's needs.

I was grateful, but when I spoke to my mother's spirit, it wasn't to thank her. Instead, I would defend myself, for the way I was handling my new jobs as executrix and trustee or for continuing to live in New York, rather than Virginia, where I could take care of Sally as she had. Where Mother had kept in constant, overriding touch with Sally, I found myself resisting asking the important questions when Sally and I spoke by phone every evening. *Are you taking your medicine? Are you going to the mental health center?* I couldn't badger her the way Mother had. Although I was thirty-eight, I was still her little sister.

Even though I knew Mother had never expected or wanted me to take her place, I felt compelled to speak to her out of my own sense of inadequacy. I would silently beam an irritable monologue toward some spot above the ceiling of my room that signified heaven. "I'll call the nurse at the center tomorrow," I might begin. "I'll mail the tax check in the morning." And finally, "This is the best I can do, Mama."

Toward morning, revved up by anxiety, I would go over the day's tasks in my head: Write to the Civil Service Commission to have Mother's annuity checks stopped; write to the neighbors who sent flowers to the memorial service; call the Treasury Department to find out how to roll over a T-bill; call the Virginia Health Department for more death certificates; call Rhonda Buckner, the social worker who looked after Sally, and tell her to go ahead and have Sally's belongings moved to the rented basement where Sally insisted she wanted to live now. I had just moved Sally's furniture out of storage and into her apartment. Now it would all have to be packed and hauled again.

Sadness would overcome me as I thought about Sally, forty-seven then, but childlike in many ways. In the weeks since Mother died, I had spoken to Sally by phone every evening, and I could hear the loneliness in her voice. She had browbeaten Mother all winter into allowing her to move into her own apartment from the same house she now wanted to return to, but she had soon found the long hours of solitude dismal. Now, without Mother to call at night and visit on weekends, she found the apartment intolerable. Her old room had been rented, but the couple who owned the house offered Sally space in their unfinished basement. She insisted it was a glorious place—full of possibilities. *Possibilities*—I knew what that meant. I had my doubts, but I wasn't there to see for myself.

Rhonda was different from both Mother and me in that she was prepared to allow Sally much more autonomy. If Sally was determined to move, who were we to stop her? For although Sally had been committed to mental hospitals against her will, she had never been put in the care of a legal guardian, and she still retained all of the normal rights of an adult. Anyway, she had been so lonely in the apartment she'd already left it for a local crisis center several nights before. No one could persuade her to go back. I finally said yes, on the condition that if this didn't work out, Sally would apply for a place in a group home.

"Fine," she said readily. "But this is going to work out. You'll see."

I knew it wouldn't, but at least I'd extracted the promise. Now it was just a matter of time before things fell apart again. I knew Mother would have argued more forcefully, but I wasn't Mother, as I continually told her ghost.

For the past six years, since Sally had returned home after a particularly bad breakdown, Mother had been Sally's mainstay, trying to provide some order in her life, trying to keep her out of hospitals. Even after Sally moved to the rented room, Mother made sure she had regular doctor and dentist appointments, took her grocery shopping, helped her balance her checkbook, spoke with her often, sometimes several times a day if she was trying to ward off a crisis, brought her home on weekends, and joined her in family therapy at the county mental health center, adjacent to Arlington Hospital, a five-minute drive from Mother's house. During the week Sally was expected to go to the center, where she could take advantage of a number of services and activities. She could see a counselor, work on projects in occupational therapy, participate in group activities such as drama therapy, and have an inexpensive and healthy lunch that was prepared in part by other clients at the center.

I wasn't surprised to hear that there were now many days when Sally couldn't find the will to go. Her attendance had been erratic even when Mother was around to nag and cajole her. When she went to the center her social worker and other staff members would tell her she was capable of doing more than she did, of doing better, of trying harder, of getting a job, perhaps. "They try to make me into someone I'm not," Sally said. Mother put it another way: "They won't put up with Sally's nonsense. They expect her to take some responsibility."

Mother had resented having to push Sally to do "what's good for her," and Sally bitterly resented Mother for her help, which she regarded as a relentless intrusion on her privacy. I sided with Mother, for it seemed to me that during those six years Sally had been relatively stable for the first time in more than a decade. Ever since Mother gave up expecting Sally to live independently (as all of Sally's doctors had urged her to do) and began, instead, to monitor her closely, there had been no midnight roamings, no sudden divestitures of possessions, no hallucinations, no delusions. There had been no police escorts, no commitments to state hospitals, no shock treatments. All of that had been business as usual, before. By the time she was forty, Sally had been a patient in psychiatric wards and hospitals more than twenty times.

t w o

....

In the early spring of 1959, when Sally was eighteen, she was taken out of boarding school and admitted to the Sheppard and Enoch Pratt Hospital, in Towson, Maryland. It was her first hospitalization for mental illness, although she had been taken to psychotherapists when she was a child. At Sheppard Pratt she was diagnosed as having "chronic schizophrenic reaction, undifferentiated type." She was "almost catatonic," my mother told me many years later. "She looked like she was sleepwalking." Sally told me recently she had simply "lost all sense of self."

I was ten when Sally went to Sheppard Pratt, and I barely noted her transition from one institution to another. Eight years apart in age, we had never been close, and because she had already been away at school for nearly two years I was accustomed to her absence. I was too young to understand, or consciously to care about, Sally's unhappiness. All I knew, and this I knew well, was that my life was easier when she was out of the home. When Sally was there, she and my mother fought incessantly, or my parents fought about how to handle her. I stayed away as much as I could—playing outside or at the homes of my friends. When Sally was gone, the house was quiet and the world was calm. Best of all, I could reclaim my parents' attention.

After she was sent to Sheppard Pratt, I was instructed not to tell the neighbors "about Sally," but that meant little to me, because I never mentioned her anyway. I was earnestly pursuing the fantasy that I was an only child.

Denying Sally's existence enabled me to concentrate on trying to make my own life seem as normal as possible, but it eventually took a toll, of course. I couldn't bear to be alone, and I was often unable to concentrate. I had always been an excellent student, but now I had trouble studying, and by the time I reached high school I could barely keep up with my classes. I suffered from a vague but pervasive sense of hopelessness that made the future seem somehow out of reach, and I was often deeply depressed.

In college, I consulted the school psychologist occasionally, but never revealed the depths of my misery. I know now that I was terrified of becoming mentally ill myself and had been most of my life. I was afraid that if I sought help in a serious way I would be "like Sally." It wasn't until I was in my thirties that I began therapy in earnest, perhaps because by then, even though I was often suicidal, some small part of me felt confident that I would get better, not worse. I was ready to give up some of my defenses.

I gradually shed much of the sadness that had been weighing me down since childhood, but I continued to suppress many of my feelings about Sally. Then one day, in the office of a magazine where I worked as an editor, I caught an embarrassing glimpse of my private iceberg.

I was idly chatting with some of the other editors while making corrections on a set of galleys. The conversation turned to families, and one young woman, a friend, complained about being a middle child—an invisible cipher, she said, stuck between two older and two younger siblings. Someone else said how different it was to be an only child. Without looking up from my work, I chimed in to agree. Yes, I said, it certainly was different.

There was a moment of silence. Then my friend said gently, "But Peggy, you have a sister."

Part of my amnesia was due to buried grief—for the older sister I felt I'd never really had, for Sally's lifelong struggle, for my own confusion and misery—and part to a fully conscious dread of the time when, I anticipated, I would have to pay attention to Sally every day. I thought of my mother, still comparatively young in her early seventies, and said a prayer of thanks that it would probably be a long time before I'd have to fill her shoes. When, a moment later, I tentatively imagined her death, and myself returning to Virginia to take over Sally's care, I instantly thought of suicide. I was convinced I would have to give up my life; I just wasn't sure which way I would do it.

three

W hen my mother died suddenly of a stroke in the early spring of 1987, three weeks shy of her seventy-fifth birthday, I was finally forced to confront the reality of my sister's illness and her needs.

In the late fifties, my parents had expected Sally to be cured by the treatment she received at Sheppard Pratt, and, indeed, she was well enough when she came home to complete high school and go on to graduate from college. But though she functioned at a fairly high level, she was not exactly well. Any added stress was apt to make her falter.

As long as she lived at home, she remained stable. When she moved out, in 1969, to an apartment an hour away in Washington's Maryland suburbs, she almost immediately broke down. For thirteen years, from 1969 to 1982, Sally was in and out of mental hospitals. Her breakdowns were precipitated by various kinds of stress—an unpleasant coworker at her job, tension with a roommate—which built up to a point at which Sally felt unable to cope with daily life. She suffered from an inability to manage the kinds of setbacks everyone has to face. For her, they were cumulative and, ultimately, overwhelming. She sometimes felt hopeless, and she made one attempt at suicide, a serious one, but as she herself would tell you, that experience more than any other convinced her that she wanted to live.

Mother clung to the belief that Sally would get "well." Each time Sally moved from an apartment to a rented room, or checked out of another hospital and into a halfway house, Mother would be filled with hope that *this* time would be the charm, *this* time Sally would "settle down."

Mother was "like Cleopatra," as she herself later admitted—"queen of denial." When Sally broke down, she would take her to the hospital, but she tried to stay away from her when Sally was better. During the years when doctors routinely blamed mothers for their children's psychoses, my mother had been only too willing to believe them. "You have to let her live her own life," they told her repeatedly, as if her attention were the primary cause of Sally's failures, and she would try, forcing herself to leave Sally alone. When she did that, Sally would maintain for a while, but eventually her life would come unraveled again, and Mother would be forced to intervene.

By the time Sally was in her midthirties, her diagnosis had been changed from schizophrenia to manic-depression, or bipolar illness. Uncertainty about diagnosis is common, despite new criteria for judging a patient's psychosis. When Sally was first diagnosed, schizophrenia was the label of choice among most doctors. Now that more is known about the different forms of schizophrenia and other mental illnesses, doctors are better able to classify a patient's symptoms. Generally speaking, schizophrenia causes thought disorders and manic-depression, mood disorders, but there is a huge gray area between the two, with many patients who show symptoms of both illnesses. Sally had manic highs and desperate depressions, but unlike those with classic manic-depressive illness, who often lead quite successful lives, she didn't return to normal when her episodes were over. Instead, she had many of the lasting deficits that are characteristic of schizophrenia, such as reduced ability to concentrate, poor motivation, and slower physical responses. She was given lithium, the primary drug for treating manic-depression, but doctors also prescribed antipsychotic drugs like Prolixin. The side effects of the lithium were bad—fatigue, constant thirst, and, at least as far as I could observe, a deadening apathy— mild by comparison to despair but debilitating nonetheless.

When Sally was sick, she might be profoundly depressed, lethargic to the point of inertia. She couldn't get out of bed and slept most of the day and night. When she was manic, her speech was pressured, she might be paranoid, she sometimes had delusions, and, at her worst, was tormented by auditory hallucinations—she heard voices. She went on shopping sprees, gave her money and possessions away, and spent day and night trying to get in touch with friends and acquaintances from her past.

For me, the worst aspect of her illness was that it was so difficult to tell where it began and ended. Sally has said angry, ugly things to me when she was sick, and although I knew it was her illness speaking, I've been hurt and angry in return. When she made what were, to me, clearly irresponsible decisions, it was hard to remember that her judgment was impaired. Even when she was in good shape, it was difficult for me to separate the disease from the person, to know what to take to heart, what to remember, what to ignore. Sally was Sally, and sick or well she had fleeting enthusiasms, passionate shifts of emotion, and imprudent impulses. She was also jolly, lazy (although this trait disappeared when she was manic), and affectionate. When I talked to her I rarely expected her to initiate topics of conversation, and to tell the truth, when she did I was a little wary. I was like my mother that way. She wanted to check in with Sally and be told that all was status quo. When all was not, it made her nervous, thinking that the possibilities for chaos were too great for comfort.

She had reason to dread changes in Sally's life, for it almost always meant another move, another hospitalization, another breakdown. Eventually, in 1980, Mother finally quit listening to the doctors who told her to stay away from Sally. They weren't around, of course, when it was time to take Sally's belongings to storage or intercede with her supervisor to plead for more time off from work, or pay another landlady for property damage. It was easier to bring Sally home than to worry continually about where she was and what would happen next.

Mother took Sally to a day program at the mental health center, and spoke often to the psychiatric nurse who became Sally's caseworker. Mother found solace in the respect she received from this young, energetic woman, something that she'd never experienced before. When she was encouraged to attend a family therapy group, she agreed, albeit with some trepidation.

The sessions were comforting in one way: Everybody there seemed to have it worse than Mother. "Some of those kids are downright *vicious*," she said incredulously. "Thank God Sally isn't like that." But the sessions were also the beginning of Mother's decline. An ostrich—and an optimist—at heart, Mother found it excruciating to acknowledge that Sally might never get completely well.

I'd tried to tell her that she had to look at the evidence and see that Sally's problems were not going to go away. "She's never going to be any different," I would say (wrongly, as it happens).

"If I felt like you, Peggy, I'd kill myself," Mother would answer. And she did, in a way. As she began to accept Sally's disability, her own natural resilience against gloom failed her. In just a few years, she was beaten, defeated, exhausted. And then she died.

f o u r

....

One question haunted me. Was I supposed to take my mother's place? I lived in New York with my two cats. I worked full-time and wrote free-lance articles on the side. Was it time to give up? I could be useful, I thought, even possibly effective, if I went back to Virginia and took care of Sally.

"What about *your* life?" my psychiatrist and my friends asked me. But what was my life? Didn't it include my only sister? If not, then who else among my circle of friends, colleagues, neighbors, and acquaintances could be expunged? I wasn't about to turn my back on Sally. I wasn't married, I didn't even have a boyfriend, and although I loved my work and my friends, some part of me insisted that I was unencumbered by any significant attachment.

Yet I was loathe to resign myself to my singleness, as if it might be a permanent condition. And I couldn't bear the thought of becoming Sally's fulcrum. I'd seen my mother's *joie de vivre* dissolve as she became enmeshed in Sally's comings and goings. I wanted to be a good sister to Sally, especially now, when she needed me, but when I tried to imagine myself moving back to Virginia, the future I envisioned was nothing but an extension of what I saw as my mother's sentence.

Mother didn't want me to feel trapped—it was my own conscience that proposed the scenario. She left the trust fund for Sally and had said a hundred times, "I don't want you coming down here and ruining your life after I'm gone." That was how we both saw our choices—escape or be sucked into the maelstrom of Sally's illness and give up all hope of happiness. To us, stuck as we were in our own blind hopelessness, there was no middle road, no possible balance between Sally's consuming need and our own lives.

Mother intended the trust to enable me to maintain my independence, and in many ways it did. The money allowed me to supplement Sally's meager disability income and to take advantage of the services of a private social work agency and have Rhonda do many of the things I would have done for Sally if I had been nearby. But the trust didn't solve all the problems. Money, wonderful as it was, didn't offer companionship or love. "When are you coming down?" was now Sally's constant, pitiable query. "I miss you, Peggy. I can't wait to see you."

I was more depressed than I had been in many years. I couldn't think of a way out, and it frightened me to find myself in despair again. But as usual, the mere thought of suicide had a calming effect, so I put it off. As a friend had said to me once, you can always do that tomorrow.

···

PART TWO

THE
FUGITIVE

· ·

f i v e

....

My memories of childhood were few and far between. The ones that did come back to me were usually set against the woods and yards around the suburban neighborhood where I grew up. One of my earliest was of reaching up to turn the handle on a screen door. It is just past dawn on a summer morning, before anyone else in the house is awake, and I can see the dewy grass sparkling in the sun. I am determined to play in the yard until it's time for breakfast. The door is locked, but I keep working at it, stretched up on my toes, struggling to make the latch give. Staring through the screen, I see a catbird picking his way through the chickweed in the lawn. I call to him desperately, "Help! Help!"

For many years I recalled this vignette as a signal of my early love of light and landscape, until a boyfriend I was leaving for flimsy reasons said, "You're still doing it—still trying to open the door and get *out.*" If I hadn't spent most of my life as an escapee I wouldn't have given a second thought to his reaction. But by the time this particular boyfriend came along I was thinking of myself as a runaway—from Virginia, from my family, from a marriage, from a vocation—and the fact that my exile was self-imposed made it worse. He was absolutely right—I couldn't deny the instant sense of recognition I felt—and I suddenly began to see the house I'd grown up in as a prison from which I'd had to escape ever after.

It always puzzled me that I had so few indoor memories—except those set at the houses of my playmates. What happened at home? Why did I block it out? I went to a psychotherapist for two years in my early twenties, when I was in graduate school in Seattle, and nothing unusually traumatic surfaced. When I had to quit (the therapist was on the school's infirmary staff, and I was finishing my degree), I was sorry, but I felt that the problems I'd brought to her were in large part resolved. I went to the last session to say thank you and good-bye.

I talked about the two great uncertainties in my life at that time, love and work—my marriage and my painting career. And then, just as I was getting ready to leave, I happened to mention Sally.

"I don't know much about your sister," the therapist said.

I began to describe Sally—how different she was from me, how alone she seemed, how sad her life looked to me. What I saw firsthand, when I was in Virginia, was a large, quiet woman who looked defeated by life. What I heard about Sally from my mother when we talked on the phone was that Sally was "feeling pretty rotten," then that she was hospitalized again, and then that she was back at her job. Mother's constant anxiety for Sally was almost palpable, and it saturated our conversations about her. These bits of talk were my main connection with my sister, for Sally and I rarely spoke to one another except in a perfunctory way. To me, Sally's life was one cycle of illness and hospitalization after another, with periods of blank depression in between. I never saw her happy. As I spoke to my therapist, I began to cry quietly.

As if I were watching a movie, I began to recall the constant, poisonous fights between her and my mother that had racketed through the house during my childhood and teens. My throat began to tighten. The therapist urged me to go on, but I couldn't bear to hear their screaming voices in my head, much less to recount what they said. Instead, I wept and wept.

Then, as I left the office, I put it all out of my mind again. It was a close call. Another session and I'd have had to examine that misery.

When I was eighteen, away at college, I'd made an illustrated book describing a beautiful place surrounded by green lawns and shaded by trees where birds sang. That's how I saw the neighborhood of my childhood, and that's how I remember it still. Our corner of Arlington was very southern, and practically the country then, in the early fifties. A family up the street kept horses. Crayfish, eels, minnows, and water skippers lived in the creek that ran through our yard on its way to the Potomac.

Now I am painfully (if liberatingly) aware of the house that I carefully left out of the picture in my book. Sunny, spacious, and comfortable, it was designed by my parents with Frank Lloyd Wright's open-plan houses in mind. There were as few walls as possible around the living areas, banks of windows to the south, and airy ten-foot ceilings. It was made for family life, but just writing that phrase makes my stomach turn with anxiety. I do not want to put the characters into this scene, for although I loved my mother, father, and sister, they did not play their parts according to the demands of my childish fantasy.

I used to think that if I described life at home no one would understand. People would react with skepticism, at least, or they would be horrified. I'm now aware, however, that much of the reality of my family's experience is also the same, more or less, as that of many others who grew up in families with serious problems. It gives me the courage to open the door, and look inside.

I'll start with Sally, who is watching television in the playroom. She is a tall, lanky teenager, but without the velocity one associates with adolescents. Her fine, dark, straight hair is limp and badly combed around a crooked part. A bobby pin holds most of it out of her eyes, but a few stray strands hang in front of her glasses. The lenses are spotted and streaked. She slumps low in the couch, her narrow shoulders rounded. She squints at the television. With a practiced gesture, she pushes up her glasses by the nosepiece with one index finger while sucking on her thumb. Her plaid shirt has come untucked at the waist. Her blue jeans ride up at the ankles, showing dark socks that have slipped into the backs of her saddle shoes. Everything about her seems somehow slack.

Our mother is thirty feet away, in the kitchen, where the cabinets block her view of Sally. She has just gotten up from the short nap she has every afternoon. She's taking broccoli and potatoes out of the refrigerator, getting ready to make dinner. My father is still at work.

It's late on a fall afternoon, and the air is getting cold. I'm six years old, playing hopscotch in a neighbor's driveway—the only paved surface in the neighborhood—where the chalk lines will show up. I've ignored the chill as long as I can, and finally run indoors to get a sweater. I'm worried that it's so late my mother will tell me to stay. My best friend, Sharon, is with me. She waits just inside but keeps the door open a crack, listening in case her mother calls her home. It's beginning to get dark.

Mother looks up. "Close that door, Honey," she says mildly, and Sharon does. But in looking up, Mother has noticed Sally. I feel the atmosphere change from neutral to negative, and I begin to hurry. "Sally, quit sucking your thumb," is how the trouble begins. Sally doesn't, or won't, hear a word. She goes on sucking, staring at the television, her face illuminated slightly blue. Mother takes offense. "Sally! Do you hear me?" Now she peers into the playroom. "Turn on a light. You're going to put your eyes out! Sit up! *And take that thumb out of your mouth!*" Sally straightens up, but she forgets to turn on a light. She doesn't watch television that often—

she's usually in her bedroom with the door shut—and I suspect that Mother has dragged her out to the playroom so she won't "be holed up" by herself. "Get out here and be sociable," is what she probably said.

"Turn on the light, damn it!" Mother is angry now. "We don't pay for your glasses to have you sit in the dark like a *moron.*" Sally responds with a deadened blankness at first. Then she seems to snap to. She stares at Mother with a steady, hateful scowl, but she never talks back, not even to say, "Leave me alone." Mother's words are unduly vicious. They spurt out as if from a boiling subterranean well of bitterness. She can't contain her irritation, and Sally, like all deeply dependent children, possibly senses that she can't win—that she does not quite dare offend her mother further.

I make it back outdoors with my sweater. I'm invisible, I think, slipping under the radar of my mother's wrath, which is fixed on Sally. In a few minutes, the streetlights come on, and Sharon's mother calls her in. When I get home, Sally has retreated to her room and Mother is trimming the broccoli in the kitchen sink. "Hi, Dumplin'," she says to me when I come in. "Where's Sharon?"

IT WAS AS if Sally and I were growing up in two different households, hers a perilous one in which everything about her seemed to irritate her mother, mine a warm, affirming one in which I could rarely do anything wrong. I was almost never blamed for anything, and became so spoiled that I was indignant whenever I was criticized, feeling it to be my birthright to be adored without reservation. Sally, on the other hand, was berated regularly. When I went out to play, she would go to her room and shut the door.

When Sally was older, she wrote a series of what she called her "If I were" poems. In helping with this book, she gave me permission to quote them. I have always found them affecting, for they seem to me to be as much about escape as about imagining. Here, for instance, is "A Grass Blade":

> If I were a tiny blade of grass,
> I'd shudder and shake as the lawnmower passed,
> And try to reach down
> Very close to the ground.

I too had difficulty with Mother. I basked in my parents' affection, but with my mother I eventually came to do so with a certain amount of uneasiness. One could not entirely relax, because it was always possible to fail. Sally knew this by heart, from experience. I knew it mainly from observation, but that was enough to provide a sharp edge of anxiety to my development.

Even as a very young child, I strained to perceive my mother's likes and dislikes, hoping to avoid her disapproval. She was contemptuous of anything "tacky," "common," or "vulgar," so that was what I most tried to avoid. In the women's pages of one of the daily papers that came to the house there were dress patterns pictured. "That's nice," she might say, glancing at the drawing of a woman in a tailored blouse. One day I saw a pattern that to me seemed the epitome of good taste—something like a Chanel suit. I spoke up. "That's nice," I ventured, pointing to my sure thing. But to my shock, Mother shrugged in mild contempt and said, "Seems kind of bland to me." My head jerked up involuntarily, and I stared at her, but she was looking the other way, going about some business. I was stunned—not because she disagreed with my choice, but because she had recognized my bid for approval, I felt sure, and had rejected it. I see now that I was too obvious. Like most people, she liked to give love freely, of her own goodwill. Like most children, I wanted to know I could extort it if need be.

I became masterly in my ability to do the right thing, and in general, my mother found me delightful. But there was a price to pay for my efforts. There is a photograph of me taken when I was five that shows me sitting primly on a love seat with my hands folded in my lap. My eyebrows are slightly raised, giving me an innocent, gently expectant look. Is it surprising that I also had a wicked temper? In the windowsill of my childhood bedroom, there are deep teeth marks where I bit the wood to keep from screaming. I unhinged a door or two during my preschool years, slamming through the house. Mother later told me she asked Sally's psychologist about my rages. "It's good for her to get it out," the therapist said mildly.

I think about my tantrums in two ways. The easiest explanation is to say I inherited my disposition from my great-grandmother, whose family name was synonymous for temper in the Kentucky town where she lived. "Don't get your Hardin up," people would say. And my great-grandfather once paid a servant to relay an apology to a man with whom he'd had an argument. "I'm afraid if I go myself I'll knock him down," he explained.

It would be pleasant to put my rage in the context of amusing family stories, but I think it was, instead, the only way I knew to express the tension I felt, which was all around me. My mother fought with my sister, and my parents fought about that. My father thought my mother wasn't strict enough with Sally on the one hand, and that she was overbearing on the other. Mother felt defensive and frustrated: She couldn't change Sally's habits, but neither could she tolerate them. At one point I asked my parents why they didn't get divorced instead of fighting so much. They stopped arguing instantly and gaped at me, then at one another. My father turned back to me and said gently, "Even if your mother and I fight sometimes, it doesn't mean we don't love each other." I think I knew that. But my intervention had exactly the effect I intended.

41

I can't remember whether my father reacted to my fits—or if he even witnessed one. Like all the fathers I knew, he was at work most of the week, and he also traveled for long periods. As an engineer with the Export Import Bank, he was often gone for a month or two at a time, studying the sites and conditions of projects that the ExIm Bank was considering for loans. We would get postcards and letters from South America, Africa, or India, and I still have a bar of soap somewhere from the Istanbul Hilton, the hotel's logo incised in a curling, fake Arabic script. He brought back wonderful dolls and toys and children's clothes from his trips, and hundreds of slides.

I can't remember how his absence felt at the time, although I have a letter of mine, to him, that says, "Please don't be gone so long this time. I miss you so much." He saved it in his sock drawer, where Mother found it after he died, along with my first homemade paper doll, valentines and birthday cards Sally and I had made for him, and a certificate from my ballet class stating I could progress to the intermediate level. Some of his longest trips occurred when Sally was away at school, so the weeks when Mother and I were alone together were peaceful, if quiet. I remember a few household crises—frozen pipes, a sick pet—when Mother said she felt helpless without him, but for the most part my recollection is of his homecomings. I would stay up late and be taken to the airport to meet his plane; he would bring presents and souvenirs, and in a week or so we would all look at the slides of his trip. "This is the great, gray-green, greasy Limpopo River, where the Elephant got his trunk," he would quote, showing an aerial shot of the African waterway. Another time, showing slides of India, he spoke sonorously of tragic death and eternal love when he got to the ones of the Taj Mahal. Everyone on his side of the family was a vivid storyteller.

He was the only one who escaped the cycles of jealousy that roiled the atmosphere in the family, probably because, ultimately, he was at the center of them. He was our hero, and we all scrambled for his attention and generous affection. He liked to sing, to tell stories, to putter in his darkroom, to work around the house. He enjoyed being at home much more than the three of us who were stuck there, year in, year out, and when he was there, the rest of us were on our best behavior. He died when I was fifteen and Sally twenty-three, which perhaps ensured our idealization of him, but I've never heard anyone speak of him with less than a kind of reverence. He was known as an unwaveringly ethical man, and when his sisters grew into old age alone, without their husbands or children, long-dead, to help and advise them, I would often hear them murmur, "If only Bob were alive."

The best thing about my father was that he was easy to please. One of six children, he'd had practice living with all kinds. He possessed a natural diplomacy that stood him well both at work, where he negotiated with people from all over the world, and at home, where his mere presence had a generally salubrious effect. I don't remember ever trying to please him, but I remember that I always did. Sally felt the same way, she said, except when Mother and Daddy were fighting about her. Whenever he sensed Sally felt excluded from the crowd of friends my age who played with me, he would dream up some special project, such as a lily pond, and ask Sally if she would mind helping him with it. The simple fact of his love for Sally was a gift to me, for it relieved the guilt I felt at being so obviously preferred by Mother.

Because I was so young and so committed to the fantasy that everything in my life was fine, I may have missed aspects of my father's character and presence that would help make him a more rounded figure here. My adult consciousness of my own unhappiness, and my determination to look back for the roots of it, began fifteen years after his death, and I've had little success reconstructing his role in the family.

In recent years, however, I find I bear him a grudge—an inchoate, unnameable rancor, of which I am mildly ashamed, because I can't explain it. Am I angry at him for dying? I think that's probably the most plausible explanation. I wonder, of course, what our lives would have been like if he had lived. As Sally's illness developed over the years, with the manic-depressive cycles beginning in her late twenties, his presence would have offered some aid and comfort to Mother, but I doubt he'd have known how to handle the crises any better than Mother did. I often feel his premature death demonstrated succinctly his inability to cope as well as she did, but I'm aware that this is hardly fair.

Although it is very cold comfort, I sometimes think that there was a paradoxical relief in losing my father, the center of our universe. There was certainly no more competition among the three of us. An aunt once told me that when I was a baby my father had confided in her that he had to be careful how much affection he showered on me. "And not just because of Sally," she said. "He told me it also upset your mother. Imagine—jealous of her own child." This modest revelation pierced my heart, for although I had long reconciled myself to Sally's envy, I'd never been conscious of Mother's. But my aunt's remark jogged memories of being humiliated by Mother and how mortifying it was to be the object of her scorn or sarcasm. I must have blocked those memories because it hurt to recall them and because most of the time I enjoyed Mother's approbation.

The episode with the dress pattern was one minor occasion when I fell from grace, and I believe such scenes were comparatively rare. Unlike Sally, I could usually elicit Mother's approval somehow, and often it came my way without any effort on my part. I remember looking up from my business in the side yard as a small child, where I might be building a snowman, picking daffodils, catching water skippers in the creek, or kicking fallen leaves over the bank, and see Mother watching me from the kitchen window, sharing my pleasure in whatever I was doing. When I dreamed about her after she died, it was to see her beaming face, smiling at me in her beguiling, irresistible way.

To the day she died, my mother was proud—no, thrilled—to introduce me as her daughter, as if to say, "See? I wasn't so bad, after all." She depended on me to clear her name—to tell the world she was capable of being the mother of a healthy child. That I was not so healthy inside didn't trouble her. I looked happy, and I genuinely liked her friends, so it was easy for her to show me off. I was happy enough for her.

My early success with my mother sprang from my ability to be outside, find playmates, and stay away from home, out of her hair, from the time I could walk. "Peggy could always take care of herself," Mother liked to say. "I never had to worry about her."

If I found it difficult to be independent, I didn't know it. I seem to have understood instinctively that to lean on Mother too much was to risk rejection. She found motherhood overwhelming, and she often said that she preferred to feel we were friends. Even now, in my forties, I can see the effects of my premature independence. I still resist acknowledging that I need anyone, especially those I love most—whom I secretly depend on, psychologically, to the extent that I feel only half alive without them. I think Mother never forgave Sally her inability to pretend that she could get along by herself.

Sally could not help making it clear that she needed extra care, help, encouragement, and reassurance. I understood Mother's frustration better in the year following her death, when there were many times I thought that no matter what I did for Sally it would not be enough. Mother felt that way from the day Sally was born, and it made her freeze with a sense of her own inadequacy. Whereas she found it easy, most of the time, to give love to me, she was unable to do the same for Sally.

Sally's illness is similar to that of others in my family; my great-aunt Maude, on my father's side, spent more than a decade in a mental institution, and my mother's uncle had classic manic-depression. Their disabilities, and the overwhelming evidence that severe mental illnesses are diseases of the brain, are partly why I don't hold my parents to blame for Sally's illness. But I do feel that my mother's anxious, frustrated response to Sally's special needs, particularly when Sally was a teenager and young adult, contributed to Sally's insecurity, and thus her vulnerability, over the years.

In fact, no one does well with a hostile, critical, overinvolved parent. I know I didn't. Mother had a repertoire of barbed remarks, and many of them were directed at me as well. When someone mentioned an attractive child, or a charming new baby, she would say, "Both my children were pretty when they were little." Another oft-heard declaration, which popped out whenever one of my boyfriends said I looked beautiful (the way any good boyfriend will from time to time), was, "I never think of Peggy as *pretty*, exactly . . ." Her voice would trail off, dropping suggestions behind it. Not pretty, but . . . what? Who can say?

These remarks were delivered in a disarmingly friendly way. Most people said I looked exactly like my mother, but she found distinctions to be made. "You have a narrow face like my cousin," she would observe thoughtfully, "—Hatchet-Faced Willie." She smiled affectionately. With her lovely, educated Nashville accent, there was a charming, musical quality to almost everything that she said in a normal conversational tone, and a surprised "My, My!" note to her exclamations. "I wonder why you're so small in the chest," she mused. "I always had a nice bosom—until I ruined it by nursing you, anyhow."

Birth and babies brought out unexpected comparisons between Sally and me. Sally had been a breach baby, and that can cause a difficult labor, but apparently in Sally's case it didn't. When Mother gave birth to me, she found the process much more difficult, even though it was a normal delivery. "If I'd had you first, I *never* would have had another," she liked to say. I think that probably the opposite was true: She found herself unable to enjoy her first child, so it took her eight years to become pregnant again ("I don't know why," she said with genuine puzzlement, "It happened right away, the first time!"), and her ambivalence about having another baby made her unable to relax while giving birth to me. Perhaps if she'd had me first, she would have had another sooner.

It wasn't just my birth that made Mother bitter, however. It was parenthood in general. "Bob and I were so happy before we had children," she used to say, dreamily remembering the early years of her marriage. As the first child, Sally must have thought the remark was mainly about her. I, however, took it literally—she said *children*, not *Sally*—so I naturally included myself as an agent in the demise of her state of grace. Mother always said such things in a benign voice—never in anger—and usually in an offhand manner, as if she herself were slightly surprised. She would be sitting with a neighbor over coffee in the dinette. The friend would mention that her son and daughter-in-law were expecting their first baby. Mother would get a faraway look in her eyes, and I would hear the words in my head before they were out of her mouth.

I wasn't horrified by Mother's comments—at least I didn't think I was. After all, I'd heard them all my life. But every so often, when I was much older, a friend would call my attention to their obvious inherent harshness. I think Sally and I heard them the way a battered child receives the occasional cuff—negligible compared to a real working over. Because my defense has always been the insistence that everything was fine, I still have trouble realizing just how damaging her asides

48

must have been. It's only in the context of some new bit of information, such as the story my aunt told about my mother's jealousy, that I am able to feel the pain of her jibes again and speculate on how it might have affected me. Part of the problem was that I also found Mother so attractive and fun, so loving—so irresistible—that it was difficult to remember her dark side, no matter how often I saw it.

During the last ten years of my mother's life, we talked a lot about her past, and about her experiences both as a daughter and as a mother, and it was then that I came to understand something of how hard it was for her to cope with the strains of raising Sally and me. As a child, she had felt vaguely estranged from her family. The older of two girls, she was studious, serious minded, and tense, whereas her sister, Irene— born when Mother was two and a half—was carefree and easygoing. My mother never got over her grief at losing her parents' undivided attention, and her normal feelings of sibling rivalry were exacerbated when her mother became ill a few years later. While she recuperated, my mother was sent away to school, but Irene went to live with their favorite cousins. Before leaving home, my mother asked an aunt what was wrong with her mother. "She's worn out from taking care of you girls," the aunt answered callously. Although she was only six, my mother resolved never to be a burden, never to need her mother again. When I heard this, I wondered if my mother had unconsciously passed on some of her stoicism to me. I also thought about other correspondences between her life and Sally's. Mother always spoke about the loving, affectionate nuns at the school she went to, which was a Roman Catholic academy. When she sent Sally to boarding school, she chose a Catholic one, unconsciously hoping, I'm sure, that Sally would find there the warmth and sustenance she couldn't get at home.

Throughout her school years my mother was an excellent, if anxiety-prone, student. She graduated from high school at the nadir of the Depression, but she managed to go to college by winning a scholarship to Vanderbilt and living at home. She was vivacious and popular, and although she had to drop out of her sorority because she couldn't afford the dues, she continued to be invited to campus parties as Kappa Alpha Theta's representative. She couldn't buy new dresses, so she would scrutinize Paris originals in Nashville's fanciest stores, then buy fabric and copy them tuck for tuck, seam for seam. The following season, she would change the look of the dress with a new collar, a jacket, or a different hemline. Use it up, wear it out, make it do, or do without. Like everyone else who made it through the Depression on a shoestring, she substituted ingenuity for capital.

When my mother was seventeen, her mother died in her sleep. My grandfather remarried a woman Mother considered an unworthy interloper, and her childhood home became enemy domain. She stayed on there because she had no place else to go.

One Saturday afternoon in 1934, she met her husband-to-be, Bob Moorman, while she was visiting a cousin of his. It was love at first sight, and they married immediately. My father was an engineer with Roosevelt's Works Progress Administration, putting in waterworks in small towns around the Midwest, and he and my mother spent the rest of the decade moving from place to place. "We just stayed on honeymoon," Mother told me more than once, smiling happily. She sometimes found work, too, and she liked to tell a story about the two of them parking their Ford this side of a toll bridge and walking the rest of the way to town because it cost two cents to cross the bridge in an automobile and only one by foot. They literally hadn't had a penny to spare, but they were young, grateful to be working, and in love.

By 1940, the Depression was lifting, and they decided to have a child. Sally was born in October. Mother loved being pregnant, and she had no reason to doubt she would be happy with her baby, but when Sally was born, she said, her maternal instincts failed her.

Mother's lack of self-confidence hurt her chances at success, but even the purest mother-love would not have made life smooth for her and Sally. Sally cried all but incessantly, the result of a painful hernia that was not diagnosed for more than five months. When a doctor finally discovered it, he bound Sally's belly with a kind of sash, and the hernia healed within two weeks. For five months, Mother had been convinced that she was a completely ineffective mother and, worse, that her baby hated her.

The hernia was not all that Sally and Mother had to endure. It was probably not even the worst. During the months when Sally cried round the clock, only nursing distracted and soothed her. But it was 1940, and doctors routinely advised mothers not to feed their newborns more frequently than every four hours. In those days, according to Dr. Spock, "physicians . . . feared that irregular schedules and irregular amounts of formula might bring on the severe diarrheal diseases that used to cause so many infant deaths." Mother was nothing if not conscientious. She waited four hours—always. Another mother might have said to herself, To hell with the doctors, but my mother didn't. She couldn't trust herself, she was convinced. There was no one to tell her to relax and do what felt natural, and it wouldn't have helped if there had been. Nothing felt natural to her. She had no mother of her own and no close friends nearby. There was not even a good child-care book for her, the excellent student, to consult. Only two years after Sally was born, Spock reports, experimenters found that babies did well and remained healthy when left to establish their own schedules. Too late for Sally, and much too late for Mother.

Mother was worn out. Worse, she was gripped by panic. She lay awake, she told me, wondering what to do. She began to doubt that she could do anything right for Sally—she thought long and hard about even the smallest gesture. One day when my father came home from work, a neighbor met him on the walk outside their apartment and told him that my mother needed a doctor. Mother had been canvassing the neighborhood that morning, going from door to door to ask how many blankets the other mothers had put on their babies the night before, and how many they thought might be needed tonight.

There were no psychiatrists nearby, but it happened that the doctor Mother was taken to knew one at Phipps Clinic, in Baltimore. Arrangements were made to send Mother there and for Sally, who was about eight months old, to be taken to live with my father's married older sister, in Charlotte, North Carolina. "When I got to Baltimore," Mother told me, "I couldn't do anything but sleep." She stayed four months, participating in occupational therapy and talking with her psychiatrist about her childhood, but she resisted admitting to herself that she had had an episode of psychosis. All she would say about her treatment at Phipps was that it was a wonderful rest.

My father's sister Peg and her husband, Lone, had a son near Sally's age. They had lost a daughter, who died in infancy, and they loved having a little girl again to take care of. "Sally learned to walk with us," Aunt Peg said when I once asked her about this time. "But she never called me Mama." Aunt Peg was probably the first to blame Mother for Sally's sad life. "There was nothing wrong with that child when I had her," she said. "She was easy to love. But your mother didn't love her, or why would she have left her that way?" Aunt Peg was close to ninety when she said this to me. I felt age exempted her from argument, so I didn't try to explain, but I felt a wave of retrospective pity for my mother, that she had been judged so harshly.

There were many years when I, too, blamed Mother for what I saw as desertion, and even now I ache when I think of

Sally at eight months, being sent away from her parents. Stress plays a large part in the onset and course of mental illnesses, and Sally's babyhood was filled with it, from the start. But because I know there are countless children who suffer worse deprivations and traumas and survive nonetheless without becoming psychotic, I would never say that Sally's early life was the cause of her later illness. Mother was conscientious and caring; she clothed and fed us and saw to it that we were schooled. She took us to church and to piano and dancing lessons, and she planned outings and vacations that she knew we would enjoy. She was there for us in myriad ways that counted. My feelings for her are in some ways permanently polarized—there is no punch I wouldn't pull, remembering how hard she tried to do the right thing by both Sally and me.

The separation that helped heal Mother was traumatic for Sally; the closeness that comforted Sally made Mother feel smothered and then guilty. Mother continued to feel unable to give Sally the wholehearted love she needed, and Sally never stopped wanting it. The strain of their relationship made it likely that Mother would later be charged by doctors and, subtly, by society, with the crime of making her daughter ill, and that she would accept the verdict. Until the experts confirmed—comparatively recently—that an undamaged brain can often fall back on its own defenses to maintain its equilibrium, while a diseased brain cannot, mothers everywhere bore the blame for the psychiatric illnesses of their children.

Sally, too, usually blamed Mother for her problems, but she was not incapable of compassion. Pondering why her arrival may have overwhelmed Mother, Sally recently formed a theory that dovetails precisely with my own ideas about the sources of Mother's insecurity—her stoicism in the face of her own mother's ill health, her resentment of her cheerful younger sister, her need for undivided love. "Mother really could not stand to have anybody depend on her too much," Sally said. "Maybe she always wanted somebody *she* could depend on. She was very dependent on Dad, I think. And when a female baby came into the house, it was a bit like . . . stealing the love. She was never very close to her own mother, and I think she may have wished she was." Sally could understand that.

After Mother left Phipps Clinic, she went to join my father in a small town in Pennsylvania where he had been sent to build a bridge. First, though, she took a train to Aunt Peg's to pick up Sally. That night they rode north in a sleeper car, sharing a berth. All night long, Sally woke up and reached out her hand. "Mama?" she said, again and again. "Mama? Hi! Mama? Hi!" Telling this story thirty-five years later, Mother wept as if her heart were breaking. How can anyone say who suffered most?

....

Every week when I was four, Mother would drive Sally and me into Washington to a small park. I sat low in the backseat of our big, black Chevrolet, looking up at the trees flying by along Canal Road. Sally was old enough to ride in the front with Mother. At the playground, Sally would disappear for a while, then reappear, and we would drive home again. I know now that Sally was in therapy at a children's psychiatric clinic. She had been troubled for a long time. By the time she was in third grade (just after I was born), her teachers were writing notes home to say she wasn't doing well. She couldn't concentrate; she had trouble making friends. When she was eleven or twelve, she began therapy at the Washington Institute of Mental Hygiene (now the Hillcrest Children's Center).

She saw a counselor named Edith Blum, a psychiatric social worker. "I went all during junior high," Sally remembers, "but I never really did talk to her much about my problems." She participated in play therapy, however, using dolls to tell a story. "It was usually a mother doll kicking a baby doll downstairs," she told me in a calm voice that struck a chill in me. I couldn't imagine Mother harming Sally, so I asked if such a thing had actually happened. No, she assured me, "But I did feel kicked around and picked on."

"I always wanted a lot of love from mother and I never could get it," she said. "I was frustrated." She said she had no such problems with our father. "Maybe it was because Dad and I were so close that I always felt closer to men than to women." She felt secure in his love in a way she could never feel with Mother. During her years in therapy with Mrs. Blum, Sally stole most of the dolls she played with, one by one, and brought them home. "And I played a loving mother who took care of the little dolls," she told me proudly—and fiercely. "There were no girls in that family, only boys. Maybe I wished I was a boy," she added pensively. "Who knows?" I wondered if maybe she wished the other "girls" in her family—her mother and sister—would disappear.

Sally loved turtles, praying mantises, lizards, frogs, salamanders, and especially snakes, and kept them as pets. A different sort of mother might have encouraged her predilections, taking them for an interest in botany and zoology, but to ours Sally's taste in animals was just another sign of her oddness and lack of femininity. Mother was a charmer—stylish and pretty—and she found it impossible to communicate with her eccentric tomboy. Perhaps Sally's boyishness was a form of rebellion against Mother, a way of demonstrating her affinity with Daddy.

It must have been difficult for Sally to accept my presence, as it is for most first children to welcome a sibling, and yet Mother insisted that Sally had adored me.

"Except when she hated me," I used to correct her.

Mother denied it. "You're wrong," she'd say fervently. "Sally *loved* you. She was always sweet to you. She was never jealous." This from someone who had suffered profoundly from sibling rivalry and had never forgotten it.

Mother was unable—unwilling—to see the complexities of the relationship between Sally and me. She remained adamant about Sally's pure affection for me until just before her death. I was home in Arlington for Christmas, and a neighbor invited the three of us over to see her toy poodle's new puppies. Sally sat in a chair while I got down on the rug with the puppies. I didn't really notice it at the time, but I remembered later that Sally was even quieter than usual as I laughed and played. After she and Mother left, I stayed to chat with our friends for a while.

When I got back, Sally was in her bedroom with the door shut, and Mother was sitting in the living room, looking thoughtful. "I never believed you," she said.

"About what?" I asked, mystified.

"About Sally and you," she said softly. When the two of them were walking back across the street, Sally had mumbled something under her breath. Mother asked what it was, and Sally had answered angrily, "I can't help seeing Peggy as the usurper."

How could Sally not have been jealous of me? And how could Mother have failed to notice?

Sally was visiting me in New York in 1980 when she said outright, "Things were fine with Mom and Dad and me until you came along." Things weren't fine, of course; I didn't ruin an idyll. But I did make life harder for her, I'm sure. Sally was an average student; I was offered special advanced classes. Sally was lonely and shy; I was outgoing.

How did Sally stand it? As far as I know she wasn't particularly aggressive toward me—no more than any other sibling would have been. She told me something else, however, that stuck in my mind. "Mom never hit me, except once," she said in a distracted way, as if she were recalling the moment.

"When was that?" I asked her.

"She came after me with a hairbrush."

"Why?" I asked.

"Oh," she answered thoughtfully, "I was trying to kill you."

Sally delivered this in a quiet voice, and with a calm, pensive expression on her face.

"Why were you trying to kill me?" I wanted to know.

"You were a baby and you were messing with my things," she said.

This conversation took place just before one of Sally's breakdowns. She looked haunted, and she spoke in jarring non sequiturs. At almost three hundred pounds, she was an imposing woman. She often scowled at me, and I found her more than a little frightening. Her words reverberated in me for a long time.

But recently I asked her about it again. This time she was on a new medication and feeling better than she had in a decade. Friendly and talkative, she chuckled as she described herself in a rage, mother with the hairbrush, and me grabbing some precious toy of hers. "You were into everything," she added. "Mischievous little devil." She smiled as she remembered. "You were cute, with your curly blond hair."

I stared at Sally. Which way had the scene really been played—as drama or as comedy? Sally had been out to do me serious damage at the time, and as a sick, suffering, jealous adult she remembered her rage and her hatred. But later, as a well, cheerful, loving adult, she could put the memory into perspective, look at its ridiculous side, and see something attractive in her baby sister.

Sally's feelings changed continually, in large part according to her mental health. And although I was often reminded of her jealousy, I knew she loved me, as well. When I was very small, she used to sing to me—"I Dream of Jeanie," "Sweet and Low," "Ashgrove," "Coral Bells"—especially on long car trips. I would trade places with the family spaniel who usually rode between us on the backseat, lay my head down on Sally's lap, and be sung to sleep as we rolled down the old white two-lane highways to southern Virginia, where we vacationed at a state park. I wished I could always remember her that way.

When, during one of those vacations, Sally lost her glasses on a horse trail, I prayed to St. Anthony (Sally was at boarding school and thinking of converting to Catholicism) for them to be found, and I felt proudly responsible when they were—muddy but unbroken. I don't know that I ever consciously loved Sally, but I hated for her to be in trouble. It wasn't just Sally's hide St. Anthony saved, it was also the peace and harmony of my day.

I wasn't always so generous. Although Sally and I didn't often play together, I can still recall the sensation of flying above her as she lay on her bed, balancing me on the soles of her feet and holding my hands. Once, we were roughhousing happily, and I screamed for help in the way children do sometimes, just for effect, to heighten the fun. But mother came running. *Trouble*. To avoid looking foolish, as someone who had yelled for no reason, I pretended to be hurt. I was the sturdiest of children; I must have fallen out of two dozen trees, headed over my bicycle handlebars twenty times, slipped on ice for a week until I learned to skate. But I persuaded Mother that I was injured, and Sally was scolded. I was sorry I'd done it, because it ruined our fun, but my treachery was worse for Sally, who was so often in Dutch with our mother.

My instantaneous impulse to point the finger may also have been my way of unconsciously living up to Mother's expectations. I was playing the good girl, and confirming Sally's role as the bad one. In another family, another parent might have told us to work it out ourselves—get along with each other, you two, or else—but that never happened with us. Because of her own lack of insight, Mother was unable to smooth the warped dynamic that drove me to implicate Sally. And because of her insecurity, she was unable to promote harmony. She unwittingly sabotaged every relationship that didn't include her, even—or perhaps especially—that between her two

eight

....

WhenI was eight, Sally went away to boarding school.
She was doing poorly in high school, and like many other
parents have done, ours decided that sending her away might
help her do better, might help her grow up. She went to a
school called Walsingham Academy, in Williamsburg.

Sally began by repeating her sophomore year to raise her
grades so she would have a better chance at college when she
graduated. When she came home for the summer, she said,
she begged our parents not to send her back, but "Mother
insisted." "I would call her and say, 'Mommy, I want to come
home,' but she wouldn't let me," she said. Sally's absence was
a relief to Mother, perhaps to all of us, so back she went for
her junior and senior years.

What was a period of agonizing exile for Sally was a time of
ease for me. Anyone leafing through the family photographs
can see how cheerful I was during my early grade-school
years, especially with my best friend, Sharon, or our other
close pal, Anne. In one picture, Sharon and I are standing on
our heads, our upside-down grins about to break into laughs.
In another, Anne and I are standing arm-in-arm in the front
yard, near the chimney of the house. I'm on tiptoe, trying to
be as tall as she is. Anne was two years older, with a preco-
cious didactic gift. She taught me how to tie my shoes, how to

skip rope, how to make costumes for plays she concocted, which we performed on a hill near her house she called the amphitheater. She and Sharon were my natural siblings in a way Sally couldn't be: I could compete with them freely, without fear of showing them up or exacting their anger. In almost every photograph of us taken by my father, my face wears a look either of complacent pleasure or impish challenge.

Sally's personality comes through in the family album, too. As a toddler, she was lovely—one of the prettiest children I've ever seen. My favorite picture of her was taken when she was about three, holding a big lump of snow and smiling at the camera. She is radiant, with the clear features of my father's side of the family. In a picture taken when she was seven or eight, she looks like Judy Garland in *The Wizard of Oz* with her dark hair drawn to the sides in tight pigtails. She's standing in a yard near a picket fence, striking a dreamy pose: Holding her pinafore out to the sides, she curtsies delicately, nodding her head just so and closing her eyes.

There's another picture of Sally, playing with me in the woods on a sunny autumn day. I'm about two, reeling with laughter, and Sally, squatting down low and wrapping her arm around me, is smiling delightedly. But she looks awkward now. Her hair is cut in a plain, unflattering style, and she's wearing a pair of glasses with homely frames. Gradually, after this picture, her demeanor changes, and she seems almost to withdraw from the scene. Her progressive sadness and alienation begin to show. The first sign that anything is wrong is the slope of her shoulders. By the time she's an adolescent, her posture is stooped. In a couple of photographs taken when she was about thirteen, she squints suspiciously at the camera, as if it were about to steal her soul. In some pictures she glares at the photographer; in one she glares down at me, five years old, half her height, standing next to her, apparently oblivious to her anger. I'm clutching a small toy rabbit and smiling tentatively at the camera. In all of the pictures, she looks out wanly from behind her glasses, but not very far.

She has begun to play her hand close, and I think of this time as her quiet period. In a picture from 1956 or 1957, just after she has been sent to Walsingham, when she is sixteen and I am eight, she looks almost ghostly. And so does our mother, I notice now, standing between her two daughters. Me, I'm smiling, and I look rather foolish for it—"happy as if you had good sense," my mother might have said. From our clothes, it must be Sunday. Sally was probably home for Easter vacation.

Sally was beginning to turn from lanky to fat. At five feet nine and a half inches, she could carry a lot of weight, but she never had good muscle tone, and whatever pounds she put on made her look puffy and unhealthy. Her complexion was fair, and as she got sick, for that's what was happening, she began to look pallid.

No one seemed to notice Sally's decline. She had always had problems, and their worsening was gradual. Instead of growing up, she grew inward. In April of her final year of high school, 1959, eighteen years old and two months shy of graduation, Sally broke down. The nuns called our parents; they suggested she be taken to a hospital. Sally stayed in her room day and night, and she cried when they tried to talk to her.

The day she came home I was playing at Sharon's house, up the street. I was ten. The phone rang, and Sharon handed the receiver to me. It was my mother. "Come home and say goodbye to Sally," she said to me. I argued with her. Why now? It wasn't lunchtime yet. And why say good-bye to Sally? She was gone all the time anyway. Mother insisted, "Come home now." I remember my outrage—a strange, inappropriate fury—at having to interrupt my fun.

I walked down the street and saw Sally, stepping gingerly down the front walk. Our father was holding her elbow gently, steering her as she walked. He led her slowly along the stone walk to the car, helped her in, and they drove off. Something in the air told me to suppress my temper. "Daddy's taking Sally to a hospital," Mother said. I asked what was wrong. "Sally's sick," she said.

"She doesn't look sick," I said.

"Sometimes you just feel bad but you don't really know what's bothering you," my mother tried to explain. "It's called depression." It was the first time I heard the word, and it made no sense to me.

••

Sally was more than depressed. When she got to Sheppard Pratt, she was also so anxious she couldn't keep food down. She would go to meals, but as she stood up from the table afterward she would be gripped by nausea and have to run to the bathroom.

Over the years, Sally had been constructing a fantasy world into which she would regularly retreat, when the ordinary world seemed too difficult or simply unsatisfying. She spent many hours each day engrossed in the imaginary exploits of her private *deus ex machina*, Flying Phyllis. Sally's Flying Phyllis was a heroine in the mold of Super Girl, Spider Man, and other contemporary all-powerful comic-book saviors, with one notable exception: Phyllis was concerned not only with justice and vengeance, but with rehabilitation and redemption as well.

Sally says that her fantasies were of Flying Phyllis saving men, and men only, and reforming them. They called her "Mommy," she says. "At least later on in my life they did." These men were all "crooks, bad hats, nuts." But under Flying Phyllis's care, they reformed, "and they got cured of all their psychiatric ailments," Sally added.

Flying Phyllis, who wore a cape "like Mighty Mouse," was a reformer who rescued a host of fantastic characters from one debacle after another. "There was the King of the Fiery Jackals, for instance, who was her ally, and the King of the Ugly Jackals, who was always getting into trouble," Sally said. Flying Phyllis conquered the "Western Outlaws," capturing them in a saloon and taking them to a ranch to clean up their act. As Flying Phyllis matured, she rehabilitated the prison system and at one point became president of the United States. Sally was unclear about Flying Phyllis's looks. "She was rather nebulous, but she always took *tender loving care* of everybody," Sally said. "I made up my own mother figure," she explained.

Sally's fantasies were her earliest escape from the tension in the family, just as going outside to play was mine. "I remember when I was younger Mother and Dad were always fighting about me," Sally told me. I remembered that, too, but vaguely, as if recalling a disturbing dream. "Mother usually lost her temper and blew up to hell, while Dad stayed calm. They fought about how I should behave, how I should be raised, how this, how that—a lot of mishmash. What I did was run into my room and fantasize whenever there was a spat, because I always thought I was the cause of it, sort of."

By the time Sally suffered her breakdown, Flying Phyllis had acquired more appeal than any actual person in her life, including herself, and she spent most of each day in her dreamworld.

I asked Sally if the fights she had with Mother had sent her into retreat. She had no memory of Mother calling her names, which, of course, was astonishing to me because that was what I remembered most clearly and painfully. But she recalled the arguments, and told me what they were about.

They fought about Sally's sucking her thumb, she said, which she abruptly quit doing when she went away to school. "I couldn't bear to do that around the other boarders," she said. "I also quit masturbating," she added casually. Sally and I rarely discussed intimate matters, so I was unprepared for this revelation. I waited to hear more, although I wasn't sure I wanted to.

"Mother used to tell me how awful it was," Sally said angrily.

"How did she know about it?" I asked.

"She used to come in my room almost without knocking."

"How much did you do it?" I asked.

"I did it quite a bit," Sally answered with unabashed frankness.

I knew that excessive masturbation was not uncommon in disturbed children. If my mother had known that at the time, she might have understood that it was a clear signal of distress: Sally was unable to take much pleasure in family, friends, school, or play, so she gave herself the only pleasure she could get. I winced when Sally told me this story because I could also imagine what it might be like to be my mother, hearing her young daughter shut her bedroom door every afternoon and knowing what was happening behind it. Sending Sally away must have been in part an attempt to force Sally to stop, and, as Sally confirmed, it worked. It never occurred to Mother to look for the root cause of Sally's behavior.

Although Sally hated boarding school, and, she said, had "a fit of wanting to come home every year," she also had some of the usual teenage experiences, such as boyfriends, including the first love of her life. "A lonely Texan who was far away from home. I met him because two of the girls went for a joy ride with two other soldiers, and they brought Tex back for me, and we fell in love with each other." Sally laughed happily as she remembered Tex. "He was a soldier, and they shipped him over to Roquefort, France, and he wrote back some of the most *interesting* letters—all about how he wanted to take care of me, and wanted me to be his sweetheart and his wife and everything."

To hear Sally describe them, Tex's letters were richly detailed fantasies in themselves. She read them again and again. "He used to draw diagrammatical pictures of all the things he'd purchase for me when he got back to the States—Jaguars in the garage and everything." Sally chuckled at the memory of Tex's Lone-Star extravagance. "I wrote to him for years until I went to the hospital," she said quietly. Then her voice rose in anger. "And then Mother wrote to him and told him she thought the letters were making me sick."

Sally thought for a moment. "And if he ever reads this book, I hope he knows that I'll always think of him with love and affection, and that Mother had it wrong," she said with a sweet combination of wistfulness and generous reassurance. Then she added, "I kept his letters for years and years after I got out of the hospital."

Looking back, it seemed to me that Mother took one of Sally's symptoms, her retreat into daydreams, as the cause of her illness. I can't be sure what she thought, however, for the morning Sally left for the hospital was the last time I heard anyone discuss what was happening to Sally until twenty years later, when I began to bring up the subject myself. In those days, even divorce carried a crushing stigma among the people we knew; mental illness was unthinkable.

Sally had already been away for almost three years. She was at the age when she might be going off to college. It seemed easy for my parents to tell the neighbors, and probably many of their other friends, that Sally was at school, so that's what they did.

The secrecy weighed on us as a family. When Sally was at Sheppard Pratt, our parents had the *Saturday Evening Post* sent to her, but because her hospitalization was so costly, they canceled our family subscription as part of a general belt-tightening. After they were allowed to begin visiting her, they would bring back her copies if she had finished reading them.

One afternoon, I was sitting in the front hall of the house near the door looking through the magazine while waiting for a friend to come over to play, when some neighbors stopped by. I invited them in, tossing the magazine aside on the telephone table and calling to my mother to let her know we had guests.

Before Mother had been in the hall for two seconds I saw a look of horror pass over her face. I didn't know what was wrong, but I sensed it was something I'd done. I couldn't imagine what the trouble was, but I racked my brain for clues. I watched her gesture toward the living room and offer her friends iced tea. As they walked out of the hall, she grabbed the magazine, glared at me, and shoved it into a drawer with the phone books. After the guests left, she screamed at me: How could I leave the magazine out, with the hospital's address showing? Did I want everyone to know where Sally was? How could I be so careless?

I didn't understand at all. Sally was Sally. She was sick and in the hospital. There were other people in our neighborhood who had been ill and in hospitals, and I didn't remember their absence embarrassing their families. My parents' secrecy made a sudden, indelible impression on me, though, and I was careful to preserve it from then on. This incident, for me, was the beginning of my feelings of shame, for Sally's illness, for my family, and for myself.

In most other ways, the eighteen months Sally was in the hospital were merely an extension of her absence and our estrangement. The only difference, for me, was my parents' anxiety, which expressed itself mainly in discussions about bank loans. My father began carrying his lunch to the office. I had to choose between art and ballet lessons, instead of taking both. Mother and I no longer went shopping for school clothes; instead, she would search for sales and bring home skirts or sweaters for me to try on. During this time, we started a program that lasted until I left for college: I would make most of my own clothes by machine, and Mother would do the handwork necessary to finish them.

After a few months, when my parents were allowed to visit Sally on weekends, they both dutifully went to Towson, even though, for a long time, Sally refused to see Mother, who stayed outside in the car or in a visitors' waiting room. Sally was in talk therapy with a psychiatrist, who encouraged her to take charge of her environment to the extent she could. Avoiding Mother, who had always been so critical of her, was a powerful way to preserve her fledgling ego, and it may also have been a way to punish the person she blamed for her unhappiness. "I couldn't stand to be near Mother," Sally said. "I had no self-confidence at all, and when Mother was around I felt worse."

I wonder how Mother felt—rejected or relieved. I imagine she must have been acutely embarrassed to have the doctors and staff witness her daughter's antipathy. On the other hand, it may have been a small price to pay for escaping, at least temporarily, the bruising business of trying to mother a child she felt she had long since failed.

There was no Washington Beltway then, and no superhighways, and the trip was hours longer than it would be today. My parents would drive up to Towson on a Saturday, and then stay overnight in Baltimore before making the trip back to Arlington the next afternoon. I would spend the weekend with our family friends Lyn and Earl, whose daughter Alice was one of my favorite playmates. While I loved having my parents to myself when Sally was away, I have to admit that these weekends were among the best times of my childhood.

There were no secrets at Alice's house. Lyn and Earl shocked me continually by talking about everything in the open. Alice and her older sister, Laurie, discussed the most exquisitely embarrassing subjects with them: brassieres, French kissing, cigarette smoking, menstruation. Lyn was nosy in the way a mother should be, questioning me about my schoolwork, my goals, even my feelings, and I was mortified every time she did. I didn't know how to talk this way. At my house, silence ruled, unless my mother was upset, when discussions took on a hysterical edge. At Alice's, everyone talked all the time without raising their voices—or, I should say, without artificially lowering them, for they said everything with a certain amount of verve.

I wished, as a child, that I could have spent a few uninterrupted years with them, but, of course, I couldn't. After the weekends, which seemed so heady with observation, activity, and interaction, I would go home.

There, I did my best to be the good daughter, the one with friends, the one who liked school, the one without problems. To succeed in this line of work, I thought I had to master the habit of avoiding anything that seemed dangerously Sally-like. And not just for my parents' sake: My fears of being like my sister were powerful. Sally put ketchup on everything; I wouldn't touch it. Sally had a pink room; I pretended to hate the color. Sally took piano; I balked at practicing and finally gave up on my lessons, although I secretly loved to play. Sally loved to sing songs, and so did I, but until very recently I suffered from a mysterious inability to remember the words to any of my favorite tunes.

One of the saddest consequences of my semiconscious determination to be different was my refusal to read. I wasn't bad at it, but except for brief bouts of bibliomania, I wouldn't be caught dead with my nose in a book. Reading was something that was done heavily in our family, but because Sally read the most, I couldn't help associating reading with her strangeness. And she wasn't the only example, in my childish reasoning, of the clear link between mental illness and the love of books. After Great-Aunt Maude's ten-year hospitalization, she went back to a job at the Akron Public Library, where she had once been head librarian.

Aunt Maude had a special affinity for Sally, which only grew stronger as Sally's problems developed. At Christmas she sent Sally boxes of children's books that had been withdrawn from her library's shelves. Some were worn, some torn; all were old-fashioned and filled with wonderful pictures. There were many years when she sent me nothing at all. As a very small child, I was quite hurt by this, but as I grew older my resentment turned to relief. "Aunt Maude feels close to Sally," Mother explained to me. That made my exclusion more bearable, for I didn't want to belong to their club. My father, Aunt Maude's nephew, was more upset than I was, fuming silently as I looked through her Christmas box in vain for a gift with my name on it. The memory is significant to me only because, as everyone's favorite, I was mystified that Aunt Maude preferred Sally.

I tried to be as different from my sister physically as I was temperamentally. Sally had terrible posture; I stood up very straight. Sally didn't bathe regularly; I got into trouble for using up the hot water whenever I showered. Sally wore pants; I wore dresses. Sally was fat; I was careful to stay thin. I never thought that there might be a fundamental difference between us—that Sally might have an illness, while I did not. My parents' inability to talk about her difficulties left me free to imagine that it might be the ketchup or the pink room or the reading that caused her problems. In 1959, my parents failed to sit down and explain what was happening to Sally. But how could they have made me understand? No one explained it to *them*.

t e n

....

Sally came home from Sheppard Pratt in the fall of 1960, my first year in junior high school. She was unmedicated— few of the remarkable psychopharmaceuticals that are commonly prescribed today were known then—but she saw a psychiatrist once a week for talk therapy. I remember that she seemed more alive than she had in years, but she still needed to retreat to her room, and fairly often. At first, Mother seemed chastened by Sally's illness. A combination of pity and something like fear kept her from criticizing Sally as vehemently as she had before, but after a few weeks, she couldn't help remarking on Sally's chronically erratic hygiene or her reclusive behavior.

In the hospital, Sally had been helped immensely, I realize now, for she could now fight back with righteous wrath, which made the new arguments between her and Mother longer and uglier. Almost every night, there would be a sudden uproar somewhere in the house. I couldn't study, sitting in my bedroom listening to it. One Sunday, walking home from church with Sally, I told her I hated her for the way she treated Mother. "You ruin everything," I said. Sally tried to argue her case with me, but I wouldn't listen. Finally she gave up. "You don't understand," she said. It was true. I didn't understand. I also didn't care if I understood or not. I just wanted Sally to disappear again so that life could be as pleasant as possible.

Sally remembers her year and a half in the hospital as a time of self-discovery. "I was distinguishing my true self from my fantasy self," she told me, "learning to like my real self, and getting to know myself as a person."

She, too, remembered our argument on the way home from church. "The reason I was fighting with Mother," she explained, "is that I was growing up. Apparently you thought I hated mother's guts, for some reason. I didn't hate her, I just didn't want her telling me what to do all the time."

Sally summed up the difference between her and me: "You were young—you hadn't started to teenage out, shall we say. You hadn't reached the age when you yourself were independent."

I loved it when Sally was on target, and this was one of those moments. For however independent I appeared to be, I was still a child, engaged in the tricky enterprise of feigning self-sufficiency so that I would be loved. I needed my mother's care, and I was not about to do anything to jeopardize my chances of getting it. Sally's presence made the house quake with animosity, so naturally I feared and loathed it.

When I "teenaged out" not long after, I began to see Sally's illness as a social liability, and my instinct to avoid her took on the creepy aspects of pack psychology. I wanted to have friends, *neat* friends, and I was afraid Sally's differentness would jeopardize my chances.

Sally was trying hard to reenter ordinary life. When she was released from Sheppard Pratt, she applied for admission to American University, nearby in Washington, and in the course of having her high-school credits sent to the admissions department discovered that the diploma she'd been awarded from Walsingham Academy was an "honorary" one. At the age of twenty-one, overweight and shy, she courageously enrolled in the local public high school to repeat her senior year.

When she graduated, she went to American University as she had planned. At first, she lived in the dormitory, but that went badly. Sally indignantly criticized her roommate for partying late and coming back to the dorm drunk, and the roommate retaliated by enlisting her friends to stand under their window at night and call Sally names. Sally moved back home before two weeks were out.

Sally was still in therapy with her psychiatrist, whom she saw once a week, but she remained unmedicated until her early thirties, when the manic-depressive side of her illness began to dominate and she was treated with lithium and other drugs. As long as she was living at home, in a relatively protected, if not stress-free, environment, she was able to function more or less normally. She was still withdrawn to a degree, and she wasn't able to make friends with great success, but she settled into a stable pattern of school and home. After the rocky period when she was first released from Sheppard Pratt, she and Mother found ways to accommodate themselves to one another, and there were few ugly fights.

A year or so after Sally returned, I began going out with a boy who was much too old for me. My parents allowed it, I think, mainly because they were not used to having to attend to me. I'd always been fine without supervision, and although by then I was showing signs of having problems myself, Mother and Daddy were so deeply involved with Sally's struggle that they simply ignored them. My grades were slipping, I went through several brief bouts of nausea so intense I couldn't keep meals down, and I had chronic insomnia. Now, at thirteen, I was seeing a college boy who was reading Ibsen and Salinger to me and talking about "physical needs."

He was a very clever young man from what is still called a "good" family—educated and well off. I was tall and looked older than I was. We met during summer vacation; fall came, and he went to the University of Virginia. I went into the eighth grade. He was surprised when he found out how young I was, but he apparently liked me enough to continue to visit, hitching rides from Charlottesville on weekends to see me.

Sally and Don were only three years apart in age, and it was natural for her to try to talk with him as a contemporary. Don would have none of it, ridiculing her behind her back and urging me to laugh at his impersonations of her. When he wrote to me he would send love to my mother and father, to the family dog, and then, in minuscule letters, he would add, "and hello to Sally."

Gradually, as Don pointed out Sally's ungainliness and made fun of her attempts to make herself attractive, I became ashamed of her.

e l e v e n

....

In spite of my efforts to disown Sally, I also couldn't help identifying with her. She was my parents' child, and so was I. We were in this together, and I must have subconsciously thought as much. Otherwise, I would never have felt so much sorrow on her behalf, or so much fear of turning out to be like her. As I grew up, I might have been able to describe her without impediment, to my psychiatrist or to my friends. My sister, myself: The revulsion I felt when I witnessed any of Sally's missteps was the flip side of a sympathy so intense I couldn't talk about it. I blocked out her pain, because, when I witnessed it, I felt it as my own.

My refusal to pay attention to Sally—or to the part of myself that felt like her—had exactly the predictable result. I was desperately unhappy. Every night, all through my adolescence, I would get into bed, turn out the light, begin to fall into a dream, and then, just as the dark enveloped me, I would start to cry.

Something was wrong, although I didn't know what— Mother's definition of depression.

As an ostensibly well-adjusted child, I was left to myself a lot, and, looking back, I realize I began to feel invisible. When allowed to date Don, the older boyfriend, I was pleased and flattered, but I was subliminally aware that I was out of my depth. I would have railed at my parents had they tried to prevent the romance, but hindsight tells me that that fight would have been as nothing compared to my confusing internal conflict. Eventually the relationship fell away of its own accord.

One night during the fall of my sophomore year in high school, after a date with a boy I hardly knew, I came home late to find Mother in a lather of anger. While Mother was screaming at me—"What do you mean you forgot to call? Don't you think about anyone but yourself?"—I shut the door of my bedroom and started to cry. My father was home, but he didn't come to my defense.

I wasn't sure if I was innocent or guilty. I hadn't done anything wrong, but I *had* forgotten to call. That seemed a tiny infraction in relation to my mother's rage. Couldn't she see how unhappy I was? I felt weary: It was too difficult for me to sort out the components of my downfall. I got up from the bed, went to my dresser, opened a box where I kept makeup and toiletries, and took out a razor blade. I looked at my left wrist very carefully and then began to make light, exploratory slices. Looking at the layers of skin, fat, and tissue, and noticing the firm round veins, I thought, This is *interesting!* I was so dissociated, I could have been cutting up a frog in biology lab.

The cuts weren't deep, but the veins quickly began to seep blood, and I was suddenly frightened. I had not exactly intended to kill myself. In fact, I don't remember thinking at all during this episode of self-destruction. It was as if an actress were playing my part, getting up from the bed, walking to the dresser . . .

I rushed into my parents' dark bedroom. "I cut my wrist," I said simply but with some urgency. There was activity as the light was turned on and a towel was wrapped around my wrist. Daddy was dressed in a flash. He told me to get in the car.

We drove all the way into Washington, to George Washington Memorial Hospital, where a young Indian doctor in the emergency room stitched me up and assured my father that he wouldn't report the "incident." He said the cuts weren't very serious. Not until just now, writing this, did I realize that if they had been, I might have died on the way to the hospital. Rather than call an ambulance, which would attract attention, my father had put me in the car. Rather than go to Arlington Hospital, where we might have run into someone we knew—after all, it was only ten thirty or eleven o'-clock at night—he had chosen to go where yet another family secret was likely to be safely kept.

Later that night, I was feeling much better. There is nothing like physical pain to take your mind off the trouble in your soul. No one said anything to me as I washed my face and went to bed, but the next day, my mother asked me if I wanted to see Sally's psychiatrist. I was aghast. After all the years I'd worked to make it clear that I was different, here she was suggesting that I needed psychiatric help—from Sally's doctor. "No!" I screamed. "I'm fine!" And I was, instantaneously—as fine as ever, that is.

From about that time until I went into therapy in a serious way at the age of thirty-two, I thought of suicide at least twice a year, sometimes for weeks on end. I couldn't imagine a future in which I would be happy. Whenever I achieved a semblance of equanimity, it would eventually erode under the pressure of my hidden conviction that misery would find me. I behaved as my parents did, pretending nothing was wrong, and I was usually able to succeed by dint of pure will. I was not Sally, I swore to myself. I wasn't *at all like* Sally. As long as I could maintain that conviction, I could keep up a good front. Sally had problems; she saw a psychiatrist. If I saw a psychiatrist, I reasoned, it would be tantamount to admitting that I had problems too. If I saw *her* psychiatrist, I would be in her boat, which, as far as I'd ever been able to see, was hardly protection against drowning. "Don't worry about me," I said earnestly. "I'm really fine."

Neither of my parents ever asked me to try to explain what had gone through my mind as I ran a razor blade over my wrist, and if they had, I wouldn't have known how to answer. Neither asked me if I was unhappy, or why. The only reaction was that my father went into a flurry of picture taking, as if to preserve a record of a daughter who might at any moment disappear. I have a number of yellowing slides of a slender, well-groomed, cheerful-looking fifteen-year-old who has white gauze wrapped around her left wrist.

t w e l v e

....

 We should have been taking pictures of Daddy, instead,
for a few months later, on New Year's Eve 1963, he died of a
heart attack.

We were all about to go out for the evening. Sally was going
to baby-sit for a family nearby, and I was getting ready for a
date. Daddy was polishing shoes in the utility room, which
doubled as his darkroom and workshop, and when he fell
there was a loud crash as the stool on which he'd been sitting
hit the hot-water heater. Our cocker spaniel began barking
frantically.

Mother, Sally, and I came out of our bedrooms, where we
were dressing, to see what had happened. I reached him first.
His eyes were closed and his face was bright red. He was
struggling for breath with loud, rasping gasps, but these
stopped after a minute or two. His face began to turn blue. I
held my hand under his nose, but I couldn't tell if he was
breathing. Then, to see if his heart was still beating, I put my
hand on his chest. This revived him momentarily—his mouth
opened and his body shook with a racketing inhalation of air.
I jerked so hard my head flew up and hit the workbench behind me. It was many years before I heard of cardiopulmo-
nary rescusitation, but when I did, I nearly fainted from the
sudden knowledge that if only I had kept pressing on my

father's chest, I might have kept him breathing. Instead, for almost a decade, I was sure my touch had killed him.

By this time Mother was at my side. I heard her saying he'd had a heart attack or a stroke. I ran to the telephone and called the operator, ordering an ambulance. Someone came on the line and said to keep him warm and support his head. I grabbed two coats from a closet, one to put over him and one to fold up as a pillow. Mother called a neighbor who was a doctor and begged him to come quickly. He lived less than two blocks away, but it was a quarter of an hour before he showed up. By that time, Daddy was dead, though I didn't know it. Then the ambulance screamed past the house, missing the address. I ran outside to catch it, wondering why Mother, kneeling at Daddy's side, was suddenly quiet.

Two attendants carried his body out to the driveway on a stretcher. I saw Mother climb into the ambulance after them, and they drove away. She didn't say a word to me. She just left. I have no idea where Sally was during all this turmoil. Neighbors were gathering, and I felt someone draw me close, hugging me. It was a girl who lived across the street whose father had died not long before. She was sobbing, but I was numb.

I walked into the house, into my parents' bedroom, and lost all strength in my legs. The adrenaline had run its course. My knees buckled, and I fell to the floor as if I'd fainted.

I don't know when Mother came home. I don't remember if she spoke to Sally and me. She told me twenty years later that it didn't occur to her at the time that we had suffered a loss that might have been on a par with hers. She knew she was devastated—her husband was the most important person in her life—but she didn't realize that we were too. "I guess it was pretty hard on you," she mused.

Mother had been given sleeping pills that night by a doctor at the hospital, and she handed out one each to Sally and me. I put the pill by my bedside and then turned off the light. I lay in the dark and looked out my window at the bare branches of the forsythia bush under the streetlight. Cars went by often—people were coming home from parties. There was a horn or two at midnight, but not much more, for most of the neighbors knew by now what had happened. I looked at the sleeping pill. I thought of the way both Sally and Mother had been immobilized earlier, when it was important to act, and I reasoned that I was the only one in the family capable of being strong. I had to hold myself together, I thought. That night I lay awake until morning, but I managed to sleep the next. The pill sat on my nightstand for more than a week, and then I threw it away. It was many years before I cried for my father, and after I began it was a long, long time before I could stop.

I never saw Mother cry, either, though I remember hearing Sally, in her room with the door shut, weeping quietly. I think she was the only one of the three of us who was remotely capable of facing life's pain. She had been in therapy for more than five years, and she had learned to pay attention to her emotions—at least to a degree: She said recently that it took her, too, many years to get over our father's death.

A family in shock, we never shared our grief, or tried to comfort one another. Only the dog pined for Daddy, howling and keening into the night—the only overt sign of mourning in the otherwise silent house.

At some point during the next few weeks, Mother stopped eating. For a month or two all I noticed was that she didn't talk. Before, I now realized, she had talked mostly to Daddy, in the mornings at breakfast as they read bits of the paper to each other, and in the evening over their old fashioneds—just one, never more—as they discussed his day at the office. She had never talked much with Sally, and it had been years since she and I had any serious conversation. Now she seemed to have nothing to say to us. One day I looked at her and saw that her clothes were much too large. She was using a safety pin to draw a thick dart in the waist of her skirt, and her blouse hung on her like a hospital gown. "Mama," I said, "You're so thin!"

"I know," she said. "Never mind."

I minded—I minded very much. Even though I wasn't receiving guidance from her, her mere presence was crucial to my well-being. Now I'd lost her attention completely.

Mother was not only grieving, she was in a panic about her financial future. She received some life insurance money, which she guarded assiduously and which eventually became the core of Sally's trust, and an annuity from the federal government, but she could not make ends meet. She had always been a great reader, so Lyn suggested she take the test for a job with the Arlington County library system. I remember the day she heard the results. She had aced the literary part, and had done well enough on the math to qualify with flying colors. No one was surprised but her. She held the letter in both hands, reading it over and over.

Within a month she started working at a small branch library. Like most of the college-educated women her age that we knew, she had stopped working after starting a family. When she and my father were first married, however, during the six years before Sally was born, she held various jobs. Although she was an English major at Vanderbilt, she became a social worker after graduating. It was practically the only vocation open during the Depression, and she loved it. She was curious about people, didn't have a snobbish bone in her body, and enjoyed her clients immensely. And working gave her stories to tell, such as the one about the woman who asked if it was possible to vulcanize a diaphragm, the way you fixed a rubber tire. Why? Mother asked her. "Oh, the baby bit a hole in it," the woman answered matter-of-factly.

A busy public library had characters of its own, and Mother quickly befriended them. Most of the other librarians were much younger than she, and their informality inspired her. She gradually became happy in a way I'd never seen. She had me cooking dinner, Sally washing dishes, both of us cleaning the house, and a regular paycheck coming in. After she retired, fifteen years later, she recalled this time as "the happiest years of my married life." I wasn't sure whether to remind her that her husband had died just before they began. Or that her younger daughter had been headed for another fall.

Sally, in contrast to me, seemed to find Mother's inattention positively bracing, and I'm sure she was glad, finally, to be indispensable at home. In any case, she somehow mustered reserves that no one knew she possessed. She continued in college, graduating in 1967. After Daddy died, Sally had offered to stop therapy in order to relieve Mother of the expense, and she continued to do well without it.

Sally majored in education because she thought she might want to teach, but after she observed some classes and told the instructors what she thought they were doing wrong, she was not allowed to do student teaching. Sally can be rigid about rules and regulations, and can't see situations in a multifaceted way, but I don't know to what extent this is a reflection of her personality or a manifestation of her illness. Her professors decided she was "too immature," and she now concurs in this assessment. "I should have kept my mouth shut," she said, and added, "I didn't have the patience to teach."

Instead of teaching, after graduading Sally applied for two clerks' positions with the federal government, and was offered both. The first acceptance came from the Department of Agriculture Library. She began working full-time, while continuing to live at home.

I was becoming desolate. Sometime toward spring, I began sneaking out to spend part of each night with my boyfriend, who lived just up the street. I would sleep soundly for a few hours, secure in his arms, and then walk back home before daybreak. It wasn't long before we decided to try lovemaking, and not long after that that I became pregnant.

My boyfriend was two years older than I was, and he wanted to get married. He seemed undaunted by the prospect of raising a child. I was barely hanging onto life, and I also knew that I was still a child myself. I decided to give the baby up for adoption.

I went away for the remainder of my pregnancy, staying in another part of the county at the house of a woman who rented rooms to student teachers. Her children were grown, her husband had recently died unexpectedly, and she and her elderly mother enjoyed sharing their large house with young people.

Whenever I was away from home I was happy, no matter the circumstances, and now I relished this sojourn with college girls, an industrious old lady whose lap was always overflowing with knitting projects, and a motherly woman who loved to cook. The house was filled with soul-nourishing smells and friendly chatter. The student teachers made me their pet, treating me with great affection. They were curious about what it was like to be pregnant, and they seemed surprised at my serious, studious nature. "How could such a nice girl be in your condition?" they would tease. "You must be faster than you look." I remember this period as one of the few times in my life I truly felt like anyone's little sister.

When it was time, I went to the hospital. The baby was born on January 30, 1965. I gave him up for adoption through the Barker Foundation in Washington, realizing, as I signed the papers relinquishing my rights, that I would never get over the loss.

I didn't tell Sally, fearing she would secretly gloat over my misfortune, and if she guessed, she has never said so.

Seventeen years after Daddy died, when Mother brought Sally home to live with her for the last time, a social worker at the mental health center asked her to write a short biography of Sally, in part to clarify details of her illness. Cleaning out the house after Mother died, I found the notebook in which she had outlined dates and events. "December 31, 1963—Bob died," she had penciled in, and after it, faintly, as if she were unsure that it could be true, she had added, "Sally did better than Peggy." I felt a curious sense of well-being. Wow, I thought. She noticed.

t h i r t e e n

···

Mother and I were no longer close. We had terrible fights during my late teens and early twenties, one of which I remember vividly. We were in the side yard, where I was mowing the lawn. Mother was dogging my steps, back and forth, back and forth, insisting that I return to college for my senior year. I kept shouting No! and, finally, as I turned the mower around, she slapped me across the face. She was that frustrated. Without stopping to think, I slapped her back. Shocked, she stared at me for several seconds before slowly backing away.

We were fighting about money, ostensibly—I had transferred from Connecticut College to a less expensive school, and Mother was threatening to cut me off if I transferred back, which I intended to do. When I told her to go ahead, that I wanted to take a year off and earn the money myself, she was furious. I only recently realized that the fight was grounded in something deeper that I didn't understand and, therefore, couldn't explain to her. The truth was that Sally had moved out of the house that year—1969—and I—unconsciously, of course—wanted to live there one more time as my mother's only child. If I took a job to pay for school, I would have to stay home to save money. After graduating, I would be off, on my own. I must have subconsciously felt that this was my last chance to cadge some of the mothering I'd missed since Sally's first breakdown.

I prevailed by dint of pure stubbornness, taking a job as a clerk-typist in the Africa Bureau of the Agency for International Development, where my father had worked the last few years of his life. I lived at home with Mother, and at work I felt like the daughter of all the engineers in my department, who had known my father well. It was a stultifying year, undemanding and wholly unsatisfying. Mother was preoccupied with Sally, who broke down almost immediately after leaving home, and we rarely spoke except about the daily business of groceries or schedules. My high-school friends were all away at college, and I was lonely and bored. The following summer, I knew there was no possibility that my pathetic regression could be prolonged without giving up all hope of a healthy life, but I knew it only in the most inchoate way. I used my savings to return to Connecticut College for my senior year, not because I particularly wanted to go but because I couldn't do anything else.

Sally had moved to an apartment in Maryland, where the Department of Agriculture library relocated that year. It was difficult for her from the start. After a hospitalization for depression, she returned to her apartment and lived there for three years, during which time she had a variety of misadventures with roommates, a spate of accidents with her car, and a series of fights with her landlady, who eventually evicted her. Sally left two cars, one of which she had damaged in an accident and the other she had bought for $60 and never driven, rotting in the apartment parking lot.

She began going in and out of hospitals with some frequency, usually suffering from a paralyzing depression brought on by anxiety and loneliness. She always returned to her job. Mother never talked to me about Sally's problems, nor did she attempt to share her own anxiety and exasperation. In fact, she hid Sally's breakdowns from me as if they might be catching. The result is that I am a poor witness to Sally's first years away from home. I only remember the strained weekend visits, when Sally stayed in her room except for meals. And I remember my mother murmuring something about Sally's wonderful boss, who always held her position for her and welcomed her back. This supervisor also switched her to part-time work when Sally decided to pursue a graduate degree in library science and kept her on a reduced schedule even after she dropped out of school. She knew that full-time work was more than Sally could handle. I know now that for the chronically mentally ill, such a supervisor is an anchor that keeps the patient moored in the community, as a contributing member of society. For the productivity lost, the savings are immense, for it costs many times more to subsidize a nonworking mentally ill adult than one who is allowed to participate to the extent of her abilities.

Back at college, I began to panic. I knew that I had to be away from home in order to grow, but I didn't know what I would do when spring came. I had majored in art because I was considered talented, but talent doesn't go far, and at twenty-one I lacked both the drive and the self-confidence to take my work as seriously as I should have. I was afraid of being sucked back into my depressed family—forever, as I saw it—but I was incapable of projecting myself, alone, into the future in any positive way. This would be true of my escapes forever: No matter how far away I was, I was in the thrall of my family as long as my feelings of love and aversion remained unexamined.

It must have seemed to me that marriage was the only excuse for not going back to Virginia, although I don't remember thinking it through. There was a boy I'd known when I was at Connecticut before who was as eager as I was to join our fortunes together, so I married him, the week before graduation. At the end of the summer Cliff and I set off for Seattle together, with all our meager possessions in our ice green

1961 Rambler, a gift from his grandparents.

Cliff was—is—fair-minded and egalitarian to a fault. He badgered me to do my best, to be serious about my work. He challenged me to be competent and independent in ways I never dreamed of trying. We both went to graduate school at the University of Washington, he for a Ph.D. in math, I for an M.F.A. in painting. The marriage might have worked had I been capable of facing up to my own psychological problems and doing something about them, but my defenses were still too strong for that.

In spite of Cliff's constant encouragement, my depressions were deepening. I continually thought of suicide and I honestly didn't know why. I simply couldn't see how to go on in life. I knew I needed some help, just to survive. I finally went to a therapist at the university for almost two years, the one who heard about my sister during our last, tear-drenched session. That should have been a turning point for me, but as I had always done before, I shut the door against thoughts that were too painful.

I eventually abandoned my marriage the same way I'd learned to abandon my family when interaction was too difficult or confusing for me, but I stayed in Seattle for six more years, teaching drawing and painting and exhibiting my own work at a gallery.

Although I felt established as a young artist in the city, I hated Seattle's dark and dreary winters, and I considered moving back to the East Coast many times. Whenever I did, I would become so anxious I would break out in hives. Twice I became so dizzy I nearly blacked out. There was no possibility of moving nearer to my family, if the thought of it made me sick. A painful awareness of my outcast state began to dawn on me. My absence from Virginia was my salvation, but it was also a penance—I felt exiled from my childhood home, hopelessly estranged from my only sister, and, in some perhaps negligible but nonetheless painful way, abandoned by my mother. I needed her to recognize my life—to second the motion, as it were. I needed it the way a small child does: Watch me, Mama!

To see my Mother, I had to go to Virginia, and if I went to Virginia, Sally came home too, at least on weekends. Sally would usually stay in her room half the day, Mother would begin to nag her to be more sociable, by evening they would be sniping at each other, and Sally would understandably retreat again after dinner. The next day would be the same. My presence seemed barely to matter.

Ever since I'd left home at eighteen I'd asked, even begged, Mother to visit me occasionally, but she wouldn't do it. "I can't leave Sally," was her answer to all invitations, from me or from her friends, many of whom had moved to such pleasant retirement and vacation spots as Southern California or Hawaii. Mother refused invitations from them even during the years when Sally was living away from home and Mother was under orders, as it were, by one doctor or another, to let her live her own life. She was too worried about what would happen if she left Sally alone, but I think she was also too depressed herself to make the effort. When she wasn't actively involved in caring for Sally, or in taking her to hospitals and mopping up after another crisis, she was still unavailable to me. "I can't leave Sally—she's doing so well," she would say. Or the opposite: "I can't leave Sally, she's feeling pretty rotten right now."

Some of Mother's attention to Sally's problems was by way of atonement for a lack of affection that she could do little to hide. But I know she loved Sally deeply, even if she didn't know it, with emotion that went far beyond affection. She did what she could for her daughter, and it was considerable. Mother did everything, in fact, but the one thing that might have helped most: seeing a therapist of her own. I encouraged her to get help, for I began to see that her relationship with Sally was based on a twisted symbiosis, oriented around one crisis after another, that kept them both entangled but angry and unsatisfied. Mother refused. "There's nothing wrong with me," she would say angrily.

"Therapy isn't to *fix* you, Mama. It's to *help* you. It's something you do because you *deserve* it, not because you owe it to anyone else."

"I deserve some peace and quiet," she'd say. "That's all I ask."

When she first learned she had high blood pressure, she was surprised, for she was slim and fit, but she was also aware that she had too much on her mind. When Sally was tested for her medication, her blood pressure was always normal. "Of course it's normal," Mother said bitterly. "What's *she* got to worry about? Wish *I* could be a lily of the field."

"So try to be a lily of the field," I answered. She shrieked at me then, screaming about how easy it was for me to say that, about how she would be the one to pick up the pieces when Sally fell apart. It was true—I wouldn't be there. But I felt Mother could do just as well by Sally, if not better, were she to learn to worry less. Anxiety is contagious. Hers was crippling, both to herself and to us.

Mother kept a fearful, paralyzed vigil and, what is more poignant, it was for the most part unconscious. She was always waiting for the next breakdown, even when she thought she was ignoring Sally, letting her "live her own life." She was caught in a cycle that began with relief, when Sally was just out of the hospital and doing well. Next she would try to forget about Sally for a while in order to enjoy her own interests—working, reading, going to the theater with friends. Then guilt would set in, followed closely by apprehension. That would usually prove an accurate predictor of the next disaster. After an exhausting spate of rescue work, the cycle would begin again.

Mother kept the worst from me. "Sally was in the hospital again," she would say after the episode was over. Only twice did she talk with me about Sally's problems as they were occurring. When, once, Sally became so discouraged about her life that she tried to commit suicide, she was found by her roommate just in time to save her life. Mother told me about it only because she was undone by the response of one of her closest friends, who said, "Poor Sally. Too bad she didn't succeed." Mother was horrified. Hours later, when she asked me how anyone could be so heartless, she still sounded shocked.

"I don't know, Mama," I answered. I didn't tell her I'd just thought the same thing. Sally's life seemed hopeless to me—chaotic, all but friendless—and I had often felt suicidal myself. I couldn't understand how Sally kept going.

The other discussion came a few years later, when Sally was hospitalized for severe depression. "Write her a letter," Mother urged me, and I did. I told Sally that I'd been terribly depressed many times, that I didn't have much insight about it or how to get better, but that I knew from experience that time would come to her aid.

"Sally told me you wrote to her and that it made her feel better," Mother said during our next telephone call, "but she wouldn't show me the letter." She was both touched that I had written and hurt to be left out of her daughters' confidence. I knew, though, that she wouldn't understand the kind of black depression that sent Sally to the hospital and caused me to feel suicidal. If she ever knew she was depressed, she didn't admit it, at least to us.

Aside from these exceptions, Mother took Sally's problems on alone. She expected me to be grateful, but her thoughtfulness had the effect of frustrating and infuriating me. I exhorted her to stop keeping bad news secret from me, for whether she told me or not, I would begin to sense when something was up. For many years, I knew almost to the day each time Sally was hospitalized. Perhaps I could tell from Mother's tone of voice over the long-distance lines. Perhaps her calls were less frequent, or more. Whatever the reason, I would feel it in my bones. It would begin with general anxiety. I couldn't concentrate on my work. I would have trouble sleeping. Eventually I would wonder if Sally might be sick again. She always was. I remember telling friends that my sister and I were weirdly connected, despite the dearth of communication between us. When I criticized Mother for trying to keep me in the dark, she said "I want you to be happy. At least *one* of us can be happy."

Happy? I thought. Who can be happy? Does she mean me? "It makes me feel like I'm not part of the family, Mother," I said.

"What's wrong with that?" she said. "Thank the Lord for small favors."

SOMEHOW I was able to persuade Mother to come to my graduate exhibition when I finished my M.F.A. degree. I picked her up at the Seattle-Tacoma airport and drove her to my apartment. Cliff and I had separated, but we were still good friends, and he liked Mother, so I invited him over for dinner. She was in her expansive form. "Isn't this apartment of Peggy's darlin'?" she asked him rhetorically, when he arrived. I smiled—I was so pleased she liked it! Then she said, "It reminds me of some of the dumps Bob and I lived in when we were first married." Whereas I once would have allowed such a remark to pass, I now found it insupportable. I told her clearly that her comment was insulting and that it hurt my feelings. "Don't be so sensitive," she shrugged. "I didn't mean anything by it." In fact, she was envious. She loved the apartment, which although old was high ceilinged, spacious, and sunny. Many years later (which was as quickly as these things worked themselves out in our family), she told me that when she saw my place she had been seized with the desire to sell her house and move into an apartment in Washington. "It reminded me of when your father and I were young and penniless," she said. "And carefree."

The visit was difficult for both of us. She wanted to be allowed to guess which paintings were mine in the thesis show, but after searching for fifteen minutes, she returned to my side and said she couldn't find them. She hadn't seen any paintings of mine for a few years, and she wasn't prepared for the abstract works facing her. When I pointed them out, she actually jumped back a step. "But those are so angry!" she said. They weren't angry at all, but they were large—five feet high and seven wide—and their colors were vivid and hot—reds, violets, brilliant golds. They were ambitious paintings for me—I might have called them "powerful" if I'd been writing my own critique—but they were joyful. "They're so aggressive," she insisted. "They make me nervous."

When we left the gallery, she was quiet as we walked. Waiting for a light to change, she noticed two dowagers on the opposite curb. "Those women look nice," she said firmly. I looked at the two ladies, dressed handsomely in their anonymous suits and sensible shoes. "Very nice," she repeated with satisfaction. Mother was in an unfamiliar place, with her suddenly unfamiliar daughter, so she seized on the most conventional sight she could find. There was nothing challenging there.

I was disgusted and furious that she could find fault with the few things I had—my apartment, my paintings—and be attracted instead to mediocrity. Now I'm older, and I pity a vibrant, highly intelligent, open-minded woman who clung to the commonplace as if her equilibrium depended on it.

In the twenty years between the day I left for college and her death, Mother traveled to see me four times. In the twenty-four years she lived after my father died, she took only two vacations for herself—one to New England to visit old friends and a short trip to Nashville for her fiftieth college reunion.

fourteen

....

In the summer of 1979, I moved to New York. I was afraid
of being just a few hours from Arlington, but my unconscious
need to resolve my feelings about my family, I believe, drove
me back east. Like many people who can't cope with a disabled family member, I felt guilty most of the time. Whenever
I was happy, I was soon to be almost rigid with anxiety. I was
sure I didn't deserve to be happy, or to strive for my goals,
and I was, therefore, convinced each time I succeeded in meeting one of them that something would happen to destroy my
achievements. I would often harden my heart—sometimes
consciously, sometimes not—trying to forget about both
Mother and Sally, but that only ensured that I would eventually dissolve in worry, and, later, in penitence.

Occasionally I made an attempt to be a better sister to Sally
and a better daughter to my mother by becoming more involved, spending more time with Sally when I was home visiting in Arlington, and going there more often. I felt I had to
atone for what I saw as my unearned freedom, but my efforts
usually left me shaken.

Sally was still living in her own apartment, and occasionally, when I was in Arlington for a visit, I would drive her
home on my way back to New York. Usually I would just
drop her off, making up some excuse for not going in. Sally

never pressed me—for anything. She had an innate sense of my limits.

One time, I asked if I could come up to use the bathroom. She enthusiastically said yes and offered to show me some crocheting projects on which she was working. We climbed the stairs to her place, on the second floor, and she opened the door.

Sally had always been sloppy, so when I saw her living room I thought of it as just one step—albeit a large one—beyond what I already knew of her habits. The apartment smelled. The mattress of the sofa bed where she slept was bare except for a few grimy, twisted sheets and blankets. Dirty clothes were kicked into piles, with a few items strewn about. In the kitchen, bags of garbage spilled onto the floor. The countertops were sticky with spilled food.

Sally pointed out skeins of yarn piled on the chairs and tables, and on the floor. Everywhere I looked there was another bundle of bright acrylic. She described the ponchos she was busy crocheting and the ones she was planning for the future. When she was finished, she would have a matching poncho outfit for every day of the week—or month, or year, perhaps, from the look of it. There was going to be an Easter Egg Poncho, for example—white for the nougat, brown edging for the chocolate, and colors for the fruit bits. She had bought fabric to sew pants to go with each of the ponchos.

If I hadn't been so terrified—of Sally's strangeness, of my family's depression, of becoming sick myself—I might have had the objectivity to think, This is too much, even for Sally; something is wrong. But I couldn't consider Sally's behavior with any objectivity, because I didn't know where to draw the line between Sally's condition and my own. I was no ace housekeeper—was I really so different from her? Instead, I reacted viscerally and did what I'd always done: I tried to ignore what was staring me in the face. I decided not to smell the fetid air. I decided not to hear Sally as she mentioned that someone was trying to break into her mailbox. I went into a holding pattern, vamping until I could leave, making polite noises, pretending to admire the yarns of many colors, waiting to make my getaway.

Two weeks later, Sally was in the hospital, and Mother was demanding angrily how I could have failed to tell her about Sally's apartment—*didn't I see* she was getting sick?

I hadn't seen. It was all the same to me, for my denial prevented me from distinguishing between Sally's day-to-day disorganization and the chaos that clearly signaled a shattered inner state. I didn't want to see that Sally was getting sick. And, too, I didn't want to add to my mother's misery, for she had begun to seem as depressed as Sally.

Although its condition was a far cry from the turmoil of Sally's apartment, Mother's house was also deteriorating badly. The tile floors were cracked, the walls were cobwebbed, the kitchen cabinets were coated with a layer of grease. At first, Mother seemed surprised when I pointed out that the place seemed to be falling apart. She seemed as if she hadn't noticed its frayed, untended look. Then she became angry. She blamed Sally and me for not helping her, but I felt that she should hire a cleaning person from time to time. She could afford it, I knew, but that wasn't the issue. "I wouldn't want a stranger to see this place," she finally said in disgust.

My visits were so painful for me by now that I either drank while I was there—it didn't take much to numb me, because I hardly drank otherwise—or I would take a Valium to calm my nerves.

In 1979, Sally was admitted to Spring Grove State Hospital in Maryland, almost paralyzed by depression. Before long, she requested electroconvulsive therapy, or shock treatments. She had had them once before, and while they had the bad effect of erasing some of her short-term memory, they were effective in treating her profound despair.

I went to Arlington, and Mother asked me to go and see

her. I wrapped up a lunch of cold fried chicken and potato salad to take to her. When I arrived at the hospital, Sally was in her room. At first, an attendant went to get her, but after a while he returned and asked if I could follow him to her room instead. I found her sitting on the edge of her bed, groggy from sleep. She managed to say "Hi, Peggy," but then she lapsed into silence, rocking slightly and looking at the floor. I felt immediately that she would prefer to be alone, but I couldn't be sure if I was being sensitive to her needs or to my own desire to flee. When I gave her the fried chicken, one of her favorite foods, she thanked me and began to eat, but she was so far from the present that she hardly seemed to know what she was doing. At one point, working on a piece of breast meat, she bit through the rib bones. I expected her to spit them out, but she went on chewing. She crunched for a while, and then swallowed. I thought of taking the chicken away from her, but instead I said, "Don't eat the bones, Sally." She made a murmuring sound, *hmmm*, to show she had heard me, which I appreciated. I waited until she finished before leaving. When I got to my car, I sat on the front seat and left the door open, leaning my head down between my knees. I wasn't sure if I was going to faint or vomit. I did neither. Instead I cried, sobbing and shaking for a minute until I collected myself.

In 1980, after another severe breakdown, when she was committed to a hospital by police, Sally was forced to retire on disability from the library. For almost two years after losing her job, she lived in various apartments, halfway houses, and rented rooms in the Washington area. Finally, in 1982, Mother decided that Sally had exhausted her possibilities for independent life. Sally had tried living alone, living with roommates, living in a group home with constant supervision, and living in a rented room. None of the places had suited her, and she would either leave them or be asked to leave by her landlords. Mother had moved her so many times she was worn out from the effort, and although she hated having Sally under her roof, she thought it might be easier to keep track of her, to help her remain stable, if she moved home.

It was a move that every doctor and social worker who had ever seen Sally inveighed against. They seemed to give Mother no credit for the immense amount of genuine help she offered. Instead, they told her repeatedly that Sally would "never grow up" if she kept "meddling." They made her feel that she was poison for her elder daughter. So whenever Sally herself asked to move back, Mother would dutifully explain that the doctors said it wasn't a good idea.

It was true that the relationship between them was never a healthy one. Sally was continually in a rage with Mother, even as she needed her desperately. "Mother never let me be me," she often said. "She never let me be independent." When I reminded her that it was she who entreated Mother to allow her to move back home, she answered, with utter guilelessness, "That was because she said I couldn't."

Back in Mother's home, Sally was relatively stable, but she was also depressed. There were times when she was so low she had trouble functioning on even a rudimentary level. She would shuffle when she walked, her hands shook, so that food would fall from her fork as she ate, and she would go to her room to sleep whenever she could. Some of her problems were the side effects of medication, but others were due to depression. It was impossible to determine how the cycle of depression began. The drugs, particularly lithium, seemed to make Sally listless, but when she rested, her inactivity ultimately seemed to feed the depression even more. Except when mania made her wildly industrious, Sally was characteristically lazy around the house, making it even harder to discern the causes of her withdrawals. Mother nonetheless began granting Sally more privacy, allowing her to stay in her room to rest for long periods, although she always encouraged her to come out when old friends stopped by, or when I was home and neighbors would invite us to drop in.

Some mentally ill people, tortured by their illness, terrorize their families with violent rages. Others are tormented by voices and can't help talking to them aloud. Sally was never that sick in my presence. Embarrassing non sequiturs were her worst social fault. Once when I was visiting, we were sitting in the backyard of a couple who'd asked us over for drinks. They were old friends: Ed had worked with my father and given me my first job. He and Pat, his wife, had a son who'd been a friend of mine in high school. The talk was pleasantly desultory, meandering from politics to family news and back again. Sally was deep inside herself; she hadn't said much. Then, during a lull in the conversation, she seemed to wake up. "Mother," she said, breaking in abruptly, "Dad and I slept together when I was little, didn't we?"

I remember the bright pink of some impatiens that spilled over a low rock wall, and the clink of a piece of ice in my glass. Mother just stared at Sally, but before she could say anything, Sally went blithely on. "Remember? On Saturdays sometimes, when he took an afternoon nap on the living room couch? I'd lie down and go to sleep too." Everyone laughed, nervously. Mother was mortified, but she eventually learned if not to shrug at such interjections at least to react mildly. They were rare enough.

Occasionally Sally and I were able to enjoy one another's company. Where Mother hated the holidays, especially Christmas, which she found both depressing and burdensome, Sally and I loved them, in spite of their inevitable disappointments. Every year I would wear myself out buying gifts, hoping to bring some cheer to Arlington. Sally loved it. "Peggy always makes things happy," she announced one year. All that Mother could see was the work involved. If I cut holly to make a wreath for the front door, she would try to discourage me because she would have to take it apart again after New Year's to save the circular balsawood form Daddy had carved thirty years before. I gave up trying to buy a Christmas tree; it was too much for Mother to have to carry it outside when the season was over. Sally would probably have done it if asked, but that was beside the point. Mother would have to nag her to do it, and that by itself was too much trouble. Often Sally and I could ignore Mother's scroogery and just go ahead and celebrate, and Mother would usually go along with us, making a delicious meal for Christmas dinner and saying, at the end of the visit, that she had enjoyed all the fuss after all.

Most of the time, though, it was Sally's unhappiness with which I identified. Her illness had isolated her and made it impossible for her to fulfill her dreams; while my life was a social whirl by comparison, I somehow felt alone. Whatever I did I did halfway, while the part of me that identified with Sally—that *was* Sally—waited for the ax to fall. That part insisted that I was sick, too, and didn't deserve to succeed or embrace life fully. No matter what my accomplishments, I had the feeling my life was a charade.

In 1981, I began therapy in earnest. One morning I described a dream to my psychiatrist, Fiona: I was riding on a crosstown bus that stopped to pick up passengers just before entering Central Park. A small black child climbed on the bus with his grandmother. He was retarded and crippled with some sort of palsy, and the other riders on the bus startled and stared as he lurched down the aisle to a seat at the rear. I felt my heart ache as the stylish passengers grimaced and recoiled. Then, as the bus entered the park, the boy began to sing in a high soprano voice, clear as a bell. The others sat absolutely still, listening to him, deeply moved by the beauty of his song.

"I think that child is you," Fiona said.

I considered her suggestion, but while it appealed to me, it didn't quite ring true. Then, suddenly, I knew the little boy's identity. "No," I answered, "It's Sally."

FROM TIME to time I would try to be more of a sister to Sally, but I was so inexperienced that I didn't know what to expect of her. I never knew whether to treat Sally as a child or an adult, as a dependent or someone capable of taking responsibility for herself. I had little sense of her internal life, except its changeability. It was impossible to be on intimate terms with someone whose emotions were constantly in flux. But the larger reason I was at a loss to know how to talk with her was that I had never wanted to be privy to her thoughts and feelings—I needed the distance that ignorance automatically provided—and, therefore, didn't know her well enough to gauge her reactions to what I said.

I could never seem to talk with her as an equal. Conversations were one-sided, with me asking questions and Sally telling me what she was doing. Or, more often, there was an awkward silence. She almost never asked me about myself in any way that seemed appropriate. And her questions about other subjects left me tongue-tied. "Tell me, Peggy," she might begin in a hearty voice. "When do you think it's all right to have sex with a man?" Taken aback, I would reel with the implications of the question. Should I ask her why she wanted to know? Should I talk to her about birth control and venereal disease? Maybe the question was as out-of-the-blue for her as it was for me, and she simply wondered what I thought, on a purely philosophical level. Should I tell her what I really thought?

On that occasion, as it happened, Sally was setting me up. She was involved with an ex-convict who was also attending the mental health center, and Mother had been arguing against her pursuing a romantic relationship with him. By asking me in a seemingly innocent, objective tone about a vaguely defined subject, she got me to answer in a way that bolstered her side of the fight. After hemming for a minute or so, I said awkwardly, "I think it's an individual thing, Sally." We were in the backyard, where I was putting away gardening tools. Sally walked into the house, told Mother what I'd said, and Mother, without realizing that I knew nothing about the ongoing conflict, thought I'd told Sally, in effect, that she should do what she wanted. Later that day, after weathering one of Mother's blistering attacks, I repacked my weekend bag and headed back to New York early.

I can remember only one conversation from these years in which my part was natural. I was driving Sally to a doctor's appointment, when she asked how large my paintings were. I was instantly elated. This was a question I could answer, and it was about my life, without being too personal. I told her they were fairly large, at least five feet in one dimension.

She paused, then said, "They must be hard to transport with your little Volkswagen bug."

I was flabbergasted, thrilled to be recognized by Sally as an independent other and to have her consider me and my life in a thoughtful, sympathetic way.

"I have to borrow a friend's truck!" I exclaimed, with an excitement that must have puzzled her.

f i f t e e n

....

As the years passed and my therapy progressed, I gradually became less afraid to examine my feelings about both my sister and my mother. These seemed to ricochet between anguished sympathy and cool disdain—between love and hate. One day I would cry to think of their unhappiness, and another, I would cry for myself. There were times I wished I could do right by them, and times I wished they would disappear. The latter wish always shocked me, and I could tell it only to Fiona. I was even more bewildered when Mother said, on two occasions, that she'd thought of getting a gun, killing Sally, and shooting herself. She said it in a light, offhand way, as usual, but I think the plan had crossed her mind and that in a moment of despair she had taken it seriously.

She was in bad physical pain with arthritis, and the constant torture was not only depressing, it made taking care of Sally even more onerous. Mother was trying to be more tolerant of Sally, and toward the end of her life I often saw her hold her tongue rather than criticize small faults. Sally took full advantage, pouring ketchup on her eggs in the morning, or "resting" in her room whenever she wanted to. As Mother calmed down, the tension between them lessened, even though there continued to be many times when they seemed as angry, resentful, demanding, and depressed a duo as ever.

But even when they were at odds, they were also enmeshed with one another, in what I saw as a sick symbiosis.

Each caught my heart at different times, but as my own depression began to lift, my feelings about Sally changed. I probably stopped identifying so much with her sadness, and, perhaps unfairly, I gradually became impatient with her. She, however, had not changed. She couldn't live with or without Mother. She seemed always to be caught in a cycle of high optimism and resigned regret. Eventually, my sympathies shifted, but not only because of my perceptions of Sally. I began to take the other side because, in a way, I was preparing myself to take Mother's place.

The prospect of doing that, however, was enough to send me back into despair. I watched Mother as she allowed Sally's illness to define her life, using it as an excuse for all that she could not bring herself to do. I recognized the same tendency in myself and hated the thought that I might do the same. Mother was depressed and exhausted, and worry had leeched her of her natural buoyancy. She was too stubborn and too proud to get help for herself, and I finally stopped exhorting her to try therapy, but I resolved to do things differently when my turn came.

IN THE spring of 1981, I invited Sally to visit me in New York. I was working full-time for a news magazine, so I took a day off and invited her to come for a long weekend. I was back on my feet after recuperating from mononucleosis, which I'd contracted the summer before, at the end of my first year in the city. When I was sick, I could hardly walk to the corner grocery without having to sit down on someone's front stoop and rest. Six months later, I went out to dinner with a friend and noticed I felt strange. I relished my ability to walk up subway stairs without clinging to the banister, and then I realized that I was healthy again. I'd forgotten what it felt like.

I had been teaching art history part-time at a university, without a contract, when I got sick. I had no health insurance, no sick leave, no disability pay, no vacation time. When I was well enough to work again, my savings were gone, and I was insecure in a way I had never been before, from chronic ill health. I began looking for a job that would provide me with some benefits, and found one at *Newsweek* magazine, where I began working in late 1980 as a letters correspondent, composing replies to critical letters from subscribers. I worked in a large, sunny room with eighteen witty, friendly others. The conversation at the office was buoyant and silly, serious and literary, and always entertaining. Our supervisor was a brilliant woman who did her best to teach me how to put a paragraph together, and her encouragement gave my life a dimension that had long eluded me.

I'd wanted to write since I was a teenager, but didn't have the nerve. After my father died, I'd submitted a poem about his funeral to the high-school literary magazine. I thought it was good then, and a decade ago, when I happened to come across it in a box of mementos, I thought it was even better than I'd remembered. When it had been rejected, I was not just disappointed, I was devastated. Many things had come easily to me, without bringing me much satisfaction, and then, at the lowest point of my life, I failed at the one endeavor I then cared about. The job at *Newsweek*, however lowly in the eyes of the higher-ups on the masthead, made me swell with a sense of accomplishment. It was probably the crutch that enabled me to hobble into therapy at last.

For two years, I continued to paint, spending hours in my uptown studio, a geographical error far from other artists in Manhattan. I had been intensely lonely there since I'd rented it, and my work reflected my unhappiness. It became weak, almost pretty, with pastel colors and repetitive structure, and I despised it. After I began at *Newsweek*, the contemplative side of my personality all but disappeared for a while, as I enjoyed the healing company of the people around me and the challenge of new work. My paintings reproached me from the walls of the studio, making it even harder to go there. Eventually, I gave up my lease and moved my canvasses to storage.

At the time Sally came to visit, I was physically well and happy in the new job. But I hardly felt secure as a writer, and I was tortured by the loss of both the act of painting and confidence in my work. I felt strong enough to propose the weekend, but in retrospect I see that it was probably too soon for me. I was still working out too many of my own problems.

I picked Sally up at Port Authority Friday evening. As we rode the subway to my house on the Upper West Side of Manhattan, she seemed nervous, but no more so than other out-of-towners confronted with the filthy, graffiti-ridden trains that were standard in New York then. She was equally uneasy on the crowded streets. When we finally got to my apartment, she was visibly relieved. "It's beautiful!" she exclaimed happily. "I didn't think it would be so homey." I was living on half a shoestring, and much of my furniture had come from the street, but she very sweetly found it all delightful. She set about taking pictures of each room. Before she went to sleep that night on the sofa bed in my living room, she said that she would *love* an apartment like mine. "It's what I've been dreaming of," she said. She repeated this the next morning, and again several times each day. As she snapped a picture of my dining room table, a piece of unfinished furniture I'd bought used for twenty dollars, she told me it was just what she had been looking for.

I had planned the weekend carefully: pizza the first night, a matinee of *Annie* on Saturday and dinner at a friend's house afterward. We were going to take a trip to the Bronx Zoo on Sunday with a friend from *Newsweek*, a ferry ride to Staten Island the next day to see a herpetological zoo, and then dinner at the house of another friend. Tuesday morning, on my way to work, I would put her in a cab to the bus station. I wanted to show her a good time, and I also wanted to avoid the kind of sitting-around-doing-nothing that so depressed me at Mother's house. In my ruthless planning, however, there was no time for Sally to rest each day.

Before the visit I thought that being out and about would keep us on a casual, cheerful plane, but I soon learned that being indoors was not the primary cause of the trapped feeling I experienced in Arlington.

The first night, Sally looked angry when I ordered a small pizza for us at a neighborhood hangout, even though I assured her that we could never eat one of the larger ones. "I could," she said firmly, and sat with pursed lips for the twenty minutes that ticked by as we waited for the meal.

"I eat here often, Sally," I tried to persuade her. "Trust me." She couldn't relax until the waiter set down a two-inch-thick, supper-plate-size pie before us. Sally exclaimed happily, "You're right!" I had forgotten how important food was to her. She was unable to chat, to rise above her anxiety, as long as there was doubt in her mind that she would be adequately fed. As usual, she ate in silence, concentrating on her meal, but when we were done she said several times, "That sure wasn't what I'd call a 'small' pizza!"

I was grateful to my friends April and Mary Joan for their invitations to meals. I knew that they would make Sally comfortable, and I also knew that I would not be uneasy around them. The friend from work, Alison, was someone I didn't know well, and I felt somewhat shy about the trip to the zoo with her. "Don't talk about personal things when we're with Alison," I instructed Sally. "I haven't known her long, and I work with her, so I'd prefer to be a little formal for now." As if I had said the opposite, Sally began talking about an old boyfriend as soon as we sat down to our picnic lunch at the zoo. I knew some things about this man that were fairly dicey, and I was in agony until I could change the subject. When I got home, I told Sally I was angry.

"I don't tell you how to talk to *your* friends," Sally argued.

"This isn't your friend, Sally."

"I consider Alison a friend," she said indignantly.

I let the subject drop, hoping the incident was just a misunderstanding.

The weekend slowly unraveled. At Mary Joan's house, Sally told her how much she had enjoyed the meal. "I'd like to come see you again, if I may," she went on brightly. Mary Joan answered that that would be fine. Sally continued, "I'd like to visit Peggy more often, too, but she needs her space." I held my breath. "I *love* Peggy," she said, with what I could only read as manipulative, phony fervor. "She's a fabulous sister." Mary Joan looked at me with sympathy.

On the way back to my apartment that night, Sally asked how much hotel rooms cost in New York.

"Why?" I asked.

"Well, if I stayed in a hotel when I came back, I wouldn't be in your hair," she said.

At the snake zoo on Staten Island, we got to talking about the family. It was there that Sally said, "Everything was fine with Mother and Dad and me until you came along." I was so taken aback I thought I'd misheard her and asked her to repeat what she'd said. She said it again, and I was dumbstruck, but I sensed Sally wasn't pointing her finger at me so much as simply describing her own life. The Peggy she was telling her story to wasn't exactly the Peggy she blamed for her ruined childhood.

Later that night she told me she dreamed of starting a halfway house of her own—a project that had consumed her during her last manic attack. I was exasperated that she would even think of it again.

"Why don't you just take care of yourself, Sally," I answered bluntly.

Sally was appropriately offended, and I watched for several minutes as she collected her thoughts.

"You told Mother you'd always look after me," she said at last.

That was true. I'd said it many times, whenever Mother worried about what would happen to Sally after she died. "Yes, I did," I admitted.

With forced politeness, Sally ground out the words through clenched teeth, "I appreciate your concern."

But? I thought.

"But I'll have you know," she began, using a locution she favors when she feels wrongly accused, "I do not need your help."

"Great!" I said with hearty sincerity, if also some disingenuousness. I was delighted with the loophole in my contract, and I hoped Sally would drop the subject.

I was beginning to appreciate Mother's frustration, and I noticed that I was as ineffective as she was at getting Sally to do my bidding. I couldn't persuade Sally to brush her teeth—"I will," she kept saying—and after two days they were thickly coated. I had noticed she didn't take her medicine on time, and when I reminded her, she scowled at me. Now she was telling me she didn't need my help. I was angry, thinking that if no one badgered her she would fall apart at the seams. I think now that the nagging I did was my own problem. It was up to her to make herself attractive, to take her medicine, to live her own life. And, as Sally would say during a later breakdown, "It's the inner me that counts." She was only with me for the weekend, and I could have been more tolerant. But I was trying so hard, and now I was furious that she would presume to criticize me.

"You want to feel like the benevolent one," Sally accused me, with eerie acuity. She was angry, too, and I could tell she was drawing on years of pent-up resentment. "And you want to be *thanked* all the time. If you wanted to be equals, that would be another story."

"I'd love to be equals, Sally," I said.

Sally cut me off before I could deliver my reasons why that was impossible. "You think I'm not able to take care of myself," she said, possibly hoping, or even expecting, that I would contradict her.

I was in the habit of being ruthlessly honest with Sally, partly because I refused to mislead her and partly because I was sorting out my own feelings with my psychiatrist, and that made dissembling difficult. I was also involved in my own brand of denial, which meant that I could not treat Sally with the kindness and tact I would use with a disabled person. I had no perspective on Sally's half of the conversation—I wasn't able to take her part in any way—and not much understanding of my own, either. "That's right," I answered unsparingly. "You're not able to take care of yourself."

The evening was shot, and the rest of the weekend seemed unsalvageable. Sally, to her credit, kept trying. *Annie* was enjoyable, but when we went to a coffee shop near the theater after the show, Sally suddenly began talking about her old boyfriend again. "I was so glad when he broke my cherry," she said in an offhand tone of voice.

"Sally!" I hissed, stopping her short. I looked around to see if anyone had heard her. No one was near us. I was as shocked by her language as I was by her talking about sex in public. I think now that she probably had no one to talk to about adult matters. She certainly wouldn't have confided in Mother, and she had few girlfriends. She had talked to *someone* about sex, obviously, and their language had become her language. Her expression, which seemed raw to me, was perhaps simply her brand of euphemism, the way I would say "sleep with" to mean "have sex."

As we rode to April's on the subway, I tried to "make

nice," but Sally understandably was having none of it. But by the time we had been in April's apartment for an hour or so, she warmed up. As we were sitting down to dinner, Sally mentioned her "If I Were" poems. We asked her to remember a few, and we were both struck by their charm. We were transfixed as she recited one after another in a sweet, lilting voice, giving the titles and pausing a few seconds after each one. "A Little Seahorse," she began.

> If I were a little seahorse
> I'd be the seafairies' steed
> And they would ride me in and out,
> Among the green seaweed.
>
> And down the faces of coral cliffs,
> Above the waving anemones' branches,
> And finally home to my seashell stable,
> At the seafairies' undersea ranches.
>
> Into my boxstall I would go,
> Curl my tail 'round my hitching rail,
> Eat a nosebag full of oats,
> And drink sea milk from a seashell pail.
>
> Then I'd close my soft brown eyes,
> And dream the night away,
> Waiting for the dawning
> Of a bright new blue sea day.

Then, "A Weed":

> If I were a weed, I know where I'd hide:
> In a daffodil bed, so deep and so wide
> That no peeping eye
> Of a weeder nearby
> Would me espy.

Yet even if one did see me,
My roots would still remain,
Hidden away in the daffodil spray;
And I would bloom again.

"A Marble Bust":

If I were a marble bust,
I'd sit happily,
Contemplating others while
They're contemplating me.

"A Little Butterfly":

If I were a little butterfly,
I'd fly from flower to flower,
Sipping up the bright dew drops
At every lovely bower.

And after I had finished this,
I'd flutter everywhere,
Drinking in all sorts of sights,
While high up in the air.

"A Flower":

If I were a flower,
How sad I would be!
I'd be spied and
Plucked up speedily.

They'd put me in a lovely vase,
But, alas, away from my garden place,
I'd die!
So I
Would rather be
A little tree.

"A Pen":

> If I were a pen,
> I'd write now and then,
> But never give out of ink.
> Never skip, never trip,
> Never cause hearts to sink.

"A Paintbrush":

> If I were a paintbrush,
> How happy I'd be!
> For paint covers things very speedily.
> Such as mistakes.
> It takes
> A person who is very sneaky
> To play this game of hide and seeky.

"A Budget":

> If I were a budget,
> I would be
> All worked out so carefully
> That no one would complain of me.

And finally, "A Worm":

> If I were a worm, I'd keep away
> From those little boys who are fishing,
> 'Cause I can see by the looks on their faces
> That those little boys are wishing
>
> For a little worm just like me
> To put upon their hook
> And I won't be a stupid worm
> In anybody's book!

April and I clapped our hands and gave Sally our heartfelt praise. It was an exceptionally happy interlude in the weekend, and it was also much more than that. It reminded me how much I admired and loved Sally despite the difficulties we had with each other. It was the sort of moment that bound us together by more than blood, need, or obligation.

The last night of Sally's visit, she couldn't settle down. I couldn't sleep either, listening to her moving about the living room, zipping and unzipping her suitcase. By morning, I was worn out, and I was depressed about the ugly conversations we'd had. The weekend, for the most part, had been a disaster. Lying in bed and watching the room get light, I felt more trapped than ever. I was angry at Sally, but I also felt tremendous compassion for her. I idly thought of suicide, and I realized for the first time that I did so only because I could see no way out of my conflicting feelings. No matter what I did to forget about Sally, I would always be in the family with her. She would always be my sister. I would always love her enough to feel I needed to take care of her. And she would always resent it.

As we said good-bye after breakfast, I told Sally that I hoped she didn't feel bad about the fights we'd had. "Hell, no," she said heartily. Then she added, as if I might have missed her messages, "In fact, I'd like to come again!"

When I didn't—couldn't—respond, she dropped the subject and took up another. As she climbed into the cab, she said, "I'd like to write to you every day, Peggy, if you wouldn't mind."

"No, Sally," I said firmly. "I would mind."

I didn't want her to pour herself out to me. I didn't want to know the details of what was on her mind. I didn't want to be the vessel to hold her fragile self. I shut the cab door.

"But you wouldn't have to write back," she said.

"I know that, Sally," I said quietly. I callously signaled to the driver to go.

When I went to see Fiona that week, I told her about my suicidal impulses. I described the events of the weekend and my guilt at being so cruelly honest with Sally.

"I didn't realize Sally was aggressive," Fiona said thoughtfully.

"What? Sally's never aggressive!"

"Sounds pretty aggressive to me," she said. "She wants to move into your apartment, make your friends her friends, and generally make your life her life."

"But she has so little," I said.

"She refuses to make the most of what she has," Fiona answered.

Fiona's words struck a chord in me, and I never forgot them. *Sally refuses to make the most of what she has.* I was often angry at Sally, but I didn't hold her accountable for her actions. I rarely expected her to take responsibility for herself. I realize now how disrespectful—how condescending—that was. I know now that Sally is much more capable than I gave her credit for then. In a roundabout way, recognizing Sally's aggressiveness was a way of giving her credit for her own volition.

After Sally got back to Arlington, she became ill again and had to be hospitalized. She was on the edge of mania when she was with me, apparently, and the talk about sex and her grand plans for a halfway house—even for a return visit to New York—were part of it. The high soon turned to depression. "Sally said you were pretty blunt with her," Mother told me. "But she wouldn't elaborate." For a couple of years after the visit, Sally looked at me hatefully whenever I went to Arlington. Sitting in the dining room about to begin a holiday meal, I would look up and see her scowling at me from across the table.

I had learned to ignore Sally's angry or sad looks the way I'd learned to ignore Mother's, realizing that I was better off not knowing the details of what was on their minds. I could only speculate that Sally was hurt by my assessment of her capabilities and resented me for my comparatively rich life. And I had a strong suspicion that her abiding grudge, and her inability to express it, revolved around my steadfast determination to defend my privacy.

···

PART THREE

MY NAME
IS PEGGY

....

Mother seemed to grow old all at once, in the year before her death. In her late sixties, she considered having her hair tinted when a few white strands appeared, but she wasn't really comfortable with the idea—it was too extravagant, she may have felt, or too pretentious—and she never got around to it. Instead, every morning after she finished her tea, she would dab her temples with the damp tea bag, staining the gray hairs a light brown to match the rest. Slender and animated, she looked young, and because her political views became more and more lively and liberal as she aged, she seemed young as well. A whole-grain, fresh-vegetable fanatic all her life, she expected to live a long, long time.

In the summer of 1986, when she was seventy-four, she and Sally came up to the Catskills with me for a week's vacation over the Fourth of July. I'd just bought a little house, and I wanted to show it off. I invited them both together because I knew Mother couldn't refuse to come on the excuse that she had to look after Sally, and because I knew Sally would be thrilled. She needed a vacation, and she liked being in the country. I invited Aunt Irene and asked her daughter, my cousin Trenie, to come with her husband, Mark, and their nine-month-old baby. It was to be a mini family reunion. Everyone was excited about it.

I was working as an editor at *ARTnews* magazine, after holding a number of jobs in editorial departments at *Newsweek*. When my alienation from art had begun to depress me, I'd applied to *ARTnews* as a free-lance reviewer of exhibitions. A year later, my editor there decided to leave to write a book, so I applied for her position. Life felt good: I loved the job and found friends among my coworkers; I had a steady boyfriend I liked and respected; and six years of therapy had strengthened my psyche. I knew a week with my family wouldn't do me in, no matter what.

Mother and Sally arrived first, flying in from Washington to the airport at Albany. I had been painting and fixing up the house for the first week of my vacation, and I thought I was looking forward to their arrival, but on the way to the airport, I felt apprehensive. Driving north on the New York Thruway, I suddenly felt a smothering drowsiness overcome me. I was perspiring heavily; the road seemed to radiate heat. Five miles south of the airport exit, I felt myself jerk suddenly. I was halfway onto the shoulder, and another driver, next to me in the left lane, was leaning on his horn. I had fallen asleep at the wheel. I pulled over and stopped the car. After a few minutes I started the engine again and went on, this time wide awake, for I was shaken and my heart was racing.

Waiting at the gate, I saw Sally first. She looked excited, but also tense, perhaps because she didn't like to fly. Then I saw Mother walking gingerly behind her. Some small part of me refused to recognize her at first. I hadn't seen her since the previous Christmas, and in those six months she had aged years. I knew that her arthritis kept her in agony, especially at night. She looked tired, and although she almost never complained about her knees, she had begun to walk with a cane. She had always had poor posture, and now she almost stooped. That combined with the awkward jerk of her painful gait made her look like an old woman for the first time. The tea bag trick was no longer working, and her hair was frosted with white.

This first, unsettling impression lasted throughout the vacation. As I watched Mother walk slowly up the country road every morning to buy the *New York Times* at the market, I had to fight tears. Just a few short years before, she had outpaced me on the long walks we took around her hilly neighborhood in Arlington.

I loved having her at the house, though, especially because she was as taken with it as I was. Like me, she enjoyed it even more because it had cost only fifteen thousand dollars. "Why, you'd almost spend that for the garage alone," she'd say one morning, in wonder. Or I'd find her staring out the kitchen window at the wide, clear trout stream that bordered the backyard. "You couldn't get a view like this for less than a hundred thousand anywhere near Washington," she'd say. It was wonderful to see her delighting in something, especially something of mine.

Sally fell for the house too, or, more accurately, for the yard, where she spent her days sitting quietly, smoking cigarettes. She discovered a nest of orioles in the willow tree, and she spotted bats one evening swooping and dipping along the bank, catching insects. A year later I would hear her tell a family friend, "Let's put it this way—it's a place you could dream on."

Greatly overweight, Sally was having trouble breathing, and that combined with the medication she took—lithium, principally—made her drowsy. She had always slept a good part of the day, but now she stayed awake only an hour or two before nodding off again. Sometimes she fell asleep sitting in her chair, and I wondered if she might have a form of narcolepsy. She had been seen by doctors, who found nothing wrong. They told her to lose weight—she was up to 290—and stop smoking, but I doubted she would ever quit. A couple of years before she had been laid low by pneumonia. She was put in intensive care, and then in an oxygen tent for several days, and Mother said she could have died. As soon as she was released, though, she resumed her by-the-carton habit. In spite of all this, Sally was, in Mother's words, healthy as a horse. She had an astonishingly resilient constitution.

Not long after Mother and Sally settled in, Aunt Irene, Trenie, and the baby arrived. Mark had not been able to get away from work. Unfortunately, we all not only liked to have a man around the house, we were clearly dependent on one to leaven our heavy mix. Although we'd all had a good time together one Christmas, when Trenie invited us to Pittsburgh, none of us got along well this time. Uncharacteristically, Aunt Irene behaved like a princess, refusing to do so much as make herself breakfast. "When I'm on vacation, I'm on vacation," she said. Trenie had her hands full with the baby, but she gamely took care of her mother as well. Mine stopped enjoying the vacation after a day and a half. She became cranky and rigid. As if to demonstrate just how little she had in common with Aunt Irene, Mother began scurrying around tidying up, washing every dish that anyone left in the sink and complaining bitterly about "the mess all day."

Everyone was at her worst. Aunt Irene looked at Sally with horror as Sally slurped the milk on her breakfast cereal, or gnawed on the end of a chicken bone. I was reminded of my boyfriend who had denigrated Sally when I was thirteen and how seeing Sally through his eyes had alienated me from her. Now, when I saw Aunt Irene recoiling, my sympathies were entirely with Sally. I wanted to scream, "Give her a break, damn it!" But Sally didn't notice Aunt Irene's glances, and, of course, I didn't call her attention to them.

Mother harangued Sally not to chew on the bones. "I pay your dentist bills," she said angrily three or four times. Sure enough, Sally broke off a whole tooth on the knob of a thigh-bone. Mother was furious, going on at length about the cost of the repair. Sally bowed her head and tried to pretend she didn't hear. At every meal, Mother brought up the subject of the broken tooth. It was difficult to forget, because the gap showed whenever Sally smiled, spoke, or, more often, yawned.

Even the weather could do nothing right. The week was cold and rainy, forcing us to stay inside most of each torturous day. It was obvious none of us could wait for the vacation to end.

I made a point, one day, of taking Sally alone on an outing to a game farm and zoo, where she went on an elephant ride. She was the only person over ten on the huge animal, and she was so heavy that she could hardly stretch her thighs over either side. The rough bouncing hurt—she was sore for days afterward—but she had looked ecstatic in the saddle, and she insisted the ride was fun.

I couldn't imagine that Sally had enjoyed the week any more than the rest of us, but on the last day, driving back to the airport, I sensed her reluctance to leave. She was silent, sitting next to me in the car, but I could see her pinched brow and I thought I could almost hear her pleading to know when she could come again. I dreaded the actual scene and thought I might be able to avoid it if I kept up a cheerful patter. But as she was walking through the gate on her way to the plane, she turned back to look at me and said what I'd already imagined: "When can I come back, Peggy?" She gazed at me beseechingly. I didn't answer right away, but Sally wasn't waiting for me to speak. "Make it soon," she said, as if she couldn't last another year.

Her wrenching good-bye made me think, as I had years before on her awful visit with me in New York, that she had no life of her own in Virginia, at least none that she valued. Her neediness seemed bottomless to me. Although she hadn't said it, I heard an accusation in her words—that the week wasn't enough. I had the feeling that whatever I did wouldn't, in the end, be adequate, and once again, I knew that it would be a long time before I asked Sally to visit me. I just couldn't stand the guilt.

Two weeks after the trip, Sally was in the hospital. "I think she was on her way down when we were at your little house," Mother said. But I began to think that visiting me was a bad idea; perhaps it made Sally feel worse about her own life.

Mother sounded exhausted, not combative as she often was when Sally became an inpatient. She spent a lot of energy keeping Sally out of hospitals, trying to conserve the mental-illness hospitalization benefit in Sally's health insurance, which had a lifetime ceiling of seventy-five thousand dollars—not much, considering the price of care. Sally had occasionally used hospitals like spas, we both thought, checking in when she needed a serious rest or a vacation, or just some extra attention. The social workers, nurses, and doctors who saw her every day at the mental health center in Arlington refused to admit her when she was not that sick—when she was simply depressed or anxious, the way almost everyone is at times. It is now recognized that hospitalization (especially if it is prolonged) can make it harder for a competent patient to reenter daily life. If supportive care outside a hospital environment is available (a big if in many communities), it is preferable. Sally would infuriate her caseworkers, and Mother, by going over to the District of Columbia and persuading a former doctor of hers to admit her to Providence Hospital. This time, Mother seemed resigned to Sally's need to extract herself from daily life for a while. "She's really depressed," she said weakly, with a deep sigh. She could also have been describing herself.

••

I had no conscious presentiment of my mother's death, but that fall I went to a self-help group for families run by the Friends and Advocates of the Mentally Ill (FAMI), the New York chapter of the National Alliance for the Mentally Ill (NAMI), a grass-roots group started by parents that now has 130,000 members. I was the only sibling at the meeting; all the others were parents. When my turn came to speak, all I could say was that my mother was getting old, that I didn't do much to help, and that I dreaded the day the responsibility for my sister's care would fall to me. The parents looked at me blankly. No one spoke. It was as if I were talking about *their* deaths, expressing reluctance to care for *their* sick children. Faced with their stares, I felt ashamed to be so free, living far from my family and from the endless mishegoss that knotted up their lives. The leader, no more sympathetic than the rest, quickly went on to the next person. She didn't tell me there was a separate self-help group for siblings and the adult children of mentally ill parents, many of whom were not—or not yet—the primary care givers for their ill brothers and sisters, mothers and fathers. I left the meeting with a desperate sense that there was no one to talk to—indeed, that I didn't deserve help. My mother was still alive and taking care of Sally. What did I have to complain about?

What I had were my anxiety, my doubts about my own effectiveness, my uncertainty about my own mental health, and a dozen other dreads that could have used the light of discussion. Every person at a sibling and adult child support group would have understood instantly, but I didn't know that. I decided to keep my worry to myself and went home.

THAT autumn was long, warm, and sunny, but for us it was bleak. Aunt Ginny, my father's sister and our favorite relative, died in October. Aunt Ginny inspired love among her family because she gave it copiously. She had money and spent it thoughtfully but generously, and Sally was one of the people she spent it on. She laughed when Sally once came to visit her with an empty suitcase. "You always take me shopping for new clothes," Sally said practically. "This way I have plenty of room to carry them home."

Sally went to Pennsylvania for Aunt Ginny's funeral, but Mother stayed at home. She couldn't bear funerals, couldn't face her grief, and couldn't bring herself to see Aunt Ginny's house and know that she would never come back. Aunt Ginny had always been there for her to talk with, and Mother was so depressed by her death that for a few days she could hardly move, she said. "I've just been sitting in one place since it happened," she told me when I called her the following Monday.

Aunt Ginny, who had no children, had earmarked two parts of her estate to go to Sally in trust, with one part for each of her other relatives. The rest of the family were also left pieces of furniture, and as Sally watched us dividing the contents of the house, I felt sorry for her. She probably knew Aunt Ginny would not leave her anything large, for she was living in a rented room and had no place to put furniture. Looking around, she asked for a small ceramic statuette of Squirrel Nutkin, from Beatrix Potter, for a keepsake. When someone remarked on Aunt Ginny's generosity toward her, trying to make her feel less excluded, she said, with simple honesty, "I don't care about money." And, in truth, I knew that the money was left not just for Sally's benefit, but for Mother and for me, who would be forced to care about money for Sally's sake.

Mother had talked about dying for so long, I was sure she'd made every preparation of her own, but now I learned she had never made a proper will. I insisted she hire a lawyer to write one and draw up a trust for Sally. Mother had been talking to trust officers at banks for years, but she had never actually done the work of setting up a fund. As it happened, she had heard about an upcoming meeting at the mental health center that was to be sponsored by NAMI. The topics to be covered were trusts and estates and the general question of what will happen to disabled dependents whose primary caregivers have died. She went to the meeting, where a social worker named Rhonda Buckner spoke to the group and introduced a new organization, the Planned Lifetime Assistance Network (PLAN).

PLAN was started in Virginia by the parents of handicapped children, most of whom were either retarded or mentally ill, and by professionals who were allied with such groups as the Association for Retarded Citizens (ARC) to address what they called "the when-I-am-gone, or WIAG, problem." PLAN was designed to enable parents to provide for their disabled heirs all the kinds of help that social services agencies normally can't provide. A PLAN social worker would help a client shop for a winter coat, for instance, would balance the checkbook and make sure bills were paid, see that birthdays and holidays were not forgotten, and, perhaps most important, would coordinate and maintain the network of agencies, friends, and remaining family that provided the social milieu of the client. If the client needed transportation to a doctor's appointment, PLAN social workers would arrange it. If the client wanted to take a trip, PLAN would help him or her make travel arrangements and pack a suitcase. If a client needed to be hospitalized, PLAN social workers would sign the commitment papers. In other words, PLAN would make it possible for a client's life to go on much as it had before the parent or guardian died.

It wasn't lost on me that PLAN would also allow *my* life to go on. In fact, that was one of its primary goals: to relieve surviving family members of the burden of full-time care for the disabled. No parent wants a well child to have to curtail plans and aspirations, much less to jeopardize jobs and families, to take over the day-to-day responsibilities of a guardian, and no well child, however much he or she loves a brother or sister, wants that either. Under the PLAN proposal, parents who were fortunate enough to have the wherewithal to do so would open a trust fund with PLAN. The interest from the trust would be used to pay a PLAN social worker for services on an hourly basis. The trust would be established in whatever amount would generate money to pay for the number of hours needed every year, which would be projected through interviews with PLAN's staff.

My elation when I heard of this fledgling group was so acute it affected me physically. My heart sped with excitement. I felt a pervasive sense of well-being—a mysterious, light feeling I couldn't identify at first. I looked around myself at my friends, my work, and my apartment with new appreciation, as if I were allowed, finally, to commit myself to spending some part of the future with them. The intensity of my relief should have told me the truth I was still reluctant to admit: that my sister's disability was a powerful, pervasive force in my life. Yet somehow I was still unable to wrestle with that idea. I was still unconsciously looking for a way out, and PLAN was simply the best escape route I'd heard of.

Mother and I went to talk with Rhonda, then PLAN's northern Virginia coordinator, at her office, which shared space with the local chapter of ARC. "Instant karma," I would later laughingly tell my friends. "Love at first sight." A New Yorker originally, Rhonda had a no-nonsense, no-bull-shit approach, tempered by a profound respect for the feelings and opinions of others. She had an easygoing sense of humor and a warm and hearty laugh. It was hard to imagine her ruffled by anything. She inspired confidence, and she was thoughtful and quiet enough that Mother and I rattled on for more than an hour.

Rhonda made notes about Sally's interests, about her friends and acquaintances, about friends of the family who might have Sally to dinner occasionally if they were encouraged to, and about Sally's medical history and doctors. She asked Mother what she did for Sally now that would need to be done for her if Mother were no longer alive. Mother began to talk, and as she went along, the list seemed endless. Rhonda took it all down, then she looked it over and said, "Do you think Sally might be able to handle some of these things by herself? We don't try to cut corners, but we want to encourage independence."

"Of course she could," Mother answered sharply. "But she won't as long as I'm around to do it all for her." She sounded cranky—she was worn out.

"You could hire us right now, occasionally, if you wanted to," Rhonda offered. "We could take over some of the tasks you find particularly difficult. Usually that means money management."

Mother startled. "That's the worst, all right." She supplemented Sally's disability retirement pay from the federal government to such an extent—more than five thousand dollars annually—that for the past few years she had been able to claim Sally as a dependent on her tax returns. She didn't mind helping if Sally was willing to spend wisely, keep track of her money, and balance her checkbook—three things that were extremely difficult for Sally to do.

"You know, there are a lot of people in your boat," Rhonda said gently. "Maybe you'd like to go to a support group for parents. The Alliance for the Mentally Ill could tell you when they meet."

"Oh, I know," Mother said. "I just can't stand the idea of thinking about all this any more than I have to, to tell you the truth. It depresses the hell out of me as it is. I don't want to go to some meeting and talk about it when I could be watching television and letting it slip my mind for a while."

Rhonda shrugged, demonstrating that she wasn't going to press the point. But she tried to offer another word of encouragement. "I think most people feel that way at first," she said. "But they usually find the group a great relief after they start going. Sometimes it's reassuring to find you're not alone."

Mother brushed her off politely, and we soon left. I felt optimistic for the first time, while Mother was guarded in her hopefulness. She worried about the trust money—more than fifteen thousand dollars—and about setting it aside with a group as new as PLAN, and she couldn't quite bring herself to believe the PLAN system would work. In contrast, I was flying with the expectation of help and freedom. I kept remembering something Rhonda had said to me. "My sister doesn't have to help me buy a winter coat," she said. "She doesn't have to pay my bills or help me pack for a vacation. You shouldn't have to do those kinds of things for Sally. PLAN's objective is to allow you to be just what you are—sisters."

The next step was for Mother to complete a will. This was terribly depressing for her, as I suspect it is for most people. "It's like looking Death in the face," Mother said, but she forced herself to make an appointment with Gerard Rugel, a lawyer who worked with NAMI and whose office was also in ARC's suite. I told her to call me and let me know what happened.

"You'd like him," she said after their first meeting.

"Don't *you?*" I asked.

"He seems a little young to me," she said. "He rides to his office on a bicycle."

She knew me: I liked him already. And I liked her even more, for going ahead with someone who was hardly the white-haired type to inspire her confidence.

She recorded their meetings, and I still have the tapes, with her nervous southern voice asking pertinent, intelligent questions about executors, trustees, and assets and then digressing at length about how impossible it was to imagine what would happen to Sally without her nagging. "She'll probably be better off after I'm gone," she said twice. Gerry gently steered her back to business.

By late fall Gerry had drawn up a will and a "spendthrift" trust. I was to be executrix and Sally's trustee. Mother had thought she would have a bank as trustee, but they required a minimum amount in the trust, and their fees were comparatively high. Gerry persuaded her to name me instead—I had told her I was willing to do it—as a way of saving money. This way, all of the trust's income could go toward making Sally, and not a bank, happier and more comfortable. Since that time, I have heard stories that have made me even surer that we did the right thing. A woman I know whose sister was left her parents' entire estate in trust is now suing the bank that handled it. After ten years of dealing with her sister, who will not take her medication or cooperate with her social workers, the bank began to dispense the trust money almost indiscriminately, and our member's contention is that the trustees are trying to use up her sister's money as quickly as they can so the bank will be free of the onerous responsibility of dealing with her. Mother, hating to think of me saddled with the job of managing Sally's money, included a clause stating that I could name another trustee to take over if I wanted, and that I could become trustee again any time I changed my mind.

The clearly worded purpose of Sally's trust is "to provide for the beneficiary's needs, over and above the benefits she otherwise receives or might receive, in her own right, from any local, state, federal government, or private agency," and not to be a substitute for those other benefits. It is supposed to "make the beneficiary's life as pleasant, comfortable, and happy as feasible."

As trustee, I am specifically directed not to pay for the "prohibitive" costs of hospitalization or care by any "public agency." The trust's income and principal are "not to be considered income to, nor assets of, the beneficiary for any purpose, including but not limited to the determination of income or assets as stated in any rules and regulations set forth by any local, state, or federal government or agency," which means, for instance, that Sally cannot be disqualified from applying for low-income housing. The trust is not to be liable for "any present or future debt of the beneficiary to any creditor, public or private," which protects Sally's money from lawsuits, and as trustee I have the right to terminate the trust "as though the beneficiary had died" if a court determines that the trust is liable for "basic maintenance, support, medical, and dental care that would otherwise be provided" by social service agencies.

After the trust was completed, the only item of business that remained was a list of Mother's assets, all of which would go to fund the trust, except her house. She and my father had designed and built it, I'd grown up in it, and I didn't want to be forced to sell it if she died. Gerry suggested she divide her estate to provide the largest possible share for Sally, because she would need it more than I. Mother agreed in principle, but, she said, she wanted me to inherit too. She wanted me to "have some fun," she said. I told her I would have more fun knowing that Sally was taken care of. Her other assets totaled much more than the value of the house, so she decided to leave them in trust and leave the house to me. She sent me the trust documents, I signed them and sent them back, and that was that.

"Don't you feel better now that it's done?" I asked Mother.
"I guess," she said, sounding uncertain.
"What's wrong?"
"I feel like I might as well go ahead and die."

e i g h t e e n

....

There was a bad storm the night before Thanksgiving, five weeks after Aunt Ginny's death, so I waited until the holiday to drive down to Arlington from New York. The early morning was wet and bright, and there was little traffic on the Jersey Turnpike. I made the trip in record time, so I slowed down on the last stretch, the George Washington Memorial Parkway, which leads to my mother's neighborhood from the Washington Beltway. I rolled the window down and let the moist air rush through the car. A thick, smoky fragrance carried me back to childhood for an instant. It was the smell of wet oak leaves, and I suddenly recalled how they had felt slipping under my shoes as I tried to get off the old rope swing in the side yard on a fall day. *Let the cat die down*, I thought, remembering how I would have to wait for the swing to stop moving before I could climb off.

I'd been grieving for Aunt Ginny the whole month long, and this tiny madeleine scene was a blessed reprieve. Such memories often greeted me when I went home, and even though my visits usually turned tense, I couldn't help thinking how much I'd loved the Potomac landscape.

The pleasure of hazy recollection evaporated during the afternoon, but not for the usual reasons. We were all laid low by Aunt Ginny's death, and we didn't fight or argue. Mother was oddly silent, still in shock. I left the next day to drive back via Pennsylvania, where I picked up a carload of furniture Aunt Ginny had left to me.

Mother seemed more depressed, not less, as the weeks passed. She always said she dreaded the holidays, and this year her disgust was obvious. She didn't want to see anyone, though we usually had our neighbors Donald and Betty to Christmas dinner. Betty was an old friend—she and Mother had known each other since high-school days, in Nashville. Not to invite her and her husband, Donald, was almost like not inviting me and Sally. And in early December, Mother had begun saying, "Don't buy me any presents. I *mean* it. There isn't a thing I want from anybody." When I arrived home Christmas Eve, she seemed distracted and distant. "I'm sick of cooking," she announced, so I said I would make Christmas dinner, but when I woke up the next morning I could smell the onions sautéing for the stuffing. "Never mind," Mother said petulantly when I got to the kitchen. "I'll do it. I don't want a mess in here all day." When we opened our presents there were only a book for me and some plastic storage boxes for Sally. The rest of the gifts were ones I'd brought from New York. "I told you not to," Mother said angrily.

Not long after I arrived, Sally began talking about finding an apartment. She was tired of living in her nearby rented room, where she had moved after living at home for a couple of years. She had applied for, and been accepted into, a Section Eight housing program. This would enable her to rent an apartment at a reduced rate; the federal government would pick up the remainder of the tab. Mother couldn't bear to hear of it. It was too much for her to conceive of now. All she could think of were the headaches for her: getting a mover for Sally's belongings, paying for a telephone to be installed, making sure Sally paid the utilities, and, in the worst-case scenario, closing up the apartment or paying the rent herself when Sally eventually broke down and went to the hospital. Sally had never made a long-term success of any living arrangement. Mother had no reason to believe this time would be any different.

"She's determined to do it, though," I said.

"I know she is!" Mother shouted. "What does she care if it drives me to an early grave!"

"Can you stop her?"

"Of course I can't!"

Sally had been given a list of eligible rentals. One was on a direct bus line and within walking distance of the mental health center. If she was going to move to a place of her own, this apartment sounded ideal. She called the superintendent and made an appointment to see it, and then took out a bus schedule to map out her route.

I was doing nothing much, and I had my car, so I offered to drive her over. It seemed like the natural thing to do. But as soon as I spoke Mother began raging at me, screaming at me to mind my own business, accusing me of siding with Sally against her, of not caring a damn about her. I tried to plead that we could do nothing to stop Sally from living where she wished. Mother was in a frenzy, worse than any I'd seen in a decade, shouting about the money she spent on Sally year after year, about the fact that no one would be around but her when it was time to pick up the pieces after Sally "wrecked everything" again. "I should have made her my ward years ago," she cried. "I should have just taken over."

Sally simply ignored Mother, going to her room whenever the fighting began. She was not really concerned, anyway, as Mother had managed to focus her wrath entirely on me. Every time I entered the room where she was sitting, she would be at me again. I finally left the house, took the car, and drove around Arlington for hours. When I returned, I told her if she kept up the abuse I would leave immediately. After that, she sat on the couch in front of the television and cried quietly while watching a football game.

Sally moved into the apartment just after Christmas, and suddenly Mother was filled with enthusiasm. "What a nice place!" she exclaimed to me on the phone. "I'm so glad you took her to see it. What if someone had snatched it out from under her? Why, anyone would love it—all that light. I told Sally maybe I'd get an apartment in the same building some day. She could take care of me when I'm old and gray!" I could imagine how Sally received that daydream.

I was furious at having been put through hell over my small role in helping Sally make her move, even more now that Mother was so chirpy about it. I coldly refused to join in the joy.

After a month, Sally began to feel lonely. There was no one to talk to all day, and when she got home in the afternoon from the mental health center, she would go straight to bed for a long nap.

A busybody neighbor—even lonelier than Sally—knocked on her door day after day, hoping Sally would prove a willing ear for her long monologues, but Sally wasn't interested in making a friend of her. Sally liked to attach herself to someone stronger, I thought, someone who could inspire her—someone, I used to say, whom she could body snatch, entering into their personality and making it her own as much as possible. For several years she had rented a room from a couple named Tammy and Mike, and for much of the time she'd lived with them she had been half in love with one or the other—usually Tammy. "She's the mother I never had," Sally announced once in a family therapy meeting, at which Mother got up and left the room.

Tammy and Mike were not people who commanded our respect. They were often in financial trouble, and their ugly fights over money and other touchy subjects occasionally turned violent. They seemed genuinely to like Sally, however, and to admire her—besides having good character, she was much smarter and more educated than they were—but they also appeared to use her as much as they could. Sally had told Mother and the workers at the mental health center stories about them that led everyone to suspect them of taking advantage of Sally, personally and financially. "They stop short of anything they can't rationalize," Mother said, but she was appropriately wary of them. Nothing she said, however, could sway Sally's affections until Sally's infatuation finally wore itself out and she decided to leave.

When Sally first took the apartment, she was thrilled to have her own place. She invited her best friend, Franklin, over for meals, and she enjoyed being ruler of the roost. After loneliness set in, though, she began making occasional visits to Mike and Tammy's house, hanging out in their kitchen sipping instant coffee, listening to the radio, and watching their busy lives unfold like a soap opera. Every night, she would call Mother on the phone. "I really haunted her, I guess," she told me later.

I heard about Sally's loneliness only from Mother. In all the years I lived away from Arlington, Sally never called me on the telephone. When I think of it now, it seems bizarre not to have communicated more often, but I never questioned our modus operandi. It was just one of many dysfunctional patterns that seemed normal to me.

W hen I returned to my office from lunch on March 2, 1987, the receptionist handed me a message saying Sally had called several times. My immediate thought was that something had happened to Mother.

I reached Sally at her apartment, where she was waiting for my call. "Mother's in intensive care," she said. "She's had a stroke."

"How bad?" I asked.

"She's not responding to anything but pain," Sally said, repeating something she had been told by a doctor. The words echoed in me, and although I knew they described a simple physical test, they signified more to me. Mother had had to respond to so much pain in her life. I knew she wouldn't regain consciousness. I knew she was dying. I had absolutely no hope.

I ran from the office to get a cab to the airport, unable to hold back the tears. By the time I got to Arlington, I was almost sick from crying.

I went straight to the hospital. In the intensive care unit, the nurses seemed to stare at me slightly. They, too, knew that she was dying—had died, in fact, although she was kept breathing with the help of a respirator—and they looked as if they wondered how much would have to be explained to me.

She looked serene, lying in the white bed, breathing gently through the tube that pumped oxygen into her lungs. She also looked beautiful, in a way she hadn't for a while. There was no tension in her brow. Her countenance was calm. The room was almost silent, except for the hum of the machines, and I took her hand.

"Can she hear me?" I asked.

"Probably not," the doctor on duty said. "She's suffered massive brain damage."

I felt stricken, and he must have sensed it, for he hurried to say, "You can always try."

He left the room and I talked to her for a long while, leaning close to her ear to tell her how much I loved her, telling her I admired her more than anyone I knew, that I didn't know what I would do without her. "Mama, Mama," I whispered. "Oh Mama, please don't die."

Lyn and Earl appeared in the hall outside her room, and Lyn walked to the bedside. She took Mother's hand and said good-bye, then they led me to their car. We picked up Sally at her apartment, and they dropped us off at Mother's house. When I'd spoken to Sally earlier in the day, she'd said generously, "I'll stock up on groceries and you can stay with me at my place!" I cut her off cruelly. It was a kind offer, but unimaginable to me. I couldn't accept Sally's largess, couldn't let her be the one to take care of us. "We'll stay at Mother's house," I said curtly. Now we were there, and I wondered for a second if it was too late to change my mind.

One of the joys of my childhood was the sure knowledge that whenever I came home, Mother would be waiting for me. And one of the joys of coming home as an adult was her excitement at seeing me when I came through the door. Her face would beam pleasure, and she always struck me as particularly young at the moment when she caught sight of me. Tonight the house was dark, and so quiet that I jumped when the refrigerator motor clicked on.

I turned on lights around the house—in the kitchen, the living room, and hallways—and then I asked Sally what had happened that day.

In the morning, she told me, Mother called her to say she was on her way over to the apartment. Sally went outside to wait for her on the sidewalk in front of her apartment building, but when Mother didn't come, she went back in and lay down. Much later, she realized something must be wrong, so she called Donald and Betty and asked them to go by Mother's house and check. They found Mother sitting in her armchair. She had been putting on her shoes to go out, and apparently had had the stroke while sitting down. She was conscious, but weak and confused. "I feel so strange," she kept repeating. Then she said, "Someone call Sally." Betty had interpreted this as a mistake, assuming she meant to say, "Someone call Peggy"—that someone should telephone me in New York. She thought Mother was looking for help. But I knew it was exactly what she meant. She knew Sally was waiting for her. She was dying, but it didn't stop her from worrying.

Betty called an ambulance, but Mother lost consciousness before it arrived.

Sally told what she knew matter-of-factly, as if the enormity of what had happened had not hit her yet. She soon went to bed, but I stayed up for a while, calling my closest friends. I was calm now, but I couldn't shake a sensation of being cut off from everything around me, even the air. A year later, I would hear someone describing her own grief after her brother died in an accident. "I feel like a fly trapped in a glass," she said. "Everything is distorted. I can't even hear what's going on out there."

I reached my friend Elizabeth in Seattle. "I'm going to fly out tomorrow," she said instantly. "I'll be there by evening." Somehow the promise of her immediate presence was enough to dispel my desperation. I felt strong enough to tell her to wait—she was in school, and I knew her finances were tight. I could get along, I said, and if I couldn't I promised I'd call her right away and say so. Near midnight, I went to bed too.

As I had done more than twenty years before, on the night my father died, I lay in the dark telling myself to be strong. I was overwhelmed by the knowledge that my life would never be the same, and that from this day on I was no longer anyone's child. Sally snored loudly in the room next to mine—so loudly I couldn't sleep. At two in the morning I dragged myself from the bed and put on my coat. I slipped out the front door and into the yard.

It was lovely there. The branches of the enormous old oak tree made shadows by the light of the street lamp. Just above them, the moon was nearly full and shining so brightly it made a second, fainter set of shadows across the lawn. I stood still for fifteen minutes or so, shaking, although I didn't feel cold. The words of an old Burl Ives song filtered through my mind. *Down in the valley, the valley so low, hang your head over, hear the wind blow.* Sally had sung it to me when I was a baby, and all I remembered was the one verse. Hang your head over, hear the wind blow.

I finally went back inside and slept until morning.

....

The next day, I woke with a start. Sally was still asleep. I knocked on her door.

"Sally?" I said. "Get up and I'll make breakfast. You take a shower, and I'll take mine later."

"Okay," she answered with uncharacteristic speed. She was up in moments and in the bathroom.

I seemed to feel that keeping Sally on schedule was the most important thing in the world, for I insisted she go to the mental health center as usual. I heard myself ordering her around as if I were Mother, and I watched her respond as if it was a comfort to her to have me riding herd on her. It wasn't like me to treat her this way, and yet I couldn't help myself. I think now that I was trying to *become* Mother, not just because I thought I needed to step in as Sally's overseer, but also because it was a way of keeping Mother alive. For a little while, it worked well for both of us.

We drove to the hospital, Sally went to the center, and I went upstairs to the intensive care unit to wait for Mother's doctor. Sally didn't ask to come with me—I never gave her the chance. When the doctor arrived, he reminded me that Mother had left a "living will" asking that no extraordinary measures be taken to keep her alive. I remembered—Mother had been adamant about it and had left copies with practically everyone she knew.

Sally came up to Mother's room during the morning to say good-bye. Without me to choreograph her movements, she'd had time to think, and she soon realized she had to see Mother too. She sobbed by the bed, and I put my arms around her. I think she hadn't realized until then that Mother could not be revived.

"The doctor is going to remove the breathing tube later today," I told her. "I'm going to wait for him, and then I'll pick you up when I leave the hospital."

Sally went back to the center. "I'll be all right," she bravely reassured me.

I suddenly felt more alone than I could ever have imagined feeling, and it frightened me. I had an old friend from high school who still lived nearby, but his number was unlisted. I called another friend and asked desperately if he had Tom's number. Within half an hour, both men were at the hospital. I was grateful beyond words, but I couldn't help noticing that their kind presence didn't dispel this new sense of isolation I felt. I became even more frightened. This was what I'd been running from all my life—from a grief or a sadness that cut me off from the world around me.

My friends offered to stay with me, but after a while I told them to go. The doctor would be coming soon, and I knew I had to be alone with Mother when the life-support machines were removed. When the doctor arrived, he advised me not to stay in the room after he disconnected the tube. "There's no reason to," he said, but I insisted. I held Mother's hand, covering her wrist lightly with my fingers, and felt her pulse slowly, slowly stop. After a few minutes, it was over. I looked at her face and felt myself give a start. I had forgotten how a body looks after the life has gone from it. I'd only seen it happen once before, and seeing Mother brought it back to me with a force I hadn't reckoned on. It was my father's face as well as Mother's.

I called the funeral home from the hospital, somehow understanding that they would know what to do next. Then I called the cemetery where Daddy was buried, and the church up the street from Mother's house where she had sung in the choir years before. I called Rhonda at PLAN just to let her know, though there was nothing for her to do yet for Sally, and I called Gerry Rugel to ask what to do about Mother's will. "Just deal with your grief for now," he said softly. I thought: This is how I am dealing with my grief, making telephone calls one after the other.

I picked up Sally and drove home. She had seemed stunned the day before—she was efficient and calm, but somehow removed. Today she was agitated, crying intermittently and smoking cigarette after cigarette. Next to me in the car, she began to rock slightly, staring out the window. I noticed her glasses were filthy, the lenses covered with greasy fingerprints and dirt. I didn't tell her to clean them. I didn't think it mattered, if she was feeling the same way I was, whether she could see or not. At one point she turned to me and moaned. She sounded anguished.

"Are you all right, Sal?" I asked her.

"Oh, Peggy," she said. "What if I'd called Betty and Donald earlier? Mother might still be alive." She looked at me, hoping for comfort.

"It wouldn't have made any difference, Sally," I told her, trying to sound authoritative, although I'd wondered the same thing myself. I'd thought of Sally going back to bed and napping while Mother was sitting paralyzed, but awake, in her armchair. I'd fought the thought, unable to bear the implications. It didn't make any difference *now*, anyway. Later that day, I spoke with the doctor, and I told him what Sally feared. He said the words that I'd spoken instinctively. Mother's hemorrhage was so massive it took hours for the draining blood to damage her brain, but there had been no chance of saving her once the stroke had occurred.

At home, I walked around the house aimlessly for a few minutes. Sally went to bed. I decided it would be a good idea to eat something, because I hadn't had a meal since lunch the day before. In the refrigerator I found lettuce, mushrooms, broccoli, carrots, tomatoes, cabbage, yogurt, cheeses, skim milk, brewer's yeast, bran—everything healthy and fresh. I made myself a salad and sat down at Mother's desk, an old home-made one that sat in the kitchen. It was perfectly neat—completely unlike any desk of mine. The pens and pencils were stuck in a holder. A stack of notepaper was placed to one side of a clean blotter. A plastic tray held stamps, paper-clips, Scotch tape, a jar of correcting fluid, and address labels. Mail was stacked in the middle of the blotter.

I opened the top drawer and saw a white, letter-size enve-lope with my name on it. It was unsealed. Inside, there were three pieces of lined notebook paper, each with a heading. "People to call in case of my death." "Assets as of January 1, 1987." "Important phone numbers and addresses."

It was as if Mother had been expecting to die.

I began telephoning her friends, many of whom had already heard the news. Each one without exception offered to call others, and I gratefully let them. The second sheet of paper, a list of U.S. Treasury bills and bonds, stocks, and savings ac-counts, with the amount in each, was a mystery to me. The third sheet told me where her banks were and that her will was in her safe deposit box. Years before, she had given me the second key to her box, and I'd put it in a safe place—the kind that is impossible to recall later. I had no idea where it was now.

I left Sally a note and drove to the bank, which was nearby. A woman named Mrs. Porter was keeper of the vault, I learned from the nameplate on her desk. I sat down and waited for her to finish a phone call. When she hung up I looked at her and found that I could not speak. It was the first time I'd had to tell a stranger what had happened, and my throat locked shut. As I began to cry, she handed me a Kleenex and told me to wait until I felt better. Finally, I told her why I was there. "What's your mother's name?" she asked. I told her. She seemed startled and looked at me more closely. "Sara?" she said. I nodded. She shook her head and said she was so sorry. She asked me when it had happened, and we talked for a few minutes. Then she thought of something. "What about your sister?" she asked. "How is she taking it?"

I was not prepared for her solicitousness, and I began crying again. I told her I wasn't really sure yet, and she nodded again. She said Sally often came to the bank with Mother. "I know her," she said simply, by way of telling me she knew this would be particularly hard for Sally.

I told Mrs. Porter I had no idea where my key was, and that I didn't know where Mother kept hers either. She described what the key looked like and began suggesting all the places where Mother might have put hers. "Try her dresser drawers first," she said.

I went home, opened the top drawer of the huge old black chest in Mother's bedroom, and began to sift through the handkerchiefs, stockings, and underwear. I felt a box and lifted it out. I recognized the doll-size tea set Sally had brought Mother from Williamsburg when she was in boarding school. I somehow also recollected, against my will, Mother's ironic look when she had opened the gift. It was something made for a child, or a collector of chotchkes. And yet she had kept it all these years. I opened the box to look at the tiny cups and saucers, and there was the safe deposit box key.

For the next two days, I worked from morning to night, making lists of things to do and people and agencies to call and then ticking off the tasks one by one as I completed them. In the evening a different friend or neighbor would invite

Sally and me for dinner. After the meal, I would take Sally back to her apartment.

I knew how lonely Sally had been before Mother's death, and I should have insisted she stay at the house with me, but I was worried that she would have a harder time returning to the apartment the longer she stayed away from it. It was stupid of me, and insensitive, but Sally put it right. "Can't I stay at Mother's while you're here?" she asked one day.

The next morning, she asked what would happen to the house, now that Mother was gone.

"I think I'll try to rent it for a while," I said.

I could see her thinking this over. "Did Mother leave you the house?" she asked.

I said that she had, and Sally was silent. I told her that everything else Mother had, all the money she'd been saving over the years, was going to fund a trust, so Sally would never need to worry about keeping a roof over her head. She didn't answer. What is a trust fund, I imagined her thinking, especially one over which you have no control, compared to the house you grew up in?

We talked about a memorial service, because Mother had always had a horror of funerals. She wanted to be cremated and "dropped in the ground," she used to like to say, with her usual bluntness. As Daddy had always answered, I told her that was one time we'd get our own way, but now I decided not to have a graveside service. That was what she most abhorred. We planned one instead to take place at the church, so that all her friends and neighbors could come, and another one, with just Lyn and Earl, and Donald and Betty, at the cemetery with us to bury her ashes. Mother had always wanted to have a party for her friends, so I invited them all back to the house for a buffet lunch.

I called the minister to talk over our ideas, and he came by the house. He didn't know us or Mother, but apparently he had heard that we were old members of the church and once active in the congregation, and he treated us with a gentle respect that suggested he felt like a newcomer by comparison. Sally chose the hymns. We didn't spend a lot of time talking, except to ask the minister if he would open up the service at the end to anyone who remembered Mother and wanted to speak, the way they might at a Quaker meeting. Although he seemed slightly uncomfortable with the idea, he readily agreed.

Sally seemed more withdrawn each hour, and began to spend more and more time in bed. My heart was with her, but I found it a strain to be living together, even temporarily. The worst thing was that I was exhausted and couldn't sleep. Her medication made her urinate frequently, and I would hear her get up several times a night to go to the bathroom. I was so jittery every sound woke me up. I would listen as she opened her door, padded back and forth, and settled into snoring again immediately. It would take me a while to get back to sleep every time. In the morning, when it was time for her to get up to go to the center, her alarm would ring. I would jump awake, instantly thinking of everything I had to do that day. It was hopeless to try to go back to sleep, so I would pull myself from the bed and go into Mother's bathroom to take a shower and dress.

Sally didn't seem to be keeping herself clean or changing her clothes, and soon her room began to smell. When we were in the car together, I had to open a window. I finally told her she had to take a bath. I told her she had to wear clean clothes. I harangued her continually, and after a day or two she accidentally called me "Mom." Although she didn't appear to notice, I was electrified by her slip.

We were sitting in the car in the driveway, and I told her I was going to go to New York the next day, put my desk at work in order, and then drive back in the evening. I was overwhelmed by the amount of paperwork I had to do to transfer Mother's accounts into the estate and, after that, the trust, and I knew it would take time. I thought I would bring my two cats and stay in Virginia for a couple of weeks so I could do as much as possible in person.

When I told Sally, she turned toward me and looked straight into my eyes. "Promise you'll drive carefully," she pleaded. "What would I do if anything happened to you?" Her face crumpled and she began to sob.

"Nothing's going to happen to me," I promised her.

The next night, however, driving down Interstate 95 from New York with the cats sleeping in their carrier in the back seat, I somehow lost my way. Depressed and fatigued, I had been staring at the road and gripping the wheel, forcing myself to pay careful attention, because I could feel my mind drifting. I had to concentrate to stop at the toll booths, to watch the gas gauge, to press the gas when the speedometer fell below forty-five, and to let up when it went over sixty. I wasn't doing well at all. Suddenly I found myself, not on Interstate 95, but on an old four-lane highway somewhere in rural Maryland, without a road sign for miles to tell me where I was.

It was like a scene in "Twilight Zone." I drove on for a half hour, absolutely alert now, waiting for the lights of a filling station or a restaurant to appear. Nothing. There were no turnoffs that were marked by route numbers, only road names that meant nothing to me. I knew I was south of Baltimore—I remembered going through the tunnel. Washington had to come next, unless I was somehow headed inland, in which case I would be in Appalachia before the night was over. I didn't have a map to figure out what I'd done, and I couldn't quite imagine how the interstate could fork into something like this, but it had, apparently, and I had unconsciously taken the exit.

I remembered Sally's words: *What if something happened to you?* and for the first time I was terrified that something would. I drove and drove, down the empty road. It was midnight on a Thursday, and there seemed to be no one else out driving this late. Then, ahead of me, I noticed the moon, the lovely moon that had comforted me three nights before. It was in the same part of the sky where it had been as I'd stood in Mother's yard, wondering if I would ever sleep, and it was in the same relation to Baltimore, I figured, as it was to Mother's house. I steered for it, tracking south and west, taking a side road that looked as if it might go straight to it. Before long, the countryside gave way to strip developments of tire stores and discount centers, and I knew I must be near Washington. Then I was in the city, but I wasn't sure where. I couldn't see the sky for the buildings, and I suddenly felt fogbound at sea. I could be going in circles for all I knew. Stopped at a light, I rolled down my window to ask directions of a young couple out for a late night stroll. "Can you tell me how to get to M Street?"

They looked at each other. Then the man said, "This is it, Lady. You can make a left, or you can make a right."

In a minute I was crossing Key Bridge into Arlington, and soon I was pulling into Mother's driveway. Murmuring "Thank you," I nodded to the moon.

The house was quiet, except for the sound of the cats galloping softly through the rooms, getting used to a new place. I found a pencil and notepad and lay down on my bed on top of the covers, thinking of all I had to do the next day.

I woke up the next morning to find the blank notepad resting on my chest and the pencil on the floor next to the bed.

....

Aunt Irene came from Knoxville that morning, and Uncle John, my father's brother, flew in from Chicago. Trenie drove down from Pittsburgh, leaving the baby home with Mark. My friend Rick came from New York and helped drive people to and from airports and train stations. Western Union delivered telegrams all day from Mother's cousins in Nashville, and from old friends of the family who had been called by the neighbors. I was comforted by the activity, glad to be overly busy making up beds and answering the door, but Sally became quieter and quieter. She sat in the living room with Aunt Irene, Uncle John, and Trenie for a while, but soon excused herself and went to her room to lie down.

Just when I was beginning to be distracted by tasks, a man called from the funeral parlor to ask if I would come there and identify Mother's body. They could not cremate her remains, he said, until she was identified by the family, and there was also the paperwork. . . . I could barely listen to him. His voice lacked the unctuousness I was expecting, and although I thought it was probably preferable that he speak normally, I found myself unsettled by his brisk, businesslike tone. There was nothing to do but say I would be there, so I told him I would come at two that afternoon.

After lunch, as I was leaving to go to the funeral home,

Sally asked if she could come with me. I hadn't told her that mother's body had to be identified, and I was worried that it would upset her, so I told her I needed her to stay at the house to take care of things there. That, of course, was exactly what she needed to 'get away from. I was trying to include her as much as possible in the arrangements for the memorial service, but looking back, I see that I excluded her from aspects of Mother's death that she had a right to experience. I was treating her like a child, as Mother had, when I should have acknowledged that she was at least my equal in this passage of our lives. And Sally had always proved stronger than any of us expected, especially in the face of momentous events. She could face facts better than anyone I knew. When I saw Mother's body, covered with a sheet on the gurney, I realized that I was hardly in good shape myself. My knees buckled, and I had to lean down my head and breathe deeply for a minute before I could follow the funeral director to his office to sign the necessary forms.

MARCH 6 was one of those unexpectedly hot early-spring mornings that seem to renew the world. At ten, Donald and Betty and Lyn and Earl met us at the cemetery, where the minister was waiting. I went to the small brick house at the gate where I picked up Mother's ashes. The metal box was only as big as a tea canister, but when I took it in my hands my arms dropped with the weight.

Mother had asked to be cremated, and because I wanted the same for myself eventually, I hadn't considered defying her wishes, although when we went to my father's grave and I saw the hole that had been dug—a foot and a half square—I cringed from the inappropriateness of it all. So small a spot, so small a container, for the remains of such an important person. I wanted to run away, take the ashes, and spread them on my garden Upstate, so that all the flowers that would come up later that spring could be enriched by Mother's clay. Even though I was terribly upset, Sally was crying, and something in me automatically became strong—artificially so—whenever she seemed to falter. I put my arm around her shoulders.

The minister spoke. I asked Sally if she wanted to put the box into the grave, but she recoiled and shook her head. I placed it into the dark earth and stood up. I had brought a handful of flowers from a bouquet sent by Aunt Peg, but Lyn had to remind me to put them into the grave. Startled, I handed some to Sally. Sally wept openly. I was numb, fighting off the crazy thought that I must fill in the grave with soil or someone might take the ashes. I knew that the cemetery employee who had met us at the gate would have the dirt filled in immediately. I could even see the man who was going to do it, waiting at a discreet distance. But the little box of ashes looked so vulnerable, so exposed, that I had trouble tearing myself away.

I had set the time of the memorial service for one o'clock on a Saturday so that Mother's young friends who worked could come. At about twelve-thirty I began to see the neighbors step out of their front doors and walk slowly up the hill to the church. When we arrived, the sanctuary was filled with people, many of whom I hadn't seen for many years—my grade-school principal, all of Mother's coworkers from the county library, church members I'd almost forgotten. There were social workers who had known Sally years before, and nurses from the mental health center.

Sally and I walked to the front pew with Uncle John, Aunt Irene, Trenie, and Rick and sat down. I noticed that the organist was playing one of the hymns Sally had chosen as a processional. I knew Sally wanted to sing the words, not just hear the music, and I felt her disappointment. I wished the minister had explained his intentions to her, but I knew that this sort of thing happened often to the mentally ill. They are strung along in countless small ways by people who inno-cently imagine that they won't notice.

When it came time to open the service to the congregation, several people stood to speak. Lyn went first, saying that Mother had always been a boost to her ego, that she'd always made her feel good about herself. An old friend who had been a Girl Scout leader with Mother talked about how Sara had been so competent, knowing how to do everything, from making the right amount of tunafish for a crowd of hungry campers to organizing the annual cookie sale. A man from the church stood up to say that when Sara quit the choir after starting to work again, choir practice just wasn't fun any more.

Speaker after speaker mentioned Mother's frankness. "You could count on Sara to tell you what she really thought," they said, and everyone chuckled. "You always knew Sara's true opinion." What had been so difficult for Sally and me—mother's obdurate honesty—had clearly charmed her friends. In the gentle southern milieu in which she lived, her utter forthrightness had been refreshing.

I stood up and told the gathering that Mother was espe-cially blunt with people she cared about. Her friends smiled. Sally shifted nervously in her seat, then stood up and talked about how much Mother had done for her. "I always wanted her to be proud of me," she said, choking back the tears. There was a long silence.

I put my arm around her. "Mother *was* proud of you, Sally," I whispered. I knew it was true, but I doubted Sally believed it.

The minister ended the service with a prayer, and then the organist played another of Sally's chosen hymns as a reces-sional. It didn't occur to me that I treated Sally the same way, querying her for her opinions and desires out of politeness, and then running the show my own way. "Shall we have mother's friends back to the house after the service?" I'd asked her two days before, even though I'd already called a caterer and ordered the food while she was sleeping. She had said yes automatically. She wouldn't have argued about it. She was used to going along with plans made by other people.

After the service, we walked back down the street to the house. I looked around at all of Mother's friends, and I thought that I would probably never hear of many of them again.

The luncheon didn't last long. People had to get back to their Saturday tasks. Most of the guests had left when Sally came to me with an angry look on her face. I asked her what was wrong. "There are two girls who brought their *dog*," she said disgustedly. "I have a good mind to tell them to leave."

She was talking about my friends Debbie and Andrea, whose wire-haired terrier was cavorting happily in the side yard, having spent the church service penned in the back of their car. "They drove all the way down from New York, Sally," I told her. "It's a new puppy, and they didn't want to leave her in a kennel."

"Oh!" Sally said. "I didn't know that." Then she added, "They drove all the way from New York for Mother's funeral?"

"Yes," I said. Sally seemed to ponder this. "Did they know her that well?"

"Debbie did," I told her, "but I think they came mostly for my sake."

A half hour later Aunt Irene remarked on the number of mourners at the service. "You all sure do have a lot of friends," she said.

Sally looked up. "*Peggy* has a lot of friends," she said, as if to correct her. "She and Mother."

twenty-two

···

The days that followed were surreally beautiful. March turned out to be a warm, slow, sunny month, and every morning I would prop the storm doors open to let the breezes blow through the house. As I sat at Mother's desk making telephone calls or writing notes to myself about what to do next, I could hear my cats come and go, ecstatic to be out-doors instead of cooped up in my apartment. I was relieved to be out of New York myself, feeling the sun that streamed in to warm the high-ceilinged rooms, listening to the birds outside chastising the cats, and occasionally hearing a neighborhood child in the afternoon, after school, sloshing in boots down the creek. Hundreds of daffodils and scores of tulips I'd planted were pushing up for their second season. The air smelled sweet with buds and the wet scent of earth. Friends and neighbors would call or come by to ask how I was doing. Fine, I would tell them truthfully. I'm really doing well.

Sally would take the bus to the mental health center in the morning, and go to bed as soon as she got home every after-noon; we didn't spend much time together, except in the eve-nings. We were invited over to friends' houses every night, and although it was comforting, it was also tiring for her. Each night we left a little earlier. Sally would eat in silence, and afterward fidget or sit so still her tension was palpable. Now and then she would say, "I think I'd better be getting home," but usually I picked up the signal before she had to speak.

At odd times, Sally surprised me. One afternoon as we were driving in Mother's car I noticed it was almost out of gas. "Again!" I sputtered. "My Honda gets at least twice the mileage of this car."

"Yours is a standard transmission, though, isn't it?" Sally asked.

"So what?" I answered.

"Well, automatics always take more gas," she said.

I'd never had anything but a manual shift, and I hadn't known that. I asked Sally how she knew.

"It's just one of those things you know," she shrugged, smiling at my question.

I spent the first week changing accounts and titles to the name of the estate. Later I would have to change everything again to the name of the trust. I canceled Mother's annuities from the federal government and from Arlington County. I called credit card companies to close her accounts. I went to the courthouse to have myself officially declared executrix and to the county health department for death certificates, which I needed to change the names on her bonds and Treasury bills. There was an enormous amount of business that needed to be conducted by mail; the first week I used a roll of a hundred stamps. I had to have a way to pay bills for Sally when needed, so I went to the bank to open savings and checking accounts for the trust. I had never balanced a checkbook in my life, never bought a stock or bond, and never had more than a few thousand dollars in a savings account. Now I was handling what seemed to me to be huge sums of money, and I felt barely competent to keep track of it all. It was then that I began defending myself to Mother, telling her that I was doing my best. I couldn't have explained it, but she seemed to be close by, as if, I thought, she were taking her time getting to heaven. I imagined her reluctance to leave all this to me, and I felt her watching me and criticizing my sloppy arithmetic, my nonexistent filing system, my chaotic notekeeping. One morning I said "Quit it" aloud, and I jumped at the sound of my own voice. I was trying *so* hard, I thought. I didn't need her looking over my shoulder.

Even now, I can't say for certain that she wasn't.

ALTHOUGH I was racing to do what seemed necessary, my mind was continually on Sally. When we were together, she seemed to cling to me. She cried often. I asked her to make some notes about the things Mother had done for her that Rhonda and PLAN might now take over. The list was short—she couldn't concentrate on writing it down—but when we went to see Rhonda at her office, Sally had a lot to say. "Mother took me shopping for groceries each week," she began.

"What day would you like to do that?" Rhonda asked.

Sally decided on a day. There were other things—looking over her checkbook, overseeing her finances, making sure she went to the dentist. The long list finally ended with Sally saying, "I usually went home for the weekends, and I talked to her on the phone every night."

My heart ached at this, but Rhonda spoke clearly and carefully. "We'll have to make plans for some weekend activities," she said. "And I won't be able to talk to you every night, but you can call me at the office any time you want to." She told Sally the hours, and gave her several of her cards, with the phone number underlined.

"*I'll* call you, Sally," I promised.

Sally looked at me with a mixture of resignation and gratitude. She knew I wouldn't be much of a substitute. "All right," she said.

I wondered what we would find to talk about. Mother had been such a meddler she knew all the details of Sally's days, and she also cared about them. She was always on the lookout for trouble, and she probably listened closely to every nuance of Sally's account of life at her apartment and the center. She kept track of Sally's medication, too, and knew exactly when it was time to have her blood tested to monitor the lithium dosage. Mother was well-organized herself, and found it easy to apply her standards to Sally too. I, on the other hand, was the sort of person who depended on postcards and telephone calls to remember to make and keep doctors' appointments. Thank God that sort of reminder was now up to Rhonda, I thought, but I also felt I should get to know more about Sally's comings and goings.

Rhonda mentioned ACRI, Arlington Community Residences, Inc., a county-sponsored social services agency that had already helped Sally apply for her subsidized apartment. ACRI ran different kinds of meetings for their clients and also planned parties and outings. Sally, like me—like Mother, Aunt Ginny, and, it seemed to me, most people—didn't really enjoy organized group activities, but she told Rhonda she would look into some of the ACRI weekend dates. Rhonda reminded her that her ACRI counselor would continue to check in with her at her apartment, to see how Sally was doing there, and she asked Sally if she thought she could manage to lean on ACRI and other existing networks more, now that she really needed them. Sally said she would try.

As we left Rhonda's office, Sally was quiet. She was eating a lot, and putting on more weight. Her clothes looked as if she had thrown them on. She was wearing a hooded sweater that had been oatmeal-colored originally, but was now gray, with pulled threads poking out in several places. Her shoes were not just down at the heels, their backs were bent under. She shuffled in them as if they were bedroom slippers, allowing them to flap as she walked. She moved with her head bowed, in blind sadness.

When I said something to Rhonda later, privately, about

Sally's appearance, she said she thought Sally looked fine, especially considering what she was going through. I was relieved by her response—it showed me her priorities were in the right place—but I knew Sally's appearance was often a key to her mood, and I was worried about her. On the other hand, I had to admit to myself that improving Sally's appearance was unlikely to have an appreciable effect on her spirit, and that worrying about it was the same as worrying about a symptom without addressing the disease that caused it.

When we got in the car, I asked Sally if she would mind going with me to the bank, to close Mother's safe deposit box.

"What's in it?" she asked. I told her: the deed to the house, Mother's diamond engagement ring, information about her Treasury bills, our birth certificates, and other odds and ends, such as her sorority pin.

When we arrived at the bank, Mrs. Porter told Sally how sorry she was about Mother's death. Sally thanked her and sat down to wait for me. When I came out of the vault, Sally announced that she wanted to rent a safe deposit box herself. When I asked why, she said simply that she might want to put papers in it. I tried to talk her out of it, mainly because I was pretty sure she couldn't keep track of the key, any better than I had kept track of mine, but I didn't press her for her reasons. Finally, I relented. It was only twenty-five dollars a year, so I helped her fill out the form and paid the fee.

On our way back to the car, Sally seemed to be working up her courage to ask me something. I waited. Finally, she said, in a voice so falsely casual it sounded like a vaudeville performer's, "By the way, Peggy, could I have my birth certificate?"

"No," I answered, without asking her reasons. "I'll keep it. Mother kept it before, and I'll keep it now. It's too much trouble to replace if it gets lost."

"I'll put it in the safe deposit box," she said.

Again I said no. If she could put it in, she could take it out, and if she could take it out, she could lose it.

Then I thought to ask her why she wanted it.

She squirmed and carefully did not look at me, so I knew she was about to lie. Sally is so naturally truthful, she usually can't help giving herself away. "If I lose my bus pass, I'll need it for identification," she said.

I knew this was true, for Mother had complained about having to get it out for her once. "What else?" I pried, wondering what she was holding back.

To my surprise, she answered forthrightly. "I'd like to get a driver's license again someday," she said, careful to cast this dream in the indistinct future so as not to alarm me now. Sally hadn't driven in perhaps fifteen years. I glanced over at her. She had a slightly harried, vacant look. She rarely cleaned her glasses—the lenses were always smeared—but her gaze was so inward-turned, so withdrawn, that I didn't think it mattered to her most of the time. I couldn't imagine her peering over a steering wheel, guiding a ton of metal down the road. And the longer she was on medication, the more tremulous her hand movements became. Once she had taken a test to work in a sheltered shop, and it was found that her manual dexterity was somewhat poorer than normal. I thought it would be hard for her to muster the reflexes to handle the controls of a car. I doubted she could pass a driving test, but I couldn't be sure.

Sally's desire to drive again made sense in other ways, however. With Mother's death, she had lost an important means of transportation. If she had her birth certificate, she would be able to decide for herself when she was able to drive again, without consulting me. It was a step toward a kind of independence she hadn't enjoyed for many years. While I understood all this, I wasn't willing to take the minor chance of losing something it might be time-consuming to replace.

"I'll hold onto your birth certificate," I told Sally. "And whenever you need it for a driver's license, I'll send it to you."

This seemed to satisfy her for now, and the subject was dropped. There was still the safe deposit box key to worry about, though. I asked—no, instructed—Sally to place it in her medicine cabinet, where she wasn't likely to disturb it. She agreed. If she objected to my imperious tone, she didn't say so.

My voice was beginning to shock me. Sally grew more dependent and desperate every day, and every day I barked at her more and more. Minute by minute, I was developing a new understanding of Mother's angry tone. I was overwhelmed by all I needed to do before getting back to work, while Sally seemed to be making no plans for her own future. She couldn't—she was barely able to get through a day without crying. It was healthy that she wept—as Sally later said, she grieved for Mother immediately. Unfortunately, I was heavily committed to being busy, as if my lists and letters and phone calls could keep my own grief at bay indefinitely. Sally became almost mute with anxiety and sadness, looking at me from time to time as if to reassure herself that I was still there. I wondered what she would have done without me.

Talking to Elizabeth on the phone late one night, I said, "I don't know what would happen if I'd had a family of my own."

Elizabeth was silent for a minute. "Maybe," she said finally, "this is why you don't."

ONE MORNING I went over to the mental health center to meet with Sally's nurse, Marjorie. I thanked her for coming to the memorial service, but she waved my thanks away. "Mrs. Moorman was one of my favorite people," she said of Mother. "I'm really going to miss her." Mother had always liked Marjorie, giving her highest compliment: "She has good sense," she'd said. "She knows exactly what she's doing."

I asked Marjorie how Sally seemed to her.

She answered by saying firmly that Sally was going to be fine. "She's much more capable than she would have you think," she said. "Sally has strengths she's never drawn on." I listened with some sadness. I knew Marjorie had worked with Sally for years, and she was completely familiar with Sally's ploys and gambits. But I felt somehow that she didn't quite know Sally's tender side, and that she couldn't understand how bereft Sally was feeling now. I reminded her that Sally had lost Aunt Ginny just a few months earlier, and Marjorie said she knew that, but she insisted that Sally was doing well. Still, I was worried.

"Sally's feeling pretty bad right now," I told her. "It's going to be hard for her to go on after I return to New York." I was trying to get Marjorie to feel some of my sympathy for Sally. In fact, I couldn't imagine how Sally would get along without Mother when I wasn't around to try to take her place. "Sally needs extra help right now," I ventured.

"Sally will always want more than she gets," Marjorie said. "She will take as much as you're willing to give. She has a poor sense of self, and that makes it easier for her to soak up someone else's strength than tap into her own."

I agreed with Marjorie there, and remembered Fiona's words: *Sally refuses to do the best with what she has.* But I felt this was hardly the time for Sally to be challenged to fall back on secret reserves. I felt barely able to cope, even with my friends calling every day to offer words of comfort and affection. As I listened to Marjorie's assessment, I wanted to run and find Sally and tell her I loved her. I saw how ultimately impersonal her associations were. If she just had one good friend, I thought sadly.

There were a few people, such as her pal Franklin, from the center, whom she still saw with some regularity. But leaving the center, I thought of the many others Sally had made in her life, and wondered where they were now. Sally was fortunate not to have many of the personality problems that afflict so many people with mental illness. She wasn't generally mistrustful, frightened, or paranoid, so she wasn't hostile or combative. She was a naturally outgoing person, warmhearted, intelligent, talented, and funny, and people instinctively liked her. Why did she seem so alone now?

Some years back, Sally was engaged to be married. Mother objected because the fiancé "had problems," she said. "He's no better off than she is," she told me.

"Mother," I said, "who do you think Sally would choose? Someone who knows nothing of what she's been through, or someone like herself, who would understand?"

Mother finally agreed, and anyway, she said, Sally adored the man. When I asked Sally about him now, though, she had forgotten his name. She couldn't remember any engagement. I knew that the shock treatments she'd had erased some segments of memory, but it was unusual for her to forget anyone who had played a significant role in her past. The wedding plans had progressed to the point where Mother had made a list of family friends to invite. Now Sally had forgotten it all. I wondered if it was because of the man's disabilities that he and Sally had not kept in touch, but as I thought it over, it seemed to me that most of the other friends who had seemed essential to her throughout her life had also fallen away. There had been a woman named Vera, who was going through a divorce at the time she'd shared an apartment with Sally. Vera had been the one who found her after her suicide attempt. She had come to our house for some holiday meals, and we all liked her. I hadn't heard her name in years. And there was the family Sally had rented a room from for eight months who told Mother they'd never had a tenant they liked better. Sally liked them, but was uncomfortable with their aggressive friendliness, which afforded her little peace or privacy. She stopped up their plumbing so often they finally told her if it happened again she would have to leave. Sally lost no time in plugging up a toilet, which overflowed and ruined the ceiling of the room below it. Her landlords had been sincerely sad to see her go and asked her again and again to keep in touch. She had visited the grandmother only once, during a manic attack, to ask if she would be the housemother of Sally's group home. ("She knew something was screwy," Sally remembered later.) There were others, too, who had somehow gotten lost in the discarded past.

I thought about what it took to sustain a friendship. I was terribly lax, letting months go by without telephoning or writing to people I loved. I would eventually catch up with them, however, or they would catch up with me. It took mutual volition, I knew. Not many people would call again and again if one never called back. I understood Sally's difficulties, and when she was negligent, forgetting my birthdays, for instance, I tried not to take it personally, but even so, I found it depressing at times to be always on the giving end of our relationship, and rarely on the receiving one.

Sally wasn't always the one who let friendships slide, however. She had a coworker at the Department of Agriculture Library with whom she had had dinners out and holiday gift-exchange dates for many years. When I asked Sally how it happened that they were now out of touch, I expected her to shrug, but I was wrong. "I used to call her," Sally explained, "but she never called me back, and I just got tired of it. It's no fun when you're doing all the talking." I knew how that felt, I told Sally honestly, but without elaborating.

Sally was capable of great generosity, but I think she often reserved her short-term energy for whoever seemed promising at the moment or for those people whose affections she was uncertain of. Her attention often swung between all or nothing. She would meet someone, be uncritically pleased with them for a while, give her all to the relationship, and then sour on it when it failed to meet her expectations. It seemed to me that if she couldn't be consumed by it, it wasn't worth it to her to maintain it. She couldn't seem to grasp the idea of a social life drawn from a mixed bag of attachments, some important, some casual. So she was forced to depend, at last, on people like Aunt Ginny, Mother, Lyn and Earl, Donald and Betty, and me—people who wouldn't let her down on her birthday or at holidays, whether she seemed to appreciate it or not.

AS THE DAYS passed and the paperwork began to subside, I turned my attention to Sally's apartment. While searching through Mother's papers, I found records from a storage company in Washington that she had been paying since 1980, when she had put Sally's furniture and books in storage. Over the years, she complained regularly about paying rent for twenty boxes of books, and I knew there were a number of large items there as well—a sofa bed, end tables, dressers, and more. Sally had always wanted a place of her own; now she had it, and I decided it was time to have her possessions moved there. When I asked her if that was what she wanted, she was delighted. She had inherited a thousand dollars "mad money" from Mother. We went shopping for bookcases, and ended up spending three-quarters of her money on enough of them to line the walls of her bedroom.

I spent a long day putting the shelves together, hammering the backs to the frames and installing the shelves on plug-in supports. Sally watched me working, thanking me profusely for what I was doing. It felt good to labor, and I slept well that night. The next day, Sally said that she had seen a pedestal table advertised in the newspaper and that she would like to buy it with the rest of her money. Then she would be all set, she said. The apartment would be completely furnished. We drove to the store, she picked out the table, and we carried it back to her place.

The day the storage company was due to send its truck, I had an appointment with a locksmith to put deadbolts on the doors to Mother's house, so I couldn't be at Sally's apartment to oversee the delivery. When I called her later in the afternoon, she said that the stuff had come, but that most of it wasn't hers.

"So they took it back?" I asked her, thinking it was too bad that we would have to wait until they could deliver the right furniture.

"No, I kept it," she said. "It's really nice. There's a roll-top desk, and two gold armchairs, and another desk. I sent the sofa back with them. I didn't like it much."

I hit the ceiling, just as Mother would have. "Someone probably kept *yours* once," I screamed. "You call them and tell them to pick it up *now*." I thought for a second. "No," I said, "*I'll* call them."

The game of musical chairs—or desks—never did sort itself out. The storage company never found Sally's furniture—I doubt they looked for it—and they refused to pick up what they had delivered. It was more trouble than it was worth, they said.

Sally didn't care. The important thing was that they had delivered her books. Boxes and boxes and boxes of books crowded every square foot of her apartment, along with the oldest and most decrepit pieces of her furniture, which the storage company had managed to hang onto. What had looked like a rather neatly furnished place the day before was now a shambles. I couldn't understand why Mother stored some of the ruined tables and shelves that were now crammed into every room. They were junk, barely fit for a garage sale. I suggested to Sally that we call the Salvation Army and have them pick up what she couldn't use.

"I can use *all* of it," she insisted. I couldn't budge her, even when I reminded her that she had been thrown out of one apartment because the landlady said it was a firetrap. "That was because of my comic books," Sally said. She had been an avid comic collector and had hundreds, perhaps thousands, of them. I had forgotten all about the comics. A traitorous part of me prayed they were lost along with the sofa bed.

"Where are they now?"

"They're right here!" she said happily, gesturing to half a room full of boxes.

I had to admit that I was as much a pack rat as Sally. My apartment was full, and I was in the process of making it even more crowded by carrying home furniture from Aunt Ginny's and Mother's. I had already rented a storage bin on the outskirts of Washington in which I planned to put some of it until I could clear space for it. So I didn't feel I could criticize Sally on this point, even though she had never been able to manage her possessions without help. Did it really matter? I needed help with certain areas of my life. She needed help with her plunder.

I suggested we put the comics in storage again immediately, but Sally would have none of it. She'd been waiting for years to handle her beloved collections again, and she could hardly wait to get them out on the shelves.

For the next few days, I unpacked boxes of books, shelving them and dismantling the boxes to put out in the trash. Sally rested most of the time, lying down on her bed as I worked, but even with only one pair of hands—mine—the apartment began to take shape.

One afternoon, as Sally took a nap for several hours, I set up her stereo in the living room and arranged her records on a shelf she had designated for that purpose. I also moved the furniture around to accommodate the record player. When Sally came out of her bedroom, I could see she didn't like the new configuration. I'd been at it for hours and, as usual, was expecting gratitude, but instead she gave me an angry look. "It feels like your place, not mine," she said. "You make me feel like a failure the way you run around cleaning up."

I have to admit now that I wouldn't like someone doing the same in my apartment, but I felt that she had lost her right to autonomy by being too tired to do what was necessary. I was a juggernaut in my determination to see her *settled*. I was unable successfully to address the real issues—how lonely she was and would be, how well she was able to see to her meals, how consistently she could get herself out of the house in the morning and over to the center. For me, being settled depended on bookcases. I blew up at her, reminding her who was doing all the work, but I was being unfair. She'd never asked me to. It was my own sense of order that dictated I break my back to make her place look right—right as far as I was concerned, that is.

Thinking back to other losses in my life—my father, Aunt Ginny—I can see a pattern of willed denial that began almost immediately after my initial grief. I went into a frenzy of activity each time—*constructive* activity—so constructive, in fact, that I could easily persuade myself that it was absolutely necessary. This time, Sally was impeding my progress, and my temper began to explode regularly as she hampered my furious movement.

It was easier at Mother's house. At least there was no one to argue with me about my choices as I threw out almost everything that couldn't be sold. As I worked my driven way around the house, I was grateful to Mother for being unmaterialistic, even in a benign sense, and unsentimental. Aunt Ginny had left me the responsibility for distributing her furnishings, and I'd found it mountainously saddening, for every item in her house was precious to her, and I felt each piece should go to someone who knew how special it was. I now appreciated Mother's Formica dinette table, her Conran's coffee table, her BarcaLounger, and all the other pieces of furniture that had no stories behind them. I hired a local company to hold a tag sale for me, and rented a bin to store the few mementos that I intended to keep.

I didn't know what to do with the contents of the closets and shelves in Sally's room. Besides another ten boxes of books, including both an old set of Oz as well as scores of Barbara Cartland romances, she had her extensive seashell collection and a menagerie of thirty or more "egg people," little figurines she had made from hollow eggshells. Daddy had built in vitrines to house her shells, and the fragile objects had sat on the glasss shelves, behind the glass doors, ever since. There was no room for them at her apartment, so I packed them carefully, wrapping them in paper towels and laying them on pads of crumpled newspaper. I put them in storage, wondering when they would ever be brought out again.

Tackling the attic filled me with dread, not only because clearing it out would be harder than the other jobs I'd set for myself, but also because I loved it so. Every couple of years, I had pulled down the stairs and climbed up to spend an afternoon sorting through my own old keepsakes. There were portfolios of my childhood drawings, trunks of my party dresses that Mother had loved and saved, boxes of outfits for my Madame Alexander ballerina and my Toni doll. I had spent hours and hours looking at these old treasures.

When I finally gathered the courage to look at them now, I found they had lost their appeal. I was sick of sentiment. In a fury of pragmatism, I found myself throwing out much of what had once delighted me. I didn't have time to dwell on the past; I needed to prepare for a future that at that moment looked impossibly complicated and difficult.

The attic was also crammed with large black plastic garbage bags of yarn from the manic phase when Sally had been crocheting ponchos. Mother had threatened many times to throw the yarn away, but Sally insisted she would use it some day, and Mother always relented. In Mother's fantasy of the future there was the possibility that Sally would be well enough to live independently "one of these days" and take it all away. "It doesn't belong to me," Mother said many times. "She bought it with her own money."

The day I moved the yarn was a Saturday, and I was due back in New York the following Monday. Sally had started sleeping at her apartment again, so that her return there wouldn't coincide with my departure. I drove over to pick her up, we went out to breakfast, and then I told her she would either have to make her own plans for the day or help me work at Mother's house.

"I'll help you," she said.

We went to the house, Sally walked in, and within five minutes she said, "I think I need to rest a while, Peggy. Do you mind?"

"Do I have a choice?"

She went to her room. I watched her go with a mixture of sympathy and bitterness—my chronic reaction to Sally's disability. I needed Sally, too, but I would never have expressed that to her. I needed her just to be there with me as I worked, but I knew that she was unable to stay awake. Sally always seemed low, if not depressed, and she habitually spent a part of every day resting. Now, with Mother's death, she seemed barely able to drag herself from the car to the house, much less sit up with me while I cleaned and packed.

By noon I was only half done, and my knees ached from climbing up and down the narrow, steep attic stairs, carrying load after load of yarn. I could have called Sally to help me, but I left her in her room. It was just easier that way. It took me until midafternoon to transfer the yarn to the living room, where I stacked the bags in a pile as big as an igloo, more than twelve feet in diameter. After I was done, I called Sally to look at it, certain that she would agree with me that it couldn't possibly be kept any longer. Again, I appealed to her natural generosity and suggested that we donate it to Goodwill.

My logic fell on deaf ears. Sally was adamant.

"I want to keep it," she pleaded.

"How much of it?" I asked.

"All of it."

Again, like Mother, I couldn't dissuade her and I also couldn't bring myself to dispose of it on my own. I was disgusted at Sally's tenacity and at my own weakness of will. For many years I'd been sympathetic to Mother's frustrations with her, but, again, I now had a new understanding of her dilemma.

I still wasn't close to finished. Each morning for three weeks I had gone through a bookshelf or a file cabinet, packing away what I wanted to keep—family photographs, a folder of letters and receipts relating to Sally's illness, a few of my old children's books, Mother's beloved Wedgewood dishes, the brittle blueprints and plans for the house, an old felt fedora of Daddy's that Mother, too, had been unable to throw away—and leaving the rest for the tag sale.

Every day I would tick off the rooms I'd sorted through, and move on to the next. Sunday morning I finally got to the hall closets, starting with two near the bedrooms. I opened the one on the left, where we had kept medicines, cleaning supplies, and toiletries on the upper shelves and a vacuum cleaner in a large space below. The shelves were crammed with stock—four jars of Pond's cold cream, three bottles of Prell shampoo, five boxes of Brillo, four bottles of Ivory liquid, a dozen packages of paper towels, eight of toilet paper—all bought on sale, no doubt. I had already cleared out the kitchen cabinets, which were filled with canned goods, jars of peanut butter, and rolls of plastic wrap and aluminum foil. I hated seeing the supplies—enough for years—hoarded as if against another Great Depression. It looked obsessive, like Sally's yarn. It looked eccentric. It looked crazy.

THAT afternoon, Sally came with me to drive a load of boxes to storage. I was uneasy from the start and immediately regretted bringing her along. Mother had left some things to Sally specifically—a set of brown dishes Sally had always admired, the piano, her sewing machine—but the bulk of the furniture was mine to keep or dispose of as I pleased. As we drove, I felt an old wariness overcome me—the apprehension of Sally's envy—and I began to dread opening the door of the storage bin, where I had already moved much of what I intended to keep, for fear of what Sally would say. I was doing so much to try to help her, I felt, and I thought it would break me to hear so much as a word about what I was lucky to have, or what she wished were hers.

The day was sunny and pleasantly hot, and we drove with the car windows open. I had to barrette my hair out of my eyes, but Sally let hers blow across her face. Even so, she managed to look around a bit, commenting as we drove along Route 50 east of Washington that this was the way to Tysons Corner, a shopping center she knew well.

The storage bin company was in a new business district set in a field just off a highway that ran through the countryside in Chantilly. The meadows were broken up now, gone to housing developments and shopping centers, with patches in between that were posted with billboards listing their zoning classification and the acreage available. I hated to see the old farms disappear, and Sally agreed it was awful. I felt a million years old, far from my past and unfamiliar with my present.

We pulled off the main highway to a small access road that ran past new, empty-looking office buildings. In the middle of nowhere, surrounded by a tall chain-link fence, the storage compound looked like a prison. I punched in my code number to open an electronic gate. As we drove in, the rows of long cinder-block buildings, their windowless sides studded with door after locked door, took on the eerie character of an arid De Chirico cityscape, but without the long shadows of hidden figures. It was so quiet we could hear the car tires rolling on the macadam that surrounded the warehouses, and when I cut the engine, the only sound was the crickets' chirp from the long grass that grew on the other side of the fence.

I opened the door of the storage bin and noticed that Sally perked up. She was curious to see what I'd put there. Taking boxes from the back of the car, I watched her move tentatively among the furniture, cartons, and bags. She asked what some of the things were, and I told her. As I moved more boxes in, she stepped back to get out of my way. She seemed withdrawn, as if to acknowledge that this was my business. On her way out of the room, she paused in front of a chest of drawers that had been in my bedroom when I was growing up and idly pulled open the top drawer. I'd thrown some clothes into it at the last minute—a couple of old evening dresses, a sweater, and the fedora of my father's that Mother had left hanging on a peg in the utility room for twenty years. It was limp with age, covered with dust, and there was a hole in it.

Sally smiled for the first time in days. "Aw," she murmured. "You kept Dad's hat."

Sally wept the day I left Arlington to go back to New York.

"I'll be back every weekend," I told her.

"I know, I know, I know," she kept repeating.

I couldn't imagine how she would get along by herself, and I thought I was the only one who understood what she was feeling—the fog of sadness, the sick and helpless grief over Mother's death and her own solitude. It was as if none of the social services agencies understood mourning—the depth of it, the length of it, the way it affects the way you look at every aspect of life. Sally's eyes were so dead these days she could have been blind.

Driving out of Washington, I felt as if I were leaving myself behind, too—not just Sally. My childhood seemed to have disappeared with Mother's death. These days, I was comfortable only in Arlington, surrounded by Mother's friends and neighbors—the surrogate parents of a thirty-eight-year-old orphan. New York began to look like another place of exile to me, where no one but my cats cared if I came or went.

That wasn't true, of course. My friends made it clear that they cared about me, and every day one or another of them made a gesture of comfort or affection. My coworkers were solicitous and warm and went out of their way to see that I had company at lunch every day. My friend in the art department, Danielle, came into my office the first afternoon I was back and shut the door. She pulled up a chair close to mine. "I want to know how you are, Peggy," she said. *"Really."*

I kept insisting I was fine, and I honestly thought I was. I was still busy enough to avoid the hidden well of sorrow that would engulf me when I slowed my frenzied pace. When I saw Fiona at my usual Wednesday morning appointment, I described all I had been doing, leaving her with the inevitable impression of someone who was handling everything well.

Only at night, when I was sleeping, did my true desolation appear. I dreamed about Mother hour after hour and woke crying, the tears streaming down my cheeks. The images set before me by my unconscious were grotesquely misleading: She was always alive. In one dream, she was weak, lying in her own bed, recovering from some terrible illness. I sat beside her holding her hand and sobbing. "Oh, Mama," I said, leaning my head down to rest my cheek on her arm. "You don't know what I've been through." Or, in another, she was standing in the yard, watching me pull my car slowly into the driveway. Her face was girlish and pretty, the way it always was when she was excited to see someone she loved. As I ran to hug her, she laughed delightedly. I was trembling with relief that she was here, after all. It didn't matter that I'd been through hell. None of it mattered, as long as she was alive. Again, I cried with gratitude.

Then I would wake and know it was a dream, and weep with sadness. I missed her so much—more than at first, more than when I was in Arlington, at home, surrounded by the detritus of her life. I couldn't look at my answering machine, knowing it would never again give me a message from her. When I thought of her stylish piano playing, I was literally sick with regret that I hadn't made a tape of it. That loss kept crossing my mind, and whenever it did I would almost double over with an ache in my chest.

I looked around my apartment at the furniture I'd brought there over the last few months—Aunt Ginny's desk, Mother's gate-leg table—and it looked hideously out of place. There was only one small object, a ceramic baby bluebird from Aunt Ginny's, that seemed to be an appropriate memento. It magically reminded me of her goodness and gentleness. I had nothing like that to bring Mother back to me, I thought, until I opened a thick envelope from her that had arrived after her death. I hadn't been able to bring myself to look at it at first, but now I spilled out its contents. There was no note, just a jumble of clippings from *The Washington Post*. The one on top was an article about jobs in publishing, and it carried a chart with the names of the magazine editors with the highest earnings. "Notice *all* these big salaries are going to MEN!!!" Mother had written in pencil along the border. I folded it up again and put it in my wallet. It seemed just the right bit of ephemera to represent her intelligent, outraged memory.

Friends asked me out, but I could rarely bring myself to go. In January I had met a man at a dinner party who struck a chord in me. I'd hoped to see him again, but when he called to offer condolences and ask me out for coffee, I heard myself telling him I couldn't go. Whereas I had been holding up well at first, I now began to feel weaker; I was always on the verge of tears. It was impossible to conceive of talking, much less flirting, with someone I didn't know.

I decided to stay at home, except for dinner now and then with Debbie and Andrea—the friends whose dog had so outraged Sally after the memorial service—at a neighborhood restaurant. I'd known Debbie since our freshman year in college, and she had known Mother. I could talk about anything I needed to with them, or I could sit and say nothing. It was good to get out sometimes. Usually, I would go home and call Sally and coax her to talk to me. She often said she couldn't remember anything that had happened to her during the day, although she was careful, she said, to go to the mental health center. After that, her time was a blur. I asked her if she was eating all right, though I knew she would take most of her meals at McDonald's. She almost always ended the conversation by saying, "You're coming this weekend, aren't you, Peggy?"

"Of course, Sally," I would answer.

Every Friday I would start the drive to Arlington as soon as I could leave work. The Jersey Turnpike became as familiar to me as my own block. I knew every toll booth and rest area, every stretch of grassland, every exit. I knew the last rest stop had a Big Boy, the one past the Delaware Bridge a Roy Rogers. I had been getting thinner and thinner, although I was always hungry, and when I drove to Arlington I would stop at least once for a heavy snack to tide me over on the long drive— french fries, hot fudge ice cream cake. By the time I reached Lyn and Earl's house, where I stayed now that Mother's house was empty, it was always past midnight. They gave me a key, and I would let myself in quietly. In the morning I would pick up Sally and we would go out for lunch, or for a drive, or to visit Donald and Betty. Lyn and Earl always asked us for a meal or tea, and we both appreciated being with them, as if we still had family. Sunday night I would drive Sally home, and head back.

One Sunday night as I approached the toll booths at the northern end of the Jersey Turnpike, I thought I saw a small white dog in the distance, crossing the highway, about a mile in the distance. I blinked, lost sight of it, and focused my eyes straight ahead. I was so worn out I thought I was hallucinating. I was driving cautiously, in the slow lane, and was dimly aware that a car was speeding up on my left. When I glanced at it as it passed me, I saw the white dog again. It was real. The car to my left hit it with a terrible thud, and I thought I heard the body fly against my fender as I went by a split second later. I began to scream and pulled off the road. Behind me, cars were stopping, and someone was directing traffic away from the little white mound on the macadam. I sat in my car crying wildly, uncontrollably, hysterically.

The next day, I called Sally and told her I needed to stay in New York for a weekend. My apartment looked like a hotel room that the maid had forgotten to clean. I never quite managed to unpack my bag, and I had no time to straighten up. I needed to reinhabit my home, if only for a couple of days. Also, I was so tired and depressed I was afraid to make the drive.

The weekend I stayed home it rained continually. Saturday afternoon it poured. I went out to do errands, and though I was wearing a raincoat and carrying an umbrella, I was thoroughly soaked when I got back to my apartment. The evening newscasts carried the story that the Schoharie Creek in Upstate New York had flooded under heavy rains and had swept away a bridge on the New York State Thruway. The Schoharie was the trout stream that ran through my property in the Catskills. When the phone rang at about seven o'clock, I knew it was one of my Upstate neighbors.

The town had been evacuated. As the Schoharie rose that afternoon, it coursed down Main Street and rolled through my little house, taking down my shed, depositing inches of mud everywhere, tearing loose my fuel tanks and carrying them downstream, and washing a telephone pole up in the yard. I couldn't sleep after hearing the news, but the next day, almost crippled with fatigue, I drove Upstate to survey the damage. The lawn looked like a sandbar; the gardens were covered with mud. Some had been ripped out completely. The basement was still full of water. The ground-level floors had buckled. Friends had found a key, come in, and moved all my furniture to the second floor, so it had been spared, but the house was in ruin.

Back in New York, I didn't tell anyone at first. I was stunned that a new kind of trouble could come to me. I was already overwhelmed by sympathy, and now I was embarrassed to need more. My Upstate neighbors told me how to file for flood insurance, but when the adjuster returned my call and said I had to get estimates for the repairs, I broke down. "I can't do it," I said. I was stretched to the limit. I couldn't do one more thing.

EASTER weekend, I drove to Arlington. I had hoped, but not expected, that someone would invite Sally and me for the holiday meal. I began to sense that while Mother's friends and neighbors were eager to help me, most of them were at a loss to know how to help Sally. I suspected they didn't want to start a relationship with her that might lead to her depending on them. They had all seen Mother struggle under the burden of Sally's needs, and they probably feared being sucked into a similar morass. Or perhaps they simply thought that a small gesture would not be enough. Two of Mother's neighbors did reach out to Sally, one to call her and one to buy her a lamp, and Sally had made no effort to respond. Only Donald and Betty and Lyn and Earl called Sally regularly. What made me saddest was the certainty that no one would begin looking in on Sally later if they weren't doing it already.

Sally and I might have had Easter dinner out with Donald and Betty, but this year Donald was in the hospital. We took him some flowers and then went alone for our meal. Sally wanted to go to a Hot Shoppes cafeteria where she and Mother had often eaten. As we went through the line, she enthusiastically filled her tray, but when we sat down she couldn't eat. She was so depressed she could only cry. "I don't know if I can make it, Peggy," she said over and over. "I really don't know if I can make it." She sounded utterly helpless against her pain.

"You *can*, Sally," I told her, though I was in so much anguish myself that I knew exactly how desperate she felt. "You have to give it time. Don't expect too much of yourself."

At the next table, a family was eating slowly, looking up at us now and then. The woman caught my eye and smiled gently, as if to put her arms around us. She radiated kindness, but I couldn't smile back. I could only sit quietly, hoping I wouldn't burst into tears.

Early Monday morning, back in New York, I called my friend Rick, who had come to Virginia for Mother's funeral. I was still trembling from a dream, and I was frightened at how low I felt. I needed to hear a rational voice. He asked about work, about what I was reading, about whether I was writing any articles. I could tell he was trying to talk about life as I'd lived it before Mother died, but I had no answers.

"Have you told Fiona how bad you're feeling?" he finally asked me.

"What difference would it make?"

"Either you call her this morning, or I will," he said. I agreed to do it.

....

twenty-four

One night during the week after Easter, Sally called me to say she was in the "Care House," a home run by ACRI as a temporary shelter for clients who needed extra support but were not sick enough to go to a hospital. "I'm not going back to the apartment, Peggy," she told me with absolute firmness, and I knew instantly that a team of oxen would not be able to move her there. I argued with her for a while, and then one of the Care House counselors came on the phone.

"Sally's talking about moving back in with Mike and Tammy," she said. "We're talking to her about what it was like for her there before, and how bad it would be for her to move back, but we're not making much headway."

I asked for Sally again, and told her I would be down over the weekend to see her. "Don't do anything yet," I asked her.

"I already gave notice," she said.

I blew up at her. I knew she'd done it so we couldn't force her back to the apartment, and I was furious that she hadn't talked to me first.

When I got down to Arlington the following Saturday, I could see Sally had had a bad week. She looked terrible. Her hair was filthy, and her clothes were wrinkled and stained. But she had an agenda now—to move—and that was comforting to her. It meant she was going forward in life, and I understood how good that could feel. Her voice sounded stronger than it had since Mother died. She planned to move into the basement of Mike and Tammy's house, as they had already rented out her former room.

She said the basement was a lovely, large room, and then I heard the phrase "full of possibilities." I knew that meant that it was not a fit place to live now, in the present. I doubted it ever would be. I had never seen it, and I wasn't going to go look now. I didn't want to know Mike and Tammy—I didn't even want to see them. And I refused to treat Sally's whim as a plan until it was unavoidable.

The Care House counselors knew all about Mike and Tammy, and about Sally's obsessive attachment to them. They reminded her that she had never received the kind of treatment from them that she yearned for, and that she had spent a couple of years of her life recovering from one disappointing encounter with them after another. They talked about how much Sally had wanted to have a place of her own at last, where she could have her books, have friends to visit, and have a bit of privacy when she needed it. They talked and talked and talked and talked, and I watched Sally's face as they did. She was cheerful and relaxed—and impassive—in the way she became when she had made up her mind to do something and knew that no one and nothing could dissuade her. She was simply waiting out this barrage of reason until she could make her getaway and do what she wanted.

I decided to make a deal with her that if it did nothing to mitigate the present circumstances would at least help me out in the future.

"You can move back to Mike and Tammy's if you're bent on it," I said, "but when that blows up, you have to go into a group home."

"Fine!" she agreed. She was the only one who lacked a presentiment of doom about her plans, so she was happy to say whatever she had to to get me off her back.

"Say it."

"If this doesn't work out, I'll go into a group home," she said in a singsong voice.

"Say it again seriously, and promise."

"I *promise* to go into a group home if this doesn't work out!" she shouted angrily.

I was satisfied. I knew I had her attention. I also knew that somewhere down the line she would be in a group home. Sally was satisfied, too, confident she'd made a good deal.

Rhonda surprised me by being in favor of Sally's move back to Mike and Tammy's. She had heard all about Sally's past there, but, she said, Sally was so deeply lonely at her apartment she couldn't go on living in it. I asked about the basement. There was a pause while Rhonda was trying to decide how to describe it to me. "You and I wouldn't want to live there," she finally said. "But we're not Sally. And she *does* want to." I had faith in Rhonda, and I thought that even if she was wrong, I would trust her to rectify the situation when the time came. She was in charge now. I tried to remember that, and to remember that that's what Mother had had in mind when she got in touch with PLAN to begin with.

A month later, as if to put me on guard against relaxing my vigilance, PLAN fired Rhonda. Rhonda called to give me the news, and I could tell that she herself was shaken by this turn of events. She said PLAN's Richmond, Virginia, headquarters had voted no confidence in her, and that she had been dismissed. When I asked her why she thought they would do such a thing, she was speechless. She had no idea, she said.

I called PLAN's office in Richmond, and spoke with someone who told me that PLAN's lawyer had advised them not to discuss "the case" with anyone, so there was nothing they could tell me. Eventually, when Rhonda filed for unemployment, which the state of Virginia does not give to employees fired for cause, PLAN responded that Rhonda had kept poor notes. She received unemployment, and I felt relieved that nothing more serious had apparently caused her dismissal. At the time she was fired, however, I had no such assurance, so although I was sure in my heart that Rhonda was the person I knew her to be, I was also cautious enough, for Sally's sake, to want to remain allied with PLAN, the only organization I knew of that was designed to provide someone like Sally with the supervision she needed.

I decided to hire Rhonda privately, so that Sally would not have to do without her at this critical point, but to keep an open mind about PLAN. I nevertheless sent PLAN a letter stating that I thought it was grossly irresponsible to let Rhonda go without notice and without hiring a replacement for her who could be eased into the job. My sister, I reminded them, was in a bad state, and they should have known that continuity was of paramount importance to her at a time like this. I waited for their reply, and when I received a nonanswer to my letter, basically stating with old-fashioned parental authority that PLAN knew what was best, I tore it up in disgust.

It wasn't until I met the social worker who was to replace Rhonda temporarily until another could be hired that I began to fear for the future—Sally's primarily, and then, unavoidably, mine. The new worker was a polite young Virginia girl, well groomed and well meaning, who spoke quietly but smoothly in a language I call clinic-ese, which consists mostly of gentle questions rather than specific answers and seems designed to float above all difficulties and all distasteful scenes. I knew that both Sally and I would shift to our best behavior automatically when dealing with her, and that no real dialogue would be possible, but there was nothing I could do about it. I could only hope that when PLAN hired a permanent replacement it would be someone with half as much backbone as Rhonda.

t w e n t y - f i v e

••

At the point when Sally and I were most depressed, I received a plane ticket in the mail from four friends in Seattle, who had pooled some funds and bought me a vacation. I was at the breaking point, and at first I thought I couldn't go. Like Mother, I wanted to sit at home and will disaster to stay away, rather than leave and possibly invite it to happen. But with the ticket in hand, I found myself daydreaming about seeing my old friends again, and I decided impulsively to go for ten days, planning the trip to coincide with my birthday.

I called Sally to tell her. "You'll be okay," I said. "It's only ten days."

There was silence at her end.

"I'll call you from there," I said. Then I gave her the number at Elizabeth's house, where I would be staying. I was feeling strange about my first birthday without Mother, who always sent me two cards, one at home and another at my office. "It's my birthday," I boldly reminded Sally. "Do you think you could send me a card?"

"Sure I could," she said.

I would have liked her to do it by herself, but more than that I didn't want to be disappointed.

In Seattle, I was removed from all the worries that dogged me in New York. I went to a baseball game at the Kingdome, to a Fourth of July picnic in the Skagit Valley, to the public market on the waterfront. Every evening I looked out the huge west-facing windows of Elizabeth's living room and watched the sun set over the Olympic Mountains, above Puget Sound.

Late one night, Sally telephoned. I took the receiver from Elizabeth with trepidation, wondering what calamity had occurred. "Nothing's wrong," she insisted. "I just wanted to talk to somebody really *good*."

We chatted for a while, with me asking most of the questions. As usual, I asked how things were at the mental health center. I was sorry as soon as I did, for I sensed some resistance.

"You're still going, aren't you?" I asked.

"Not really," she answered.

"What do you do instead?"

"I relax, Peggy," she said with obvious irritation. "Can't a person relax now and then?"

When Sally lived in her apartment, "relaxing" meant lying in her bed much of the day, going out perhaps only for food and cigarettes. Now that she was living in the basement, I wasn't sure how to picture her day.

"I like to sit upstairs in the kitchen and listen to the radio with Tammy," she said. She sounded sad, and I thought that perhaps Tammy's company wasn't all Sally had hoped it would be when she moved back to the house. There was none of the blithe determination left in her voice that had given it its vibrant timbre when she first decided to move back.

"Tell me again when you're coming home," she finally said, with an offhand energy that sounded forced.

When I hung up, I turned to Elizabeth and told her I was worried. The mental health center was the only structure in Sally's day, and also the only place she ate a balanced meal. I thought that without its regularizing influence she might begin to forget to take her medicine on time, or fail to have her blood monitored regularly for its lithium level.

Elizabeth calmed me down. "You're on vacation," she said, "And now Sally is too. She probably feels entitled."

On the flight back to New York I anxiously thought of the piles of work that were left to settle Mother's estate and of Sally's faltering mood, but when the plane touched down, I noticed I was looking forward to getting back to my apartment. At home that night, I went through my mail and stroked the cats. When it was time for bed, I realized that for the first time since Mother's death, I wasn't depressed.

The rest of the summer wasn't bad. I went to Arlington regularly, usually every other week. Sally and I went to a play once at Arena Stage, and another time we drove out to Great Falls Park for a picnic. She didn't seem much better than before, but she was more or less settled, at least for the moment, and that made me feel a bit easier. I stopped haranguing her about the center, and we actually enjoyed being together. I think this was the first time that I had felt close to Sally. I would ask her about the past, and we would reminisce about vacations we had taken, or about some of the pets we'd had, especially our dogs. She sang old songs, and I had her write down the words to some of my favorites—"Buckeye Jim," "Beautiful Dreamer," and "Sweet and Low." She always knew all the verses.

For Sunday breakfast we would go to a local restaurant that had a fancy brunch bar. If Donald and Betty were able to go with us, we would meet them there and spend an hour or two talking. Betty was trying to teach me about money management, and she had tips on good books to help me become familiar with financial terminology and strategy. Donald was interested in and knowledgeable about a wide range of topics, and he and Sally always had something to discuss. The conversation segued easily from theology to ethics to botany, and so on. I sensed that these visits were the only times Sally had a chance to discuss subjects that were intellectually challenging to her. Her friend Franklin was the only one among her acquaintances whose intellectual life paralleled hers at all, and she didn't see him often. Tammy and Mike's interests were quite different. While Sally found them fascinating on a visceral level, she couldn't exactly engage them in discourse.

I usually stayed with Lyn and Earl, who always greeted me with warmth and enthusiasm. Lyn called herself my "other mother," and always packed food for me to eat on the drive home. They kept up the invitations for dinner or iced tea in the afternoon, and once they rented a movie for an evening and we sat in their living room eating popcorn and watching *Pride and Prejudice*. That night, I went to the kitchen for a glass of beer, and on my way back caught a glimpse of Sally's face in the blue light of the television set. She was smiling at some piece of dialogue, and her face was glowing with pleasure. When the movie was over, we sat and talked about it for a while, comparing it to the book, which we barely remembered, and discussing the various forms of pride and prejudice we'd just witnessed. Sally looked so happy. She complimented Lyn on the popcorn and on her choice of films, and said how much she had enjoyed herself.

I remembered what a huge capacity for joy Sally possessed and what delight she took in pleasure. Suddenly I was filled with sadness. How could I go on living in New York, how I could dare to be happy by myself, when Sally was lifted out of her quotidian misery only by my presence and what I could offer her? Or so it seemed, for her voice on the phone when we spoke long distance was always vague, sad, and distracted.

Not for the first time, I felt myself to be on the brink of moving back to Virginia to take care of her. In a way, it looked easier than living my "own life," whatever that was, and living with guilt. And besides, I told myself, if life is a collection of alliances and incidents, Sally was my life as much as anyone or anything else. There were worse fates than that of being needed by your only sister, I thought.

In the early eighties, when I worked as a researcher in *Newsweek*'s religion section, I had loved interviewing church people, who were committed, body and soul, to the work they did. Their dedication held an intense appeal for me. I read books by Dorothy Day and others, inspired by their values and their urgency. I saw lost souls all around me, and I wished I could do something to help them. A poster sprouting on bus shelters and construction fences around my neighborhood showed an image of Jesus with the text, "How can you worship a homeless man on Sunday and walk past one on Monday?" The people I most admired couldn't. When I spoke about it to my friends, however, or even to Fiona, they looked at me as if I were losing my mind. "You identify with people who give up their own lives for a goal," Fiona said. "Let's try to find out why." Sally was why, of course—Sally and all the other people around us who need advocates and helpers.

Toward the end of August, the man I'd met in January called me again, and to my surprise I heard my voice leap with eagerness when he asked me to have dinner the next night. I hadn't been out of my own neighborhood for a long time, so I told him I would walk downtown, to his place.

Leaving work the next evening, I was doubtful again. I wasn't really much better than I had been for months, and as I walked I began to dread making conversation with someone I hardly knew. Just as I began to think of calling him to explain that I couldn't come after all, I noticed I was on his block. I happened to look up, and there he was, waving from the window of his building. It was too late.

When I'd first set eyes on Harvey, I'd decided on the spot that he was the man I'd been waiting for all my life. Although he was intensely attractive I felt calm, secure, and relaxed. As I looked at him it was somehow magically clear to me that it was only a matter of time before we'd be together forever. But after Mother died, I hadn't been able to think of romance, much less of love. In fact, I didn't expect to be able to consider it again for a long time, if ever. I had become like Mother, keeping myself on hold.

After our first meal together, Harvey and I were as close as I'd once secretly believed we would be. The next afternoon, walking down a sidewalk in the city, I felt the sun on my arms and realized I was noticing the weather for the first time since March. I was alive, after all. And in a way I can't quite explain, I was more ready than ever to fall in love. I felt vulnerable in the unnerving but thrilling way one does at the beginning, but I also knew that I had been through the worst of my life and survived. I felt strong enough to take a chance.

I told Harvey all about my sister, and he listened with sympathy and interest. He wasn't afraid of mental illness, as many people were. I told him I was still very busy with the estate, and that I had to go to Arlington frequently to see Sally. He understood. He offered to go with me, asking if that would make the trip easier for me, but determined as I was to have him know all the complications of my life, I wasn't ready to introduce him to the fray. I knew that seeing Sally with him would make it harder for me to ignore her quirks, her appearance, and her sadness.

I kept making the drive down by myself, arriving at Lyn and Earl's late on Friday nights. It seemed that I always had a slight cold, now. I would hear myself, each time, say to Lyn, "Don't get close, I'm coming down with something." She noticed it too, and she also pointed out that my sniffles and coughs cleared up as I packed to go back to New York Sunday afternoon. I had developed an allergy—I was allergic to going to Arlington. I again began to regret my desire to be needed.

Harvey and I had been keeping company for a month when he left for a three-week trip to Finland, where an exhibition of his paintings was opening at a museum. One Saturday while he was gone, I went to the wedding of an old friend, a psychotherapist, in New York. At the wedding dinner, I was seated next to a colleague of the groom's, a man about my age. We spent the afternoon dancing and making small talk. I noticed I was apologizing frequently about little things—dropping my napkin, wanting to sit out a number, looking for a waiter to bring me a cup of coffee. My companion also noticed. "What are you feeling guilty about?" he asked in his most shrinklike voice. He smiled self-mockingly, but my spontaneous answer was blankly serious.

"For being alive," I answered.

twenty-seven

....

I went to Arlington in late October to celebrate Sally's forty-seventh birthday. Lyn and Earl made a party for her, complete with candles to blow out, and I ordered in Chinese food from her favorite restaurant. She laughed a lot that night, but the rest of the weekend she seemed wan and withdrawn. She was immensely fat, fatter than I had ever seen her. She had to struggle to stand up, throwing her knees out to the side, so her stomach fit between her thighs, and rocking herself to her feet with a groan. I didn't say anything to her about it. I knew what it was like to try to fill the empty place inside. I did it with work. Sally hadn't worked since her last bad breakdown, and although Rhonda had mentioned that Sally could try to find a part-time job, neither Sally nor I took her suggestion seriously. Sally was too depressed to work, and while her isolation and lethargy contributed to her depression, she didn't have the energy to break the cycle. Instead, Sally filled up her empty place with food. She would probably go on a diet soon. She usually did, and she was capable of sticking to it if she wanted to. She had lost more than fifty pounds at least once, I knew. I felt that putting any pressure on her to reduce now would only increase her anxiety.

What worried me more was her comparative silence. I could tell she had things on her mind that she intended to keep to herself. Because she was by nature an open person, she had learned through the years to guard her secrets by keeping her mouth shut. She couldn't take the chance, it seemed, of letting fall some private bit of information, especially around Mother.

I didn't know how life at Mike and Tammy's was going, but I had a feeling Sally's enthusiasm was deteriorating. And I began to suspect that perhaps she had worn out her welcome. The week before, I'd spoken to Tammy on the phone, and mentioned that I would be there for Sally's birthday.

"Oh," she said quickly, "she needs a radio."

There was a radio in Sally's stereo system, I knew, but maybe it was broken. When Sally came on the line, I asked her.

"It works fine," she said.

It took me a few days to remember her comment about sitting in the kitchen and listening to the radio. The kitchen was near all the first-floor rooms, where Tammy spent her days, and I was sure Sally liked being there because she felt nearer to whatever activity there was in the house. Now that I knew Tammy didn't want her underfoot, I wasn't sure what to do about it. When I wasn't sure about something, I called Rhonda.

"Don't do anything," she said easily. "Let Tammy talk to Sally if she has a problem."

I learned something every time I talked to Rhonda. This time, it was to let Sally's life run its own course, at least in small ways. To remember I wasn't her keeper. The cumulative effect of Rhonda's advice, I began to see, was to relieve me of the never-ending worries that had exhausted Mother, and to allow Sally the kind of privacy anyone deserves.

Sally was still seeing Rhonda regularly, and she was also looked after by Rhonda's temporary replacement at PLAN. The replacement was nothing if not responsible. She discharged her tasks by the book, taking Sally to doctors' appointments, balancing her checkbook with her, and keeping in regular touch with me. But Sally couldn't talk to her. Neither could I, for that matter. She was "so goody-goody," as Sally put it.

I still had not funded the trust for PLAN, instead continuing to pay by the hour. PLAN tried to make me commit to them, but I was naturally reluctant, after the way they had dismissed Rhonda. Eventually, I received a long, rambling letter from the PLAN director in Richmond, urging me to make up my mind, to choose between PLAN and Rhonda.

How dare she? I thought. How dare she force the issue at a time when Sally and I needed all the help we could get? I was furious, but I knew I was stuck. I needed PLAN, for Rhonda would undoubtedly get another full-time job soon, and then there would be only PLAN to care for Sally. Instead of doing what I wanted to do—pick up a phone, dial the Richmond office, and give the woman a piece of my mind, I had to swallow my anger.

Rhonda, by contrast, was her usual cheerful self, asking me what I'd like her to do and checking in with me to find out what PLAN was doing so her services wouldn't overlap theirs. Sally confided in Rhonda, and Rhonda was careful, in turn, not to tell me more of Sally's business than I needed to know to be of help. She never spoke to me about Sally in a way that put us in cahoots against my sister. At the same time, she never condescended to me, as so many social workers and doctors had to Mother, as if to suggest that they knew Sally better than I did, or, worse, that I was getting in the way of her treatment. When it was important, Rhonda occasionally told me something that I knew Sally would have preferred remain between them, but her manner was so reassuring that it never crossed my mind to confront Sally. Rhonda always had ideas about how to take care of problems, so I left the problems to her.

Rhonda had handled Sally's move to the basement from

the apartment. With all the packing I had done, I wasn't about to take that on, too. I used trust money to pay for it, and when I saw what it cost I told Sally angrily that it would be a cold day in hell before I would help her light out for any other place. She had rejoiced at that, of course, as she had no intention of going anywhere else, ever.

I didn't see Sally's basement room for many months. It was her habit to wait outside for me when I came to pick her up. The weather was warm through the early fall, and she would stand on the sidewalk smoking cigarettes until I pulled up. When she wasn't there, I would knock on the front door, and she would come outside. It wasn't just happenstance, though, that kept me away from her place. Rhonda had told me that it was dreary and that I would find it depressing. I didn't need that. And because I was against Sally living with Tammy and Mike again, I withheld my presence, in effect refusing to celebrate her housewarming.

As the fall turned to winter, it was too cold for Sally to wait for me at the curb, and one day it happened that she wasn't waiting upstairs for me either. Tammy invited me in, and Sally called from the basement, "Come on down!"

I should have known better than to go. It was like descending into a Hades that had, finally, frozen over. The basement was frigid and dank, almost completely raw, with walls-to-be framed in with two-by-fours to make some future bedroom. Sally's furniture, piled high with debris, made a kind of barrier, but anyone coming down to do laundry was forced to walk through what passed for her living area. There was a sink in a corner, and she had bought a Porta Potti so she wouldn't have to go all the way to the second-story bathroom when she had to urinate during the night. I don't know how often she emptied the pan, but it was full now, and the basement stank of urine. Her bed was unmade, and her sheets were brown and stained. It looked as if she hadn't washed them since moving back in. Her clothes were strewn about, there was a plastic garbage bag next to her bed that was overflowing with McDonald's bags, and the floor was littered with cigarette butts and ashes that had spilled out of unemptied ashtrays.

When Sally emerged from behind the would-be partition, she smiled as she always did when I picked her up. She was happy to see me. I was struck dumb by the squalor around us. I gestured toward the stairs and we went out to the car. I didn't say a word. I knew Tammy and Mike would never evict her. The place was a hole. I couldn't believe they had the nerve to charge rent for it. What did Rhonda have in mind when she let Sally move there?

I knew that it had been early spring, bright and warm. The window wells let in enough of the sunshine to make the base-ment light, and the coolness of the room was probably re-freshing then, especially to Sally, who suffered in the tough Virginia heat and humidity much more than a thinner person would. And then Rhonda, as she herself admitted, wasn't par-ticularly sensitive to her clients' appearance, or to the ambi-ence of their homes. This was probably half the reason for her tolerant nature; the other half was her concern for what mat-tered to the client. In Sally's case, that was not exterior life.

I told myself these things, and reminded myself that Sally would have moved to Mike and Tammy's no matter what. But each time I thought of the place, I had a feeling that the dismal basement would be the perfect setting for another breakdown.

PLAN eventually hired someone to replace Rhonda on a full-time basis. Teresa was frank and open and old enough to have seen something of life. Sally liked her, and I thought she seemed competent enough. Meanwhile, PLAN had broken ties with its original Northern Virginia board of directors and moved out of the offices of the Association of Retarded Citi-zens. They took a place in South Arlington that was miles from Sally, so she could no longer easily visit them. They also cut back their office hours, and the telephone was now answered by a machine. I wondered what would happen in a crisis, and when I voiced my concerns to Teresa, she readily gave me her home number. She gave it to Sally as well. It was a generous move, and I appreciated it.

In November, Rhonda was hired to run a new organization, the Personal Support Network (PSN), begun by most of PLAN's former board of directors, and she moved back into her old office at ARC. I continued to use both PLAN and PSN, waiting to see which group survived. If both did, I would eventually drop PLAN, but for now I thought it was prudent to hedge my bets. Next to Rhonda, the best thing about the Personal Support Network was that they required only a modest annual membership fee, plus hourly fees for services, instead of the huge commitment of a trust fund demanded by PLAN (which, on the death of the client, remained with PLAN).

The conflicts between PLAN and Rhonda continued to make it extremely difficult to coordinate care for Sally. PLAN refused to allow Teresa even to speak to Rhonda by telephone, under any circumstances. That seemed unconscionably childish to me, and the conviction that they were willing to sacrifice Sally's best interests to preserve their own collective ego began to gnaw at me. But disgusted though I was, I felt obliged to keep them on.

Teresa complained about Sally's living conditions, and I agreed with her, but there seemed to be little we could do to improve them. It was Sally who finally took the important step of having a toilet installed. While helping balance Sally's checkbook, Rhonda noticed that a check for hundreds of dollars had gone to Tammy and Mike. Sally told her she was paying for the toilet Mike and Tammy had promised many times to have installed. Rhonda stepped in and negotiated a contract that provided for reduced rent over a year's time, to repay what was now called Sally's "advance." All parties signed, Sally got a real toilet, and that took care of the Porta Potti.

I also talked to Sally about how she was living, and told her she had to change her sheets and wash them regularly. She agreed, and I believe she began a new regime with enthusiasm. I don't think she ever wanted to live in grime, but it was difficult for her to find the energy to keep her own place clean, and it was also hard for her to keep to a schedule. I told her she had to do a load of laundry once a week. I wasn't sure what could be done about the general appearance of the basement. I dropped that subject for the time being. If I pointed out the damp concrete floor, the exposed pipes and studs, and the darkness of her living area, it would only make her feel worse. She was still looking at her room as it would be *some day*, not as it was now. To force her to drop her rose-colored glasses would only oppress her with the truth. She was not up to making the place better.

....

A s the holidays approached, I noticed I was calling Rhonda frequently, sometimes several days in a row, as much to hear her calming voice as to talk about Sally. One day, she mentioned that there was a special support group for the siblings of the mentally ill. She just happened to have the name and number of the group leader in New York City.

I was reluctant to try again. I'd felt more depressed than ever after the parents' meeting I'd been to the previous fall.

"It'll be different this time," Rhonda promised. "I think you should go."

November 19, 1987, I left work twenty minutes early and headed up Madison Avenue to Saint James Church for the six o'clock meeting of the Sibling and Adult Children's Network (SAC Network). I was still skeptical, but, worse, I was nearly sick with anxiety. On the way upstairs to the room where the group met, I felt nauseated. My object in life was to get away as much as possible—from Sally, from guilt—not to be sucked in further.

I was met by Gene Sinclair, founder of the New York City group, who was setting out brochures and a sign-in sheet on a long table. I had spoken with her briefly on the phone to find out when and where the meetings took place. Gene was a slender, pretty, elegantly groomed woman in her early sixties, who greeted me with a smile and introduced herself. I waited for her to ask me why I was there, but she didn't. That, apparently, was my business. Her combination of warmth and reserve was just right for me. I felt welcomed, but I was clearly not obliged to offer anything to the proceedings if I didn't want to. I couldn't have spoken then anyway, for I had a lump in my throat. I squinted and looked up at the ceiling, hoping my tears would wash over my eyes and not spill onto my cheeks.

Gene opened the meeting by telling how she had moved back into her parents' apartment ten years before, to take care of them, and thus inherited the care of her schizophrenic brother after they died. He had been seriously ill since childhood, had never lived on his own, and refused to take medication. He was delusional and paranoid—he thought the neighbors were spies, for instance—and he was often out of control, shouting angrily from the apartment window at passersby and raging at his private tormentors. He was a large man, both tall and overweight, and although he had never been physically violent, Gene was a little afraid of what he might do.

As Gene and the others talked about their brothers, sisters, and parents, I remembered my mother's horror at the abusive behavior endured by other parents in her family therapy group, and her realization that, all told, her relationship with Sally was blissful by comparison. Sally was by nature kind and loving. Her goodness, like everyone's, lapsed from time to time, but her basic behavior was polite. Unlike so many people with mental illness, she had found the courage to acknowledge hers, and it was many years since she'd gone off her medicine.

I also began to see that perhaps I was not so unlucky to be solely responsible for Sally. Some of the others had well siblings who gave them almost as much trouble as their ill ones or who were of no help at all. At least there was no one to give

Sally conflicting advice or to blame me if things went wrong.

Listening to the conversation around the table, I heard the others touch on the terrible worries I thought I alone suffered from—that I would get sick too; that no one would want me as a spouse if they knew about my sister; that if I were to have a child, the baby would inherit the disease; that for someone with a family history like mine, fraught with tension and upheaval, the chances for a happy life were slim. Many of them, like me, trivialized their own problems, in deference to the more serious ones of their sick brothers and sisters. Some of the group members had schizophrenic parents, and their stories of childhood were harrowing.

As the others described their ill family members, it dawned on me that the traits of Sally's that I found so discouraging— her lack of financial good sense; her manic generosity; her appetite for sugar, junk food, caffeine, and cigarettes; her casual attitude toward personal hygiene; and her inability to stick with a task or a project—all seemed to be part of her illness, to judge from the fact that everyone else's mentally ill sister or brother or mother or father seemed to share one or another—or all—of them.

I began to feel better about Sally. I mentally spoke a prayer of thanks to the gods that be, and for a moment I felt a kind of love for Sally that I had never expected to feel—one grounded in respect. The relative ease of my situation, compared to that of most of the others at the meeting, now made me less reluctant to speak. Before six months had passed I would see how ill-founded my complacency was, but the relief I felt that evening enabled me at last to begin to acknowledge my sister's affliction and the crucial effect it had had on my life.

It was my turn to speak. "My name is Peggy," I began.

....

A s November approached, I prayed for someone to invite us for Thanksgiving dinner, but no one called. I was tired of driving to Virginia, and I would have been relieved for Sally to come to New York for the holiday, but the memory of her two other visits, especially the memory of their aftermaths, kept me from asking her to come. I couldn't imagine her staying in my cozy, warm apartment for a few days and then being content to return to her dank basement. I was afraid to precipitate another breakdown.

I told Sally I would come down and we could go to any restaurant she chose, and she decided on a kind of half-fast-food place, where we ordered at a window but a waiter brought us our food. Rhonda suggested to Sally that she consider a fancier establishment, where we could make an afternoon of it and treat ourselves to something special. Sally asked me if I would prefer that, but I stupidly said the other would be fine with me. I didn't think it mattered.

The day was overcast and cold, and there were few other diners at the restaurant. The windows looked out on a busy road and an empty parking lot. We sat in the cheerless quiet and ordered our turkey. I was only down for the day, for I didn't feel comfortable imposing on Lyn and Earl or any of the other neighbors who had offered me places to stay, not wanting them to feel obliged to include us in their plans. Sally didn't seem to mind, or didn't say so. She was sullen, but her mood didn't seem to be connected to my visit. Completely silent, she ate her meal with alacrity, but she didn't appear to enjoy it much. I asked her questions about life at the house and what she was doing, and she answered me evasively, with either a grunt or a shrug. Finally I asked her if something was wrong.

In a loud voice, calculated, I thought, to embarrass me and to shut me up, she said, *"Nothing is wrong. Sometimes, Peggy, a person just wants to be quiet!"* I wasn't expecting such vehemence, and it made me jump. A man near us stared at me, and then at Sally.

I began to look forward to the long drive home. This was almost as bad as Easter had been, and it was only the beginning of the holiday season. I didn't have to worry about Christmas, for Trenie, bless her, had invited us both to Pittsburgh to spend it with her family, recently augmented by the birth of their second child, and Aunt Irene.

On Monday, I called Rhonda, who let me know that Mike had been borrowing money from Sally, and that Sally not only felt bad about it but was afraid I would find out and be angry with her. I asked how much he had borrowed, and Rhonda said it was just small sums. Relieved to know what the problem was, and why Sally had been defensive with me, I hung up and forgot about it. But I was still angry at Sally for the scene in the restaurant and decided that if she wanted to be quiet, I would let her. She could call me when she wanted to talk—I wouldn't call first.

PART FOUR

SICKNESS

t h i r t y

••

A fter Thanksgiving, two weeks went by before I heard
from Sally. When she called, her voice sounded weak and
shaky.

"Are you sick?" I asked.

"I have terrible diarrhea," she said. "I've had it for more
than a week."

She hadn't taken any medicine for it and hadn't been to a
doctor. I told her to buy bananas, rice, and Kaopectate, and to
drink water to replenish her fluids. "You have to call a doctor
if it doesn't go right away," I said. "Call me tomorrow night."

The next night, she sounded just as bad. "Go to the doctor,
Sally," I said. "You must have a bug."

Both Rhonda and Teresa called to let me know that there
was no heat in the basement, and that Tammy and Mike
didn't have the money to repair the boiler. They had supplied
electric heaters to their upstairs tenants, but not to Sally.
After Teresa spoke to them about it—firmly—they bought
Sally one, too, but the basement was still cold. I was worried
Sally might develop pneumonia again, but so far she had no
problems with her lungs. She just sounded depressed. I
chalked it up to what I thought was a stomach flu, and perhaps some anxiety over the impending holidays.

I was worried about Christmas too, but as it worked out Trenie's invitation was a godsend. We spent four days in Pittsburgh. Aunt Irene was there, too, and it was clear to me that she had begun to change her attitude toward Sally. I'd spoken with her on the phone several times since Mother's death, and each time I tried to talk a little about Sally and her illness, explaining Sally's disabilities as well as I could and trying to enlighten Aunt Irene about mental illness in general. I talked about how it was hard for the mentally ill to tolerate too much stimulation, and about how difficult it was for Sally to motivate herself, possibly because she had had so few successes with her endeavors. I told her Sally often felt hopeless, which was the worst part of depression, but that the medication she took also made her lethargic. She listened attentively, asking questions and expressing sympathy, and I soon realized that she had not understood, at all, what Sally's life was like. As I began to describe it for her, telling her why Sally needed to retreat now and then or explaining how difficult it was for Sally to keep to a schedule, Aunt Irene's disdain melted away and her natural kindness took over. It was a triumph of education, I thought. Later I would remember a chapter heading in a book on mental illness—"You Can Deal with Anything You Can Name." It was up to me to name Sally's afflictions for Aunt Irene: then she could deal with them herself.

The visit was warm and pleasant—the first family holiday I'd enjoyed in many years. Trenie's husband, Mark, had always been especially sensitive to Sally, and he stayed up late with her, smoking cigarettes and talking about life. Sally even liked being with the children, which was usually a strain for her. She often talked to Carrie, who was two, and admired her newborn brother, Matt. On Christmas day, Sally handed me the best present I could have received, which she had brought from Donald and Betty. Years before, Betty had recorded Mother playing the piano. This fall, she had found the old two-reel tape and had a friend convert it to a cassette. Still grieving, I was almost afraid to play it, but when I did, I found that the music made my heart soar. The tape also included a section of Sally playing her guitar and singing old songs.

The only worrisome part of the vacation was Sally's illness, which had not abated. She spent a lot of time in her room resting, but what bothered me was that her diarrhea was still violent, and worse, she couldn't bring herself to eat Christmas dinner. Turkey, stuffing, and gravy were great favorites of hers. When she also told me she had been losing weight, I told her to see a doctor as soon as she got back to Virginia.

When I called her after Christmas, she sounded frighteningly sick—and she sounded as if she, too, were afraid she might be seriously ill. She had been to a doctor, who was running tests, but he had found nothing obviously wrong.

"You might feel better if you went to the mental health center," I told her, "just to get out of the cold house every day and to get a healthy lunch."

Sally had already thought of that, which made me realize how desperate she must be. "I sleep in my clothes," she said pitifully, "so in the morning I don't have to think about getting dressed in the cold. I can just get out of bed and go."

I should have stepped in at this point to force Sally to honor her promise to move to a group home if things didn't work out at Mike and Tammy's, but Sally was adamantly opposed to the idea. She had lived in one once and was unable to meet the expectations of her counselors there, who insisted she do her part of the chores and honor other house rules. I had forgotten about the Care House, which would have provided the ideal respite, for it was more than nine months since Sally had been there. Teresa didn't know about it, and Rhonda was not seeing Sally enough at this point to realize she needed serious help.

Sally sounded as if she might cry. "When are you coming to see me, Peggy?"

I could feel my heart go into a knot. It was less than a week since we'd been in Pittsburgh.

"I can't come right now, Sally," I told her. "I need to stay here for a while. I need to spend some time at home."

A week later, Sally called to say she was going to check herself into the psychiatric ward of Arlington Hospital. "I *need* to, Peggy," she said. "I really do."

I argued vehemently. She was not psychotic or suicidal. She needed internists, not psychiatrists. I wouldn't hear of it, and neither would her counselors at the center or her regular psychiatrist. I told her for the second time that she had to find out what was causing her diarhhea. "Anyone would be depressed if they'd been sick as long as you have," I argued. "You're *physically ill*, Sally. If you're going to the hospital, go to the medical section, not the mental ward."

Sally had begun to call on Teresa when she needed help, instead of Rhonda, although I didn't quite realize it at the time. All I knew was that Sally's situation was worsening—the news I was getting was bad news. Before I had a chance to think constructively about Sally's condition, Teresa had taken her to a private hospital. They had gone first to Arlington Hospital, but the psychiatric intake staff refused to admit her, telling her she should be treated on an outpatient basis. Seriously worried about Sally, Teresa had found a hospital that would take her in.

I'd forgotten how determined Sally was when she had her mind set on a goal. I called Rhonda, who asked why Sally hadn't been taken to the Care House first. The ACRI counselors who normally would have advised Sally to go there hadn't seen her recently. Teresa had taken over as Sally's counselor, they said. She duplicated their services, and they weren't going to spend their time on a client who didn't avail herself of their resources. I knew Teresa was spending more time with Sally, for the bills I was getting from PLAN were much higher than they had been with Rhonda—hundreds of dollars a month. They were stretching the resources of Sally's trust to the limit.

I wrote a letter to PLAN complaining about the hospital admission, and then I called the hospital. I spoke with the social worker there, who said Sally was throwing up several times a day. She couldn't keep anything down, and they had her on a liquid diet. They attributed her sickness to anxiety, but I insisted she be seen by a regular physician.

"She's very angry with you," the social worker told me. "She goes to group and tells everyone how you wouldn't support her need to be hospitalized. She's really mad."

I hung up without thanking him for this information, and then I packed my bag for another trip to Arlington.

When I got to the hospital, my mood of resentment changed immediately, and I understood why Teresa had taken her there. Sally was terribly sick, and although she wasn't psychotic, she was very depressed. I had resisted this hospitalization because I knew she didn't need inpatient psychiatric care, but when I saw her I realized that her physical condition had deteriorated badly, and with it her spirits. She cried continually, saying she felt like "an April fool." I didn't understand what that meant, until she reminded me she'd moved back to Mike and Tammy's house the previous April. She lay in her hospital bed and wept. When I asked her to tell me more, she said that Mike had promised her he would leave Tammy and marry her.

I understood immediately that this was his idea of a joke, but Sally had taken him seriously. I didn't know what to make of that, for she had never expressed any interest in Mike, but I was sure that she had been particularly in need of affection the past months, and I wasn't surprised that she had grasped at the hope that someone might care for her.

I sat on the edge of the bed and held Sally's hand. She cried softly as she told me how sick she felt, how frightened she was. "I looked at the wall of my room one night," she said, "and I thought there was something written there on the cinderblocks. I didn't have my glasses on, so I couldn't read it. Then it seemed to move." I didn't know what that might mean, but it showed me how confused she was.

Sally was also much thinner than I had seen her in years. Her eyes looked puffy and swollen, but her face seemed almost thin, it was so gray and flaccid. Every half hour or so, she would stand up abruptly, go into the bathroom, and retch. Her stomach was empty, but she couldn't stop vomiting. She had lost more than twenty-five pounds in just a few weeks.

At first, the diagnosis of anxiety seemed plausible to me, considering what Sally had been through in the past year and a half. Sally herself seemed to think this made sense. "It was like this when I first went to Sheppard Pratt," she told me. "After I got to the hospital I couldn't even look at food. I threw up all the time the first month." But I instinctively felt the problem was physical. Sally was infinitely more resilient, psychologically, at least, than she was at seventeen. She'd been through hell since then, with no recurrence of this kind of nausea.

I drove back to New York wondering if Sally might have cancer. I had heard that lack of appetite was one of the warning signs, and I wondered if the vomiting could be caused by a blockage of some sort.

Back in the city, I was more depressed than I had been since the spring. Everywhere I looked, innocent misery stared back at me. Leaving Harvey's loft one morning with a dollar for the subway in my hand, I was asked by an old, unshaven man on the Bowery if I could help him out. He needed seventy-five cents for a roll and a cup of coffee, he said, and held out his hand. There was a quarter on his palm. When I handed him my dollar, he tried to give me change.

"Please keep it," I said.

"I only need seventy-five," he insisted.

"Keep it for *later*," I told him.

"What? Oh! Sure! Later! Thanks!" He bowed deeply and wished me a good day.

God bless those who can't conceive of a future, I thought. God please bless a man on a cold winter day who doesn't hoard his quarters for the next cup of coffee. I went into the subway, made it to my office, shut the door, and hung my head to cry.

That night as I lay in bed, drowsy but sleepless, I thought about how sick Sally really was. As if I were reading the mind of someone else, I observed that my mood changed from sadness to relief. All at once, I felt full of love for Sally, consoled by the certainty that the future would not be an endless stretch of sadness punctuated by crises. I finally felt free of my anger and guilt, free to care for Sally wholeheartedly.

Then I realized that I felt relieved because I expected Sally would die.

I used to think of my own death with relief when I had felt trapped and helpless, but imagining Sally's in the same wishful way was too much. I climbed out of bed, and although I'm not a particularly religious person, I got down on my knees and prayed for help never to do it again.

The next day, Rhonda and I began discussing nursing homes. Sally couldn't go back to Mike and Tammy's, and she was too sick for an ordinary group home. The hospital had decided her problems were physical, not psychiatric, despite her depression, but no one had been able to pinpoint the cause.

Months later, I read in Dr. Fuller Torrey's well-known book, *Surviving Schizophrenia: A Family Manual*, the following paragraph: "If the lithium level goes too high, it can be a serious, even life-threatening, situation. Symptoms of toxicity include vomiting, diarrhea, weakness, confusion, stupor, staggering, incoordination, slurred speech, dizziness, blurred vision, convulsions, and coma. Lithium should *never* be given to a patient with any of these symptoms . . ."

219

It turned out that Sally was indeed suffering from lithium poisoning, but somehow no one happened to think of it at the time. Instead, she was sent to Georgetown University Hospital, where a group of doctors was conducting tests for sleep apnea. Sally had snored loudly for many years, and her breathing was always difficult. Her internist, having checked her for every gastrointestinal disorder he could think of, finally sent her to the sleep apnea clinic because he didn't know what else could be causing her ailments. While all these tests were being conducted, she stayed in the private psychiatric hospital, remaining there for nearly a month, at an enormous cost. Finally, the doctors decided to take her off all medication. As the social worker explained it to me, they felt that Sally had been medicated for so many years, it might be a good idea to "clean out her system." Then drugs could be reintroduced as she needed them.

That sounded fine—until I learned that they also planned to release Sally.

The social worker agreed with me that that was not a good idea, to put it mildly. But over my protests and those of their own social worker, Sally was discharged without a prescription. She was asked to draw up a "contract" saying that she would go to the mental health center every day. Supposedly the doctor there, who had known her for years, would determine whether she was able to cope drug free.

I could feel Mother's spirit cringing in horror. I called Sally's doctor at the private hospital, who thought he was reassuring me when he said Sally would be monitored carefully. Nothing I said persuaded him that his plan was dangerous. "It's probably the lithium that's making her nauseous," he kept repeating. I didn't object to that belated diagnosis, only to his releasing her without any substitute medication. "We can't keep her when she's not sick," he said.

"And where will you be when she is?" I asked. He didn't answer.

thirty-one

••

S ally didn't return to Mike and Tammy's basement. Instead, with Rhonda's help, she went to the Care House for the
time being. I called her almost every night. She was feeling
much better, and she was able to eat a little. I felt heartened by
that, but I was nonetheless tense, wondering what else would
happen as the residual medicine was slowly eliminated from
her system.

Sally was still seeing both Teresa and Rhonda, although
since the hospitalization I'd had Rhonda, instead of Teresa,
coordinate Sally's living arrangements and doctor appointments. She was also trying to encourage Sally to use the services of the ACRI counselors rather than depending on PSN
and PLAN so much. For the moment, Sally seemed to have
forgotten that Teresa was her ally in her drive to be hospitalized. She knew that I was dissatisfied with the way PLAN
handled her illness, and perhaps that alienated her affections
somewhat. At any rate, she seemed to shift her allegiance to
Rhonda, even though she still met with Teresa once a week.

Just as I was feeling that life was nearly on an even keel
again, Rhonda had a skiing accident and tore the ligaments in
her knee. Laid up at home, she could keep in touch with both
Sally and me by telephone, but she couldn't see Sally in person. Once again, I had to rely on PLAN for that.

One afternoon at work, I got a call from Teresa. Sally had missed an appointment with her, and when Teresa called the Care House, the counselors said Sally hadn't been there all afternoon. I hung up and began telephoning the house every hour. The counselors were concerned but not yet worried. "Sally's feeling fine," one of them told me. "I'm sure she's all right."

When she returned to the house later, she phoned me to say she was back.

"Where were you?" I asked. "You missed your appointment with Teresa."

"Oh *that*," she said dismissively. Then she caught herself, as if remembering how much she liked Teresa. "I'll call her," she said.

"Where *were* you?" I repeated.

"At the International House of Pancakes."

"All this time?" I was incredulous.

"Yes," she answered firmly. "I was writing letters. I've written you a very long letter, Peggy, and I hope it doesn't make you angry."

I had a pretty good idea that it would, especially if Sally thought so first. I didn't answer.

"Do you want me to send it, or are you coming down soon?"

"Why don't you hold on to it for now," I said. Or forever, I thought. I assumed the letter was about how I'd tried to keep her out of the hospital, but I couldn't be sure and had no interest in finding out.

Sally sounded hearty for the first time in months. She was keeping most of her meals down, she said, and feeling much better. She had little appetite, but I figured that was normal considering that her stomach must have shrunk during the weeks when she couldn't eat at all. There was a robustness in her speech that not only made me hopeful for her recovery but also released me from guilt. Just a few days before, I had felt love and pity for Sally, but now my emotions ricocheted. She was suddenly full of verve, and she also seemed slightly angry at me.

"I'm not angry with you, Peggy," she said elaborately, as if she had read my mind. "I just want to talk to you about our relationship. I want to try to improve things. I want us to be friends."

Whenever I sensed Sally was angry with me, I felt an odd mixture of freedom, because she wasn't begging me for more love and sisterhood than I could offer, and fury, because I was usually already giving more of my time to her than I wanted to. I know this must have frustrated Sally, for the unspoken agreement I was counting on was extremely patronizing toward her: I will be kind and attentive, Sally, and you will be docile and appreciative. Sally, like any adult, wanted to have a relationship with me that was based, at least to some extent, on equality. I was incapable of that.

Sally wanted to have the kind of dynamic conversation that takes place either naturally, between good friends who want to be closer to one another, or unnaturally, as in a family therapy group, where the well person withholds negative emotions and observations so that the ill person can vent his. I wasn't about to let myself in for that. Sally and I could not talk as equals, because although she could feel free to say she wanted to be treated like an adult, for example, I could hardly say that in my opinion she didn't behave like one. If I did, it only hurt her. I was expected to be like a good therapist, drawing her out by asking such questions as, "What does it mean to be treated like an adult?" but I couldn't bring myself to stand back from our relationship to that extent. To my mind, that would be more patronizing than talking to her the way I did. I wanted to treat Sally as an equal. I wanted to *see* her as an equal. But as long as my half of our conversations took so much effort, it would be impossible.

"We'll talk when I come down next," I said in a squelching,

managerial tone that must have discouraged Sally. She agreed, though, and we hung up.

The next night, I had to call her again, this time about the tax statement for her disability retirement pay. I was trying to gather receipts, W-2 forms, and canceled checks to send to an accountant who was going to file returns for the estate, the trust, and Sally. Sally reminded me that the statement had probably been sent to PLAN, and then she asked, "So when are you coming down so we can talk?"

"How are things at the Care House?" I asked, changing the subject abruptly.

"Great!" she answered. She had no trouble making the switch. She described her roommate, the others in the house, the counselers, and the meals in detail. She went on and on enthusiastically.

The verve I'd noticed the day before had turned to urgency. There was something unhealthy, I thought, about her enthusiasm—something manic. "You sound . . . energetic, Sally," I said.

"I'm *great!*"

I made plans to drive down for the weekend.

The next day I called the mental health center. Marjorie was no longer there. The nurse or social worker with whom I spoke told me that Sally had been writing about the important people in her life, and she had also been writing long letters to those individuals to explain herself to them and discuss their relationship with her. The counselor approved of this. "She's examining her life," she put it.

It sounded manic to me, and I told her so.

"We've known Sally for years," she answered, as if that would pull rank with me.

"I've known her all my life," I countered.

"Have you ever seen Sally when she was in a manic state?" she asked.

She had me there. "No," I admitted. "I haven't."

"You've never known Sally when she wasn't heavily medicated, have you?"

"Not in recent years," I was forced to acknowledge.

"Well, we think she's showing a wonderful ability to examine her feelings. We think she's making progress."

I paused for a moment. I'd said what I had to say, and if I tried to respond to her pleasure in Sally's achievement I thought I would choke on the words. There was only one way out. "Good-bye," I said.

I called the counselors at the Care House. They, too, were comfortable with the way Sally was pulling herself together. If I'd been face-to-face with these confident people I would have gaped; by telephone, I fell back on the aural equivalent and was speechless.

"We'll make a note in her file," I was promised. "And if we notice any manic behavior, we'll be sure to see that Sally gets checked by her doctor."

I told Teresa my suspicions, but she was cool to me. She was resentful that I'd complained about her admitting Sally to a private hospital, and, I supposed, she was also miffed that Rhonda was again my main agent.

Finally, I called Rhonda. I didn't want to, because there was nothing she could do from her bed, but I needed to hear her reassuring voice. I described Sally's speech, and told her it sounded strange to me. I said I'd never seen Sally manic, but that's what I thought was happening.

Rhonda said something I'll never forget, something for which I will be forever grateful. "Your instincts are probably right," she said. "You know Sally better than anyone." If only every family member of a mentally ill person could hear those words now and then. *Your instincts are probably right.* Nothing could have made me feel better at that point, in spite of what it portended.

Rhonda called the Care House and Sally's regular counselor at ACRI. All said to her what they had said to me. Sally seemed all right, but they would monitor her carefully.

The next day was Friday. I drove down to Arlington after work. I let myself into Lyn and Earl's house and went to sleep slowly. I didn't know what to expect in the morning.

THE CARE House was a two-story brick house on a residential street near major roads, a shopping center, and a Metro stop. It was never a fancy neighborhood, and now that new commercial development was springing up around it, the houses were looking a little down at the heels. The Care House always looked trim, though, and the counselors took pains to see that visitors didn't disturb the neighbors by clogging the street with cars or blocking driveways. As I parked, a woman came out and asked me to move my car to the other side of the road. I turned and parked again, not minding the two-minute postponement of my meeting with Sally.

I was barely in the front door of the house when Sally came rushing up to me. She didn't look at me or say hello, but gripped my arm—something she had never done before—and propelled me into the counselors' office at the rear of the first floor. "Thanks!" she called to the counselor who'd directed my arrival. Apparently she had planned our talk in advance.

I say "our talk," but it was mainly hers. We took two chairs, catercorner from one another (Sally imperiously directed me where to sit), and I listened in dumfounded silence as she expounded on everything from her feelings about Mother and Dad to her resentment that I'd tried to keep her out of the hospital. She told me she wanted to have a relationship with me that was based on mutual respect, not on my helping her. She didn't want me to meddle in her life any more. She planned to start her own halfway house, and to do that she would need my assistance, but not if it meant being subordinate to me. "You have experience with the media," she said.

I didn't understand, but she explained. She needed funds for the halfway house, and she would have to get some publicity before she could hope to raise money. She knew that someone with my background in journalism would be helpful, she said, as she had no idea how to place stories in newspapers "around the country." She hoped I would be able to rise to the occasion and give her my best advice without treating her like a child.

I listened to her ramble on, feeling bombarded by her chatter. She didn't look at me, keeping her eyes on a point in the air a few feet from her face, and whenever I tried to speak she asked me between clenched jaws, but in a singsong voice, if I would *please* not interrupt her. It clearly tried her patience to have to listen to me while she was struggling to unfurl the banner of her independence.

While I now knew for certain that Sally was manic, I had to admire her intentions. She was always a generous person, without much to share, and she always wanted to be an effective person, even though it was difficult for her to manage her own life well. In every film I've ever watched on the mentally ill, the most touching segment, for me, is the one in which one of the subjects talks about how important it is to feel like a contributing member of society.

Sally talked about the last time she had wanted to embark on such a venture, and how Mother had had her committed before she was able to realize her goals. I could see her wrestle with this memory, forcing herself to suppress her anger. She was obviously determined to remain cheerful. "I can work with people better if I express myself clearly," she said several times. "I don't have *any* need to be angry with people. I just have to make them see my point of view."

There was a rote quality to what she said, as if she had memorized her lines in advance. In a way, she had. "I've written all this down," she said, "in my letter to you." She gave a brief sigh and shrugged. "Only I can't put my hands on it at the moment."

I told her sincerely that that was all right with me.

She waved away my comment. "Just let me continue, Peggy," she said, and she began again to talk about the future, when she would be the effective person she knew she truly was. She never seemed to pause for breath, drawing on some wellspring of verbal energy.

I sat and listened, sat and cringed, sat some more and wondered what I could do.

I had an idea.

"Have you had lunch?" I asked. "Want to go over to McDonald's?"

Without pausing, Sally stood up to go. "All right," she said firmly. As she had on the phone the night before, she shifted her attention instantaneously, almost as if the idea had been her own.

I wanted to talk to a counselor, but I couldn't find one in the few seconds it took Sally to go upstairs for her purse.

She came back down, this time without her upper plate in. She had to have her teeth pulled after breaking the one on the chicken bone in the Catskills a year and a half before. Her mouth was in such bad shape there weren't enough strong teeth to anchor a bridge. She had adapted to false teeth beautifully, and they looked natural. I asked her where her teeth were, but she said she didn't need them. "They pinch," she said. She had lost so much weight in the last six weeks, her plate no longer fit, but I didn't know that then. I asked how she expected to eat without it, and she said, "Oh, I can eat, all right," so I let it drop. She looked strange to me, and very old, like the toothless octogenarians in tintypes with their fixed gazes and shrunken lips.

Sally was talking when we left the house, and she kept talking as we drove in the car. At McDonald's she talked while

washing down two cheeseburgers and fries with a large Coke.
I went to the ladies room on the pretext that I had to wash my
hands, but I really needed to get away from her for a few
minutes.

When we left the restaurant, I told her I had to fill my gas
tank. She nodded, but didn't pause in her speech. She was
talking about the halfway house where she had lived in Washington years before, and how she had hated it, about Mike
and Tammy and other landlords she'd had, about Mother's
efforts to prevent her from moving back home with her.
When I got out of the car to work the pump, I could hear her
talking softly to herself while she sat waiting for me. Then as
we rolled through a carwash attached to the filling station, I
could see her lips moving, though the din of the hoses and
brushes mercifully drowned out the sound of her voice.

When we were back on the street, Sally turned to me and
said carefully, "You interrupted me when I was telling you
something important back at the house, Peggy." She smiled
but clearly had to force herself to. She was practically clench-
ing her jaw. "I could have gotten mad at you, but instead I'm
telling you about it. There's *no reason* to get mad." I was more
frightened of this new, open, honest Sally than the old one
who glared and seethed at me from time to time.

Teresa knew I was coming to Arlington, and she stopped
by the Care House that afternoon. The counselors were using
their office, so Sally directed Teresa and me to follow her to
the basement, where she set up a chair facing us and continued her monologue. This time it included information on
her sexual history, including what she did and didn't enjoy.
She explained that she had not gone to bed with every Tom,
Dick, and Harry—only with men she had been in love with,
and those had been few. She told stories about invitations
she'd received to sleep with other men, and how she had refused.

The minutes ticked away, and Teresa never said a word. I

was acutely aware of the time she was spending listening passively, for I knew the trust would be paying for it. Finally, I said it was getting late. Teresa said she had to go, and Sally hopped up from her chair as if we had been keeping her.

I told Sally I would walk Teresa to her car. On the way, I said something along the lines of "See?" I was sure Sally's mania would be apparent to her.

Teresa seemed not to have noticed. Her answer was, "Well, she certainly has a lot to say."

Was I losing my mind? Why did no one else see what was happening?

I gathered myself together to say a polite good-bye. It was that or scream. I walked back to the house, marveling at Teresa's interpretation of the ranting she had just heard.

I told Sally I had some errands to do and that I would pick her up later. "Good," she said quickly. "I'm tired." She left the room and disappeared upstairs. For me, it was as if the police had finally confiscated a nuisance radio. Sally's boom box was silent. Peace, at least for the moment.

I was trying not to panic. It was Saturday, and I suspected there was little anyone could do until the mental health center opened again on Monday. Sally could then be seen by her doctor. I didn't have much faith that that would help, though, for everyone at the center had seen Sally winding up to this pitch. And, as they had told me repeatedly, Sally seemed fine, fine, fine to them. I went in search for a Care House counselor.

The one I found listened calmly to my account of Sally's previous breakdown, when she had also talked about starting a halfway house. "You're saying she could be signaling," he suggested.

"What?"

"Signaling."

I could guess what that meant, but I asked anyway, just to make sure I had the jargon straight.

"Using phrases and ideas that she reveals only when she's getting sick," he explained. "Which gives the signal that she may be in trouble."

She'd been signaling all week by writing reams of letters, I thought, but I didn't press the point. I wished I were talking to Rhonda, with whom I never held back. She didn't require kid-glove treatment. She had my respect, and if I said something short to her, she chalked it up to worry or exhaustion. But I felt I had to watch myself with everyone else. My irritation was just under the surface, and I worked hard to keep it there.

I asked the counselor to please call Sally's doctor as soon as he could, and he said he would make a note in her file. I left him writing on a page in a manila folder that had Sally's name on its tab. I thought of PLAN's complaint about Rhonda— that she had not kept adequate notes—and I wondered if the note the counselor was now writing was going to do Sally or me any good.

LYN AND Earl invited us over to their house to play bridge after dinner. I warned them I thought Sally was getting manic, but they said they would love to have us anyway. They knew how upset I was, and I think they wanted to see Sally's behavior for themselves, so they could possibly give me the moral support of agreeing with me. I didn't know how to play bridge, but they said I could pick up the rudiments without too much trouble.

Sally was on full steam by evening. She began explaining the rules of bridge to me on the way to Lyn and Earl's, going through the details of how the cards were dealt, how to arrange your hand, how to open the bidding, how to respond to your partner's bid, and so on. I finally asked her to wait until we were actually playing, so I could learn as I went, instead of getting it all at once before I had any way to apply the information. Her voice was growing stronger and stronger, and when she went into a monologue, it got louder as well. I was feeling shell-shocked by the time we arrived.

As we sat at the table in Lyn and Earl's living room, Sally began again to give me all the details she had ticked off in the car, plus dozens of others. Again and again, I asked her to slow down. She would be silent for a moment or two, then begin to wind up again. Soon she was at full throttle, talking nonstop as if reading from a book. I finally lost my temper and told her I couldn't learn that fast.

Sally stared directly at me with an appraising look. "Tell me something, Peggy," she began. "Do you think you're a creative person?"

"What do you mean, 'creative'?" I asked. I was still trying to talk to her more or less normally.

"Well, I'm a creative person, and you know, Cliff was a creative person too," she said, speaking of my ex-husband. "I was thinking that the reason your marriage probably didn't work out is that Cliff was imaginative, while you're stuck in the day to day. You care about what's *real* to the exclusion of *fantasy*. You see, I understand you *very* well, Peggy. *Oh* yes. Very well."

I was boiling over inside, and probably simmering openly at this point, but I had no answer for her. What I wanted to say was, If you could manage to mire yourself in the boredom of the quotidian, Sally, the rest of us might have a chance to soar now and then too. I didn't say it, of course. Why try? I already regretted being engaged with her blather to the point of anger. I know now that this was exactly the time when I should have thought to myself, This is the illness speaking, not Sally. But it is terribly difficult not to bristle when someone close to you speaks insultingly about a major failure in your life. If Sally had not been sick, I would have found it unforgivable.

During a break from the game, Sally began talking about

Flying Phyllis. I hadn't heard of her for many years, and in fact I had never heard Sally speak of her. It was Mother who had told me a little about this fantasy life of Sally's. Sally had always been mum on the subject. Now I heard her detail the exploits of Flying Phyllis to Earl, who was asking her questions about Phyllis's life and times. Earl was a journalist, and he knew how to get answers. As I listened, I heard about Flying Phyllis's powers to save the downtrodden, and about her miraculous work with prisoners. I also heard Sally's voice, animated with pleasure, enter into Phyllis's world with alarming ease.

Sally had been talking for about two hours straight when I finally said I was too tired to play bridge any more. I'd forgotten just how much I hated card games, and this evening had sealed my distaste. I told Sally it was time to go back to the Care House, and, as she had been doing all day, she hopped up to go as if she'd been thinking the same thing. We drove back half in silence—mine—and half in a whirlwind of speech—hers. She continued to analyze my marriage, and at one point I found myself wanting to swat her. Instead, I said good night and promised to pick her up in the morning. We had invited Donald and Betty to brunch.

When I got back to Lyn and Earl's, Lyn was waiting up for me. She sat me down on a stool in the kitchen and poured me a beer. "Sally's *manic*," she said immediately. She shook her head and raised her eyebrows. *"Wow."*

SALLY's anger at me grew as the weekend went on. I wasn't having any of what she was saying, and it showed. That frustrated her. She had had in mind exactly how the visit would go, with her explaining to me all the ways I'd misunderstood her and treated her inconsiderately, my apologizing and changing my ways, and the two of us drawn closer at last. I threw a monkey wrench in the works by taking offense at her criticisms and showing no remorse and no inclination to be closer to her than I had to be.

Sunday morning, Sally's speeches began to fray at the edges as she struggled with her disappointment. Her syntax took on a challenging note. She began every other sentence by saying, "The trouble with you, Peggy," "One thing you'll never understand is," or "I'll have you know. . . ."

On the way to meet Donald and Betty I finally lost my temper. I yanked the steering wheel to the right, the car veered to the side of the road, and I slammed on the brakes. "Shut up, Sally," I shouted. "Just shut up!"

"All right," she said in a baldly insincere, obliging manner. "I'll completely stifle my true self *just* so you can be comfortable."

"*Good,*" I said firmly.

We drove the rest of the way in silence, but before we went into the restaurant, I told Sally not to steamroll the conversation. "Let someone else get a word in," I said.

At brunch, Sally became sweetly polite, conversing rapidly but not forcefully, asking questions of Donald, and generally appearing to have a good time. Afterward, I thanked her for making the meal so pleasant.

She smiled in a disturbing way, with an expression I hadn't seen on her face before. It was almost a sneer. "You don't have to thank me, Peggy. I didn't do it for you," she said. "You see, I'm perfectly capable of speaking any way I want."

It was as if another Sally had emerged. In many ways, she was much more adult than the one I had known, at least so it seemed to me, with adult pride and independence. She was no longer docile, and I realized that she was right about one thing: Our relationship up to now had depended on her submissiveness. I had loved the old Sally, much as I'd longed to be released from her neediness. I was intimidated by the new one, with her honest appraisals and projectile speech. I didn't like her at all. And without her teeth, she didn't even look like the sister I remembered.

I dropped her off at the Care House, wondering what would happen the next day when she went to the mental health center. Driving back to New York Sunday night, I was grateful for the absence of her voice. I left the car radio off, listening with appreciation to the soft, impersonal sounds of the wind and traffic.

MONDAY morning, I got a call at work from Rhonda. Sally had gone out Sunday night and not returned to the Care House. I had a feeling she was back at Tammy and Mike's, and so did Rhonda, who opened the conversation by saying in a jocular tone, "I don't think there's anything to worry about, but I have to tell you . . ." We talked about the weekend, and I described Sally's behavior. She listened incredulously as I told her how many professionals had thought Sally was "fine," and then she let out a little laugh. "I have a feeling," she said, "that everybody's about to develop some respect for your diagnostic skills."

Sally was, as we suspected, at Tammy and Mike's. I called them and asked if they would please watch for signs that Sally needed to go to the hospital, but my plea fell on deaf ears.

"She is so smart!" Mike told me. "We were up all night talking, and the things she said—! She understands me so well! Better than anyone ever did before!"

I thought Sally was out of the house, but suddenly I heard her shout, "Let me talk to her!" She grabbed the phone and began screaming.

"Stay out of my life, Peggy!" she began.

I interrupted to shout back, "You're manic, Sally. You need medication!"

"I don't need medication!" she screamed. "What I need is

none of your business. Just leave me alone! I don't need you and I don't want you meddling in my life *ever, ever again!* And don't you *dare* call Tammy and Mike behind my back!" She was sputtering as she shouted; I could hear her suck in her saliva now and then. Next, she excoriated the counselors at the Care House, the other ACRI counselors, and the therapists at the mental health center. "Don't expect me to go back there!" she screamed. I wasn't sure which "there" she referred to, but I didn't ask for clarification.

I was amazed by her fury, for I'd never witnessed it. Or, if I had, it had been long ago, perhaps when she had first been released from Sheppard Pratt. So this is what the fights were like between her and Mother, I thought. No wonder I had trouble with those memories.

In spite of my fear and my own anger, which at this point was considerable, I was afraid that if Sally cut me off along with all her counselors there might eventually be no one with whom she communicated. I braced myself and interrupted.

"Sally," I said. "Wait a minute. I just want you to know that I love you."

"I love you too!" she screamed angrily, and hung up on me.

....

he owners of *ARTnews* looked the other way as I now
began an extensive program of long-distance telephone consultations. Large chunks of my days were spent dialing, talking, or waiting for someone to call me back. It meant that I
took my work home every night, but I had to communicate
with Sally's social workers during business hours, the only
time they were available.

No one could keep track of Sally at first. "She's on the go!"
Rhonda said, a little too cheerfully for me. I could see that
while Rhonda was concerned for Sally, she also enjoyed her
new energy. Sally continued to meet with both Rhonda and
Teresa once a week, but she was now closer to Teresa because
she had been seeing her while Rhonda was laid up. Sally confided in Teresa, who began telephoning me often to report on
her condition. Whereas Rhonda protected me from information that would only upset me, Teresa let me know exactly
how bad the situation was.

One day Teresa told me that Sally was planning to sue me
for her trust fund. She had told Teresa to keep it a secret,
because she wanted it to be a surprise.

I immediately called Rhonda. "Oh that," she said.

I was put off by her manner. "Easy for *you* to say."

"Tell me, Peggy, how is Sally going to sue you for her trust fund?'' Rhonda spoke patiently and quietly, waiting for me to calm down. "And besides, even if she did find a lawyer willing to take on such a case, didn't your mother have Gerry Rugel draw up the trust? Doesn't it dissolve if it's sued?"

As usual after a word with Rhonda, I felt better.

A counselor at the Care House predicted Sally would peak—and then crash—within a couple of weeks. "The longest I've ever seen anyone go is three weeks or so," she said. A nurse at the mental health center said the same—a couple of weeks, maximum. I braced myself for what I assumed was an imminent fall.

In the meantime, Sally was busy, busy, busy. She went looking for old friends to help start her halfway house, opened a bank account to be used for the project, and managed to spend all of every day away from Mike and Tammy's. And, by the way, she made plans to get married.

I heard the news from Sally, who happened to answer the phone when I called her one day. Usually she was out, but I tried regularly and finally caught her.

"Who's the lucky fellow?" I asked.

She told me his name—Richard—and it rang a bell.

"Isn't that the man who was in jail?" I asked, my mind racing back to an incident she'd related to me some months before. I couldn't remember the details now. It hadn't seemed important at the time.

"No," Sally said. "Not the same man."

I was sure she was lying. I took the wedding plans in stride, having learned from Rhonda that not all dreams come true, but the lie hurt me. It wasn't like Sally.

"No?" I asked again. "It isn't the same man?"

"You don't know anything about it, Peggy."

Gratified at the implied truth, I dropped the subject. I could find out more about Richard from Rhonda.

Thinking over our phone conversations one afternoon, I remembered Mother staying at home year after year, unwilling to take a vacation for fear a delicate balance would shift and cause Sally to falter. I thought of my decision, after Christmas, to stay in New York for a while. My barely conscious thoughts now went: If I hadn't turned my back, Sally wouldn't have gotten sick. It was a long time before I could tell myself that Sally didn't get sick because I wasn't there. She got sick because she wasn't medicated. I didn't do it to her. And she didn't do it to herself.

As Sally deteriorated, I began to feel strangely alone. I wrote a few notes to myself about what was happening, as a way of keeping track, though usually I found it too depressing to see it all described on paper. It looked so permanent, it frightened me. But one day I wrote, "It's just a year since our mother died, and now I'm losing my sister, too. Not that I had her, exactly. But there's no chance now of even the merest mutual understanding. I miss her. Or I miss family. I feel lonely—how selfish. Think of orphans, of refugees. My lot is not so bad. Maybe it feels worse because I had a chance at family and now I don't. Or a chance at the fantasy of family. That's my only loss. Loss of a fantasy."

SALLY would call me at work now and then. I listened to her talk, waiting until she was through before asking how she was. "Fine!" was always her punctual, vehement answer. She now opened conversations in a chillingly friendly voice. "So how's my little sister?" she began one day. I waited to see what was on her mind.

"By the way," she began, and I steeled myself.

She wanted to move her piano to the house of a friend, she said. We had thought of moving it to storage after Mother died, but then the family who rented the house offered to keep it as long as we needed them to. Sally could get it whenever she wanted.

"Whose house do you want to move it to, Sally?" I asked.

"Some friends'" she answered evasively.

"Are you moving into their house, too?"

"I might, and then I might not."

"Well," I said, "Talk to Rhonda about it." I didn't say so, but I wasn't going to do anything on a whim of Sally's while she was manic, knowing that when she was well again, she might have changed her mind. It wasn't fair, really, because the piano was hers, but I reasoned that it was my responsibility as trustee to decide whether to release the money to move it. By telling her to talk to Rhonda, I was unfairly shifting the problem, but it was a way to gain some time.

"And let Rhonda deal with the renters in Mother's house. I don't want you calling them," I said nervously.

"I know, I know," she answered lucidly. "You don't want me anywhere *near* them."

Another day Sally called and asked where I'd put a painting that belonged to her. I didn't know what she was talking about and told her to describe it. The painting she wanted was a landscape of the valley view from Aunt Ginny's dining room window that our grandmother had painted and given to Daddy.

"I have it," I said curtly. "And it isn't yours."

Sally insisted it was, but I knew exactly where it had come from and to whom it had been given. Even if it had belonged to Sally I wouldn't have let her take it, because if she lost or damaged it I would never have forgiven her. I wasn't about to increase my reasons for being angry at Sally later. As it was, I wondered if I would ever be able to forget the nasty side of her personality that she'd revealed to me.

We argued back and forth, but this time I didn't pull any punches.

"I want the painting to give it to Richard's father," she finally said. "He's in the hospital, and it would brighten the walls."

"I'm not letting you give away Granny's painting, Sally," I said. "So just forget it!"

"You'd let an old man suffer alone in his room with nothing to cheer him up? Is that what you're saying, Peggy?"

"Yes, Sally. That's what I'm saying."

Sally's voice turned ugly.

"I have a mind to come to New York and get my trust money," she snarled.

"I don't have it here, Sally," I said honestly. The trust money was in Treasury bills and notes, and the interest was in a checking account in Virginia.

"You don't?" Sally's tone had done another quick change, from threatening to disappointed.

"No."

"Where is it?" she asked, sounding bewildered.

I thought for a moment. I was still in the process of filing estate accounts with the court in Arlington, and although I was legally able to use money from Mother's estate to pay the expenses of the trust, I hadn't officially transferred most of her assets.

"It's tied up in court, Sally," I told her as honestly as I could.

Sally let the subject drop, and that was the end of the conversation. I was drained. And I was frightened by Sally's aggressiveness. I called Rhonda and told her I was afraid.

"What do you think Sally's going to do?" she asked me.

"I don't know," I said. I really didn't. I just knew my heart was pounding and my hands were damp.

"Do you think she's going to come to New York and kill you?"

Hearing Rhonda voice the worst-case scenario relieved me immediately. It did sound vaguely ridiculous. I was also relieved because it exactly voiced the fear I couldn't quite identify.

"Maybe," I said, thinking it over.

"It's not going to happen, Peggy," Rhonda said.

"She hates me, Rhonda."

"She also loves you."

"Not right now, she doesn't."

Nothing Rhonda said could shake my anxiety. I couldn't believe I was actually worrying about Sally attacking me, but somehow it didn't seem farfetched. She'd had reason to resent me my whole life, had often expressed her envy, and now that she was in the position of having to depend on me for money, I could imagine that she felt humiliated as well.

As I was thinking about our relationship, I realized that much of my fear arose from my own sense of guilt at always having had so much more than Sally. Something in me expected her to get back at me because I didn't quite believe I deserved the blessings I had—friends, job, apartment, and now, with Harvey, even love. I couldn't separate the fear that sprang from my guilt from the fear engendered by Sally's aggressiveness.

At lunchtime I went to a nearby deli for a takeout salad. Sally called just after I left, and had apparently talked to the editorial assistant for the fifteen minutes I was gone. As I passed his desk, he handed me a sheet of typing paper and said, "You just missed a call from your sister. I'm not sure I got all of this straight. She was talking really fast."

Deciphering his handwriting, I read. "Peggy . . . Sister Sally. . . . Painting by our grandmother . . . Lehigh Valley. . . . True was Daddy's . . . *but* . . . Mother gave to me after he died." The message went on for another paragraph about Sally's right to take it and the injustice of my refusing to give it up.

I went to my desk and called Sally back. She sounded excited and happy. "I finally remembered, Peggy. Mother gave me the painting after Daddy died. She said I could have it. Honest."

I could tell from her tone it was the truth. "Sally," I said,

"You've done without it all these years. You can have it some day when you're well again. You need medicine. And don't ask anyone here at my office to take long messages again."

Sally was silent for a second, then she hung up.

My office mate, Fred, was quietly working away, but when he looked up I could tell he'd heard this latest conversation. "Anything I can do?" he asked.

I shook my head.

"What did your mother do?" he asked. "How did she handle Sally?"

My answer was out of my mouth before I could stop myself: "She died."

ONE NIGHT at home the following week, I was awakened by the telephone ringing. I had been sound asleep, but the faint light at my window told me it was almost morning. I jumped to answer the phone, thinking that no one would call me at that hour unless it was an emergency.

I picked up the receiver but before I had a chance to say hello I heard Sally's voice say brightly, "Hi, Sis!"

I asked her if she knew what time it was.

"Six o'clock!" she answered. "Listen, Peggy—"

I cut her off. "Sally, I was sleeping."

"Oh, *I'm* sorry," she said with her new false, exaggerated politeness. "I waited until morning to call. It's light out."

"Barely."

"Peggy, I have something important to tell you." She was impatient and couldn't be put off, so I listened. She said she had been to the sleep apnea clinic at Georgetown University Hospital and a doctor there had told her not to take any medicine.

I challenged her. What doctor? What was his name? When had she seen him? I didn't believe a word of what she was telling me, and I said as much. She insisted it was true. I was

243

furious. "You're manic and you need to see a doctor," I shouted at her. "You need to get medicine!"

"I'm telling you, I saw a doctor and he said not to take any!"

Sally was so insistent, I realized she was telling me the truth, at least as she knew it, so later that morning I telephoned Georgetown University Hospital. After several transfers, my call went through to a doctor whose name was similar to the one Sally had given me. I explained the situation to him, and he said that indeed, he had examined Sally, and he had told her that it was possible that the medicines she'd been taking had interfered with her sleep.

"She took your word as an excuse to stay off medication," I said. I wasn't accusatory. I knew it wasn't his fault.

He was sincerely apologetic. "I thought she was under the care of a psychiatrist," he said.

"That's okay," I said. "So did I."

I called Sally and told her I'd spoken to the doctor she'd seen. "I'm sorry I didn't believe you," I said, "But it doesn't change what I keep saying. You're not well, Sally. You're manic. You need to go to the hospital."

Sally was silent for a minute, then she answered me slowly, with absolute clarity. "You don't understand, Peggy. The medicine only masks all this. These feelings have been in me all along."

thirty-three

....

Three weeks went by, with Sally becoming more manic by the day. "She's lost her teeth," Teresa told me in mid-April. "And she talks about sex all the time." Teresa had seen her earlier in the day. They had driven somewhere—to McDonald's for lunch, or some other small outing—and when Teresa took her back to Mike and Tammy's house, Sally wouldn't get out of the car. "She just kept talking and talking and talking," Teresa said. "I couldn't get her to open her door. There's a convict in Italy, or something like that, and she's desperate to get in touch with him. She's really sick, Peggy."

As usual, her report left me feeling rotten. *I* knew Sally was really sick.

When I spoke with Rhonda I asked her about Sally's conversation, and she said it was true Sally had sex on her mind. "It's a common symptom of mania, Peggy," she told me. "It's to be expected. I talked to her about birth control, and I don't think she's active, even though she's interested."

Sally was beginning to talk openly to Rhonda again, and I was glad about that, if only because Rhonda wouldn't automatically relay what she said to me. Rhonda didn't mind Sally's pressured speech—she enjoyed her energy even while keeping a watchful eye on her mood, knowing it would change.

Rhonda made a decision not to argue with Sally about medication. She had recently heard a report suggesting that the
aftermath of commitments was worse when the episode of
illness had been fraught with tension. It didn't shorten the
episode for therapists and family members to harangue the ill
person to get help or take medication, and patients felt embarrassed and bitter when they inevitably lost the fight. "There
will be fewer bridges to rebuild later, I think," Rhonda said.

While I respected her decision and admired her for her
self-restraint, I couldn't help bringing up the subject of medication almost every time Sally and I spoke. It would have
been more effective to hold back, as Rhonda was doing. It
would have saved Sally and me some fights, and it would have
kept her speaking to me. But I still wasn't capable of taking a
therapeutic stance toward my sister. I think now that it
showed a lack of maturity on my part, but at the time it
seemed more honest to mention reality—that she was sick
and needed medicine—rather than pretend that I thought our
conversations were normal. For me they were unbearably
strange, with Sally's voice and mood changing from minute to
minute, and with her galloping speed wearing down my
nerves. For Sally, I think, they were disappointing, frustrating, and ultimately infuriating. Eventually, as I could have
expected, she stopped calling me. After that, I relied on reports from Teresa and Rhonda to find out how she was and
what she was thinking.

I began to send Sally's spending money, two hundred a
month, to Rhonda instead of directly to her. That way, I knew
she would get it and I wouldn't have to worry about her over-
looking my letters. It also meant she would have to see
Rhonda regularly—my insurance policy against losing touch
with her.

One maddening detail of Sally's care was that ACRI decided to drop Sally from their roster of clients. They argued
that she spurned their offers of help, which was true, and that

they could not work with her if she would not work with them. Rhonda was outraged. "I told them, she's *sick*," she said, "but they wouldn't change their minds." It was one less therapeutic contact for Sally, but I didn't spend much time fretting about the loss. There were too many other things to think about.

Sally was still busy with plans for her halfway house, and she was also spending time with Richard. Richard had no place to live, so Sally asked Lyn and Earl if he could stay in their basement for a while. They said they were sorry, but it wouldn't be possible. Sally took offense, I believe partly because she knew that their door was always open to me. One afternoon, she took Richard with her to visit Donald and Betty. Betty called me afterward, to say that Richard seemed like a nice man. "Sally looked good," she said. "She wasn't wearing her teeth, which made her face look odd, but she weighs less, and she was dressed nicely. She seems happy, Peggy, in an agitated sort of way."

Gradually, the agitation increased, and the happiness became harder and harder to discern, but weeks went by without Sally's reaching the kind of crisis point that would enable anyone to commit her to a hospital. That possibility, however, began to come up in conversations I had with both Teresa and Rhonda. Very early on, Teresa began saying Sally should be committed. "Sally's really in bad shape," she said to me many times. I noticed she didn't make an attempt to get Sally medicated, but I didn't hold it against her. No one could have done it.

I think I knew that Rhonda would eventually be the one to do the job. The only time I ever heard her sound low was the day we talked about the prospect of taking Sally to a hospital against her will. Rhonda was a long time advocate of patients' rights, and she had often been on the other side of the commitment procedure, arguing in favor of the freedom of someone who was trying to fight involuntary hospitalization.

"When it's time," she said, "It'll hurt me as much as it does Sally."

There is rarely a consensus about when "it's time," and in Sally's case the disagreement centered on the question of whether a hospital would commit her if she were brought in, not whether she needed to go. Everyone agreed that she did, but according to the law, a person has to be provably "a danger to herself or others" before a hospital is authorized to incarcerate her. Opinions vary on what constitutes dangerous behavior. If Sally could be proven to be not eating, for instance, that would be considered dangerous to herself. But because she was so heavy when her manic attack began, it would be hard to persuade a judge that she might starve, because she was still comparatively large. She was certainly not a danger to others. In fact, Sally was functioning at a high level, which is not uncommon among people who are in the up phase of their manic-depressive illness.

As Sally's illness progressed, however, the fabric of her daily life began to fray. After a fight with Mike and Tammy, Sally left their house abruptly. Tammy and Mike were "molesting her psychologically," she said, describing their actions as "emotional torture." She would never return, she said. I don't know if she took even an overnight bag with her when she left. She hoped to get an apartment with Richard, but soon I heard that she couldn't reach him. No one seemed to know where he was.

Sally still had control of the check that came to her every month from the federal government for her disability retirement, which was deposited directly into her personal bank account. Where she had always had trouble budgeting herself, now she was completely incapable of managing money. She spent the check almost instantly, and no one knew where it went. After using up her weekly allowance from Rhonda, she began calling Mother's friends to ask for money.

One day she showed up on Donald and Betty's doorstep.

She was in a taxi, which was waiting, and she said she needed money for her fare. She was dirty, unkempt and, Betty said, "frantic." Betty was alarmed and asked Sally to wait outside while she went to get her a twenty-dollar bill. When Betty described Sally, she sounded as if she had lost hope. "I don't know what's going to become of her," she said. Sometime during this period, Sally also went to Lyn and Earl to ask for help. They gave her money, but I could tell when I spoke to them later that Sally's manner and appearance had frightened them, too.

I decided to call Sally's doctor at the mental health center. I needed him, as her primary psychiatric physician, to sign a form stating that she was not competent to receive her disability retirement check. I wanted it to go to Rhonda instead, so that Rhonda could pace Sally's spending.

To my astonishment, the doctor refused. "She's an adult," he said. "She can spend her money any way she likes."

I paused about two-tenths of a second before blasting him to kingdom come, as Mother would have described my tirade. "She's on the street because she's sick—through *no* fault of her own!" I shrieked at him. "Now she's bothering my mother's friends, who are practically the only people on earth who really care for her! But I suppose it's no skin off you if she alienates everyone around her, is it?"

He was silent.

"*Answer me!*"

The doctor murmured that he would see what he could do, and that Rhonda should send him the necessary forms. I thanked him with unctuous grace and slammed down the phone. It was a satisfactory conversation, from my perspective. Clear and to the point.

I was further amazed the next day when Sally voluntarily agreed to let Rhonda handle her money. She was aware that she was out of control, I think, or else she thought it would simplify her life if all her money came from one source,

Rhonda, who would manage it better than she could.

By now, I could tell that Sally had passed the peak of her mania, and I knew that she was bound to go downhill. By the end of that week, Sally was desperate. She couldn't get in touch with Richard, and she had no place to stay.

The first order of business was getting a roof over her head, but she quickly took care of that herself. "Sally's incredibly resourceful," Rhonda said admiringly when she told me that Sally had gone to a county shelter in Arlington. She was not in good shape—her vomiting and diarrhea had returned, and she had an eye infection—but the shelter began treating her for her physical ailments. Sally needed the attention, and she thrived on it. By her own account, she liked her new, temporary home. She made friends easily, and she enjoyed the hubbub of a large communal living space. Months later, I discovered that she had liked the shelter so much she donated her telephone and her winter clothes to it. Sally was nothing if not generous, and mania only made her will toward divestiture that much stronger.

The shelter was created to be a thirty-day stopover, and when Sally entered its doors, she was asked to sign a form stating that she agreed to move to a permanent residence if one were found for her. When, toward the end of the thirty days, she was told she would have to work with ACRI and possibly go into a licensed home for adults, she balked. She was through with ACRI, she said. The shelter was forced to ask her to leave.

Rhonda was urging her to look for a place to live, but Sally had her own ideas about what it should be. "She has in mind maybe a small motel," Rhonda told me. Rhonda knew of a one-bedroom that was opening up not far from the mental health center.

"I can't take anything smaller than a three-bedroom," Sally carefully explained. "I have to think of my friends."

During this period, Sally moved around frequently, staying

for a while at a women's shelter in Washington, the House of Ruth, which she had heard of the last time she was sick. At one of the shelters, clients were invited to attend nearby church services. They were picked up and returned by bus each week. Sally loved it. "She says she's found God," Rhonda reported. Sally had always been drawn to religion, and she was now suffused with a newfound peace. She also felt a modest urge to proselytize.

"Do you go to church?" she asked Rhonda one day when she dropped by her office to pick up a check.

"No," Rhonda answered. "I'm Jewish."

At this, Sally broke into a rousing rendition of "Hava Nagela."

I smiled when Rhonda described the scene. It was very much like Sally to respect another's heritage.

I hadn't seen the sweet side of Sally's personality for some time, but it apparently remained in full force. One day, she told Rhonda, she met a homeless man in Lafayette Park, across from the White House. "He was so forlorn, I put my arm around his shoulder and tried to comfort him," she said. "I told him he was somebody special. And you know what he did? He told me I was a beautiful person." She paused to reflect. "He was speaking of the inner me."

If the inner Sally retained its beauty, the outer one was suffering from life on the lam. Teresa kept me apprised of Sally's disintegrating appearance, describing the torn hems on her pants, the smelly, unwashed blouses she wore, her matted hair. Finally, I asked Rhonda about it, and she told me the truth. "Sally looks awful," she said with an uncharacteristic sigh. The week before, when Sally had come to pick up her weekly check, she had smelled of urine. She explained that she'd needed to go to the bathroom, but she had been on the bus coming to the office and lost control of her bladder before she got to her stop.

I was mortified. "Rhonda," I said, "Maybe I should be

there." I had in mind going down to Arlington and taking Sally to the hospital myself, as Mother had done.

"Don't come down here," Rhonda said quickly. "There's nothing you can do, and it would only depress you."

WHEN Rhonda called me a few days later, I thought I could hear laughter in her voice. "You should see Sally now," she said.

Sally had run into Mike's mother, an elderly Hungarian woman, in a neighborhood where she often went to eat at a coffee house she liked. Mrs. B. had taken one look at Sally, marched her back to her place, put her in the bathtub, and scrubbed her from top to bottom. She then insisted that Sally move in with her. Sally responded enthusiastically. She went on a shopping spree, and when she called Rhonda to make arrangements for their weekly meeting, she described in detail what she would be wearing, because, she said to Rhonda, "You won't recognize me."

"Nu?" I asked.

"I would have recognized her—I *think*—but the transformation was really something," Rhonda said. Sally's hair was clean and combed, and she was wearing new clothes and a pair of stylish sunglasses. And she had on makeup—an ambitious touch for anyone in our family. "She looks great," Rhonda said. "It's a miracle."

Buoyed by Mrs. B.'s attention and the effect her "makeover" had on others, Sally was now bent on acquiring a new wardrobe for her rapidly shrinking figure. She was manic, sleepless, and had no appetite, but she was happy, Rhonda said. "And by the way," she added, "she's acquired a Hungarian accent."

I slept well that night, knowing that Sally was under the roof of someone who clearly cared about her. I still think of Mrs. B. now and then, and her activist generosity.

It was late spring, more than two months since Sally had been released from the hospital, and I was beginning to accept the hiatus in my relationship with Sally. As Rhonda kept telling me, there was nothing I could do for Sally, and if I went to Virginia she wouldn't see me anyway. She was no longer angry with me, but she felt our ties had been severed. If I had been closer to Sally, if we had ever been like some of the siblings I heard about at the group—intimates whose love and friendship were wrenched and twisted by the sudden onset of illness—I might have grieved over losing her. But I had been missing Sally practically my whole life. Except for the added component of worry, this new rift was not so different. This time it was Sally, not me, who was running away, but the effect was the same as it had always been. We didn't see each other; we didn't talk. And just as I had been vaguely disturbed many years before, now again I couldn't quite relax. Every time the phone rang, at home or at the office, I steeled myself before answering.

Mike and Tammy began to complain that they couldn't rent or use their basement with Sally's belongings tying up the space. Rhonda asked if I would like her to move it all to storage; she didn't see Sally agreeing to go to an apartment soon. She reminded me again that we didn't know what the future held.

There seemed to be nothing to do but pack up her things. I made plans to go to Arlington two weeks later, on Memorial Day weekend, when I would have an extra day off. I didn't think I should have Rhonda do the job, for it would take hours and hours, which translated into hundreds of dollars.

I hadn't been to Arlington for so long that I looked forward to the trip. Rhonda wasn't sure Sally would see me, but she gave me Mrs. B.'s telephone number and told Sally I would call when I got there. She said Sally was grateful I was going to help and that her hostility toward me seemed to have vanished in the weeks we'd been out of communication. Just knowing she was no longer angry at me made me feel better about going into her territory.

I left New York on Friday night so I could get an early start the next day. I was happy when I pulled up in front of Lyn and Earl's late that night. I stood in their yard for a while before letting myself into the house, smelling the healthy, grassy scent of the dark air.

The weather turned hot as I slept. Even the early morning was sultry and humid. As I drove to a store that sold boxes, tape, and twine for do-it-yourself movers, I tried to stay away from main roads in order to keep as much in the shade as possible. I almost looked forward to being in a basement all day. I bought forty cartons, folded and bound, loaded them in the back of my car, wiped my sweaty forehead with a bandana I'd brought to tie back my hair, and drove to Mike and Tammy's.

As I went down the concrete stairs in the outdoor well, I thought I could almost feel the temperature drop a little. I opened the door and stepped in. The basement was indeed cool, but it smelled bad. As my eyes adjusted to the light, I looked around. It was filthier than I could have imagined. Everywhere there were things I couldn't bring myself to touch. The floor was strewn with soiled underwear and nightgowns. The damp had caused them to mildew, so they were also mottled with constellations of black spots. The mattress was equally unrecoverable. The whole basement reeked of rot and damp. A blanket tossed on a couch was encrusted with something unidentifiable. There were cigarette butts piled in ashtrays and waste baskets stuffed with containers from fast-food restaurants and scores of empty Hi-C cartons.

I turned and left. I walked to the driveway and stood next to my car. I took a few deep breaths, then went to a store for garbage bags and a pair of work gloves.

Back in the basement, I began sorting through the mess. Anything I couldn't bear to examine went into a trash bag.

I separated the clothes into piles: summer things Sally could wear now, warmer clothes to wear in the fall. I looked everywhere for her winter clothes, but I couldn't find them. I wanted to call Sally, but I couldn't find her telephone either.

After I finished with the clothes, which were the least of the job, I tackled the items in drawers. There were all kinds of stuff—address books never used, boxes and boxes of costume jewelry, old makeup, new makeup, pens and pencils, three folding umbrellas, empty notebooks, notebooks with one or two pages used, ceramic figurines, packets of stationery with no matching envelopes, envelopes with no stationery, notecards, greeting cards, file cards. On one dresser were piles of yellow legal pads whose pages were crumpled, torn, wrinkled, and folded, on which Sally had been writing the long letters she'd told me about in early spring. I made a desultory search for the one to me, but couldn't find it. I didn't read the others.

Most of what I found looked like junk to me, but I wasn't sure what it represented to Sally. I put it in boxes with labels like "dresser drawers," "bedside table," or "floor of bedroom area." Some of what I found, though, I knew was, or had been, precious to Sally. There were keepsakes from Aunt Ginny's house, including the statuette of Squirrel Nutkin. I found a group of alabaster eggs that I knew Sally thought had been stolen, and a silver bracelet Aunt Ginny had given her for Christmas not long before she died.

As I packed, I thought that perhaps I loved Sally more than I knew. Perhaps we were close, after all, for I knew a lot about her bric-a-brac that no one else would guess. There were belongings that would look like junk to someone else, but I knew the stories behind them and that it was important to keep them. I also noticed that I was taking pains to make order of her chaos. I wasn't working resentfully, but with a purpose, racking my brain to decide whether to keep something out where she could find it easily or to toss it into a box that might be buried in storage for years. I knew I wouldn't do it for many other people. And I knew that if I were not there, no one else could do it for Sally. Maybe it wasn't so important, but it seemed so to me at the time.

After a few hours I was hungry, so I pulled off my gloves and went to the sink to wash my hands. I shook my hands dry. I'd had to throw away Sally's towel.

Before heading to McDonald's, I stopped at a phone booth and called Mrs. B.'s number. Sally's eager voice answered on the first ring.

"I'm *so happy* you're *here*, Peggy," she said. "I've been *waiting* for you to call."

We hadn't spoken in weeks, but she didn't wait for me to ask how she was. She got right down to brass tacks. "I've made a *list* of how I want my books *packed*," she said. "When can you pick it up?" Her speech was emphatic, but not so pressured as it had been when she was angry and anxious.

I asked her if she would like to have lunch with me.

"Oh, I'd *love* to, Peggy, but I *can't*," she said, without elaborating. She gave me Mrs. B.'s address, and we hung up.

After lunch I drove to the address she'd given me, which was in an old apartment complex not far from Mike and Tammy's. I wasn't sure I could follow Sally's directions, for she lost me in her long recitation of detailed information, but as I pulled into a dead-end street I could see her waving to me from a parking lot at the other end.

I couldn't believe my eyes when I drove up. She looked beautiful. She was wearing a pair of designer sunglasses, and she had makeup on. She looked the way she must have the day she told Rhonda, "You won't recognize me." She was still missing her upper plate, but her hair was shiny and combed, and she was wearing bright turquoise shorts and a flowered blouse. When I pulled up beside her, she rushed over and put her hands on the door to lean in to kiss me hello. Bangle bracelets on both wrists clinked against the car.

"You look beautiful," I told her. She smiled broadly,

clicked her tongue, made a jokey pose like an old-fashioned bathing beauty, and laughed. I laughed too, glad to get a glimpse of her sense of humor.

Before I could get out of the car, she thrust a piece of paper in the window. She had been clutching it, and I had to smooth it out on the dashboard to look at what she'd written. I could barely decipher her handwriting, but now and then something would come into focus: "Barbara Cartland romances," "animal stories," "natural history," "crime and mystery." Sally had broken down her library into categories to pack together. She'd made many revisions, crossing out words and scribbling others above them, or in a few cases simply writing the new category directly on top of the old one.

As I looked at the list, Sally rattled on magnanimously about Tammy and Mike, and how she was sure they would be friends again some day. She talked about Mrs. B. and shopping, and makeup, and her new clothes. "Of course, this is just the external me," she said at last, gesturing toward her blouse. "It's the *inner* me that counts."

"Well, you still look beautiful, Sally," I said.

"You're beautiful *too*, Peggy," she said excitedly. "And I'm talking about the *inner* you. You're the *best sister* in the *world!*"

I thanked her, we said good-bye, and I pulled away. I never got out of the car, and Sally was too agitated to get in.

I spent the rest of the day packing books, and the next morning I tackled the comics, sorting hundreds into boxes, marking them with their contents—Superman, Archie and Veronica, Casper—and throwing away fifty or sixty that had been damaged in a flood and were ruined.

After two days, I had all the boxes stacked fairly neatly. The basement was free of clutter, and I was satisfied that if Rhonda had to supervise the transfer to storage, she would be able to direct the moving company. Monday I drove back to New York without talking to Sally again. I was afraid to mar the memory of the exchange we'd had in the parking lot.

THERE WAS A down side to Sally's transformation, as I might have expected. She had bounced a substantial check to a department store to subsidize her new wardrobe, and she had run up a three-hundred-dollar bill at Lane Bryant on her charge card. I wasn't sure how the latter had occurred, since PLAN was supposed to hold the card for her, allowing her to use it when she needed to buy new clothes.

I called Teresa. It seemed that she had given Sally the card and forgotten to get it back. She apologized, and I sincerely accepted, knowing that Teresa had done her best in an agonizingly difficult situation.

I assumed that PLAN would take responsibility for the bill, but PLAN's director refused, saying that if I had wanted Sally not to have the card, I should have been explicit.

"What do you think was the point of having you hold the card for Sally in the first place?" I asked. I got no answer, and I decided the time had come to tell PLAN to go to hell, which I did, literally. I was sorry to base my break with PLAN on something that was technically Teresa's fault, but I doubted it would get her into trouble. PLAN couldn't afford another personnel switch, I reasoned, and besides, I knew Teresa kept good notes.

Teresa was not the kind of person who could just cut Sally off, even if she was no longer officially on the job. She was clearly still worried about Sally's welfare, and she called me occasionally to give me bulletins—that Sally was bothering another client of PLAN's who lived in Mrs. B.'s building or that Mrs. B.'s patience had worn out (Sally kept her up at night pacing around the small apartment and alarmed her by bringing home "strange men").

Just after this last call, Rhonda asked me if it would be all right for Sally to stay in a motel for a few nights, and I said yes, of course. Sally checked in, knowing it was only a temporary situation. After three days, she left the motel and returned, for the last time, to Mike and Tammy's.

I had one more call from Teresa, who had run into Sally on the street. Sally was talking wildly about AIDS. Sure that Mike and Tammy had the disease, she thought Teresa probably did too. "She was walking in the middle of the road with her head down, talking to herself," Teresa said. "She really needs to be hospitalized . . . just the way she *looks* . . ."

As I always did when I was upset, I dialed Rhonda. My equilibrium depended on her. She agreed that Sally should be in a hospital, but she didn't think there was any chance of getting her into one yet. "The law is clear, Peggy," she said. "They don't commit people for looking crazy."

When we hung up, I sat back and wondered how long it would be before Sally disintegrated to the point where she could be forced to get help. She had been manic for a record-breaking two months, and no one was offering any more predictions as to when she would finally crash.

W hen the Carlos Castaneda books were making a splash in the seventies, I didn't read them. Tenaciously in search of a way to live ordinary life, I was resolutely uninterested in anything that smacked of the occult. But I heard a friend talking about a scene in which Don Juan, the spiritual guide, instructs Castaneda to find the exact place on a porch where he should sit. The lesson, as I understood it, was about sensitivity to one's self and one's environment, and it momentarily sparked my curiosity. I, too, was trying to find my place on the porch, the spot where I would know in my heart that I belonged.

Sally's peripatetic life had always struck me as similar to mine in this way. She wanted to fit in, and to do it *as herself*, not by suppressing her personality or her history. She often thought she'd found her milieu, at last, only to discover after a while that her new surroundings were as poorly cut to her specifications as the last. She and I were born malcontents, in a way, and would be until we felt at home—accepted, valued, and protected.

At my first SAC Network meeting, I had noticed I felt intensely anxious, and it wasn't just the discomfort of revealing personal matters to strangers. It also wasn't entirely the desire to retreat from a subject that I had avoided more or less successfully until Mother died. I thought about it after I left—the way my hands perspired and my heart raced—and finally identified my emotion as fear. I had been afraid of the others there. I thought they wouldn't like me, that they would resent me—because my sister was stable or because she had a trust fund—or that they would try to get me more involved in Sally's care than I wanted to be, or that they would try to make me feel guilty for my perpetual desire to save myself.

To my surprise, no one had challenged me. No one suggested I move nearer to Sally; everyone offered sympathy when I told them my mother had died in the spring. And they expressed delight when I told them that Sally took her medicine faithfully, and that I could draw on a trust to pay for a social worker to look after her. After two or three meetings, I realized that the people in the group seemed to like one another, and that when they disagreed they did so tactfully, gently, and with the apparent understanding that we were all doing our best to cope with whatever thoughts, emotions, resources, and responsibilities we were dealt.

It took a long time for my surprise to turn to relief, and months longer for relief to turn to comfort. By the time Sally was breaking down, I noticed that just walking up the steps of the community house at Saint James Church, knowing the meeting would soon begin, made me feel better. It wasn't until I read a book by the founder of the SAC Network, Julie Tallard Johnson, that I understood the genesis of my original apprehension. A Minneapolis social worker and psychotherapist whose brother is schizophrenic, Johnson believes that to understand our relationship to our ill sibling, we have only to look at other relationships in our lives to see how our particular dynamic works. When I had first gone to the meetings, I assumed that the siblings I met there would be like my own sibling—and apparently I assumed that any brother or sister with whom I came in contact would be frightening, guilt-provoking, and envious. This was not the first time I understood that I was afraid of Sally. I'd identified that emotion many times, watching her glower at me after a fight. It wasn't the first time I realized I felt grotesquely guilty in relation to Sally. Or the first time I knew I was afraid to speak of my own good fortune for fear it would make her life seem poor by comparison. But it was the first time I identified all these feelings in the context of Sally's illness and the first time I was able to blame the illness instead of Sally.

Gradually, I had begun to think of Sally without fear, and without so much pain. I stopped tearing apart the past looking for someone, or some incident, to blame for all our suffering—hers, mine, our parents'. As I was released from my own guilt by the sympathy and approbation of others who understood exactly how I felt—how I had been feeling my whole life through—I began to feel strong. When I was at a meeting, I felt more myself—if that is how to put it—than I had known was possible. One night, I looked around the table where we sat and the phrase "my place on the porch" popped into my mind. I had found it.

I think that what I hoped for when I found the group was that the others in it would, in effect, give me permission to pursue happiness for myself. I thought that meant to continue to run from Sally and my responsibility to care for her, to avoid my feelings about her and my family. What happened, instead, was that the group gave me the strength to incorporate the less-than-happy parts of my life with the happy ones—in other words, to get real.

Real meant facing the worst, not running from it. I remember, early on, listening to one woman whose sister lived with her describe the abuse to which she was subjected. Her sister constantly screamed at her, threatened her, and refused to get treatment. The ill sister was a heavy smoker, and often fell asleep with a cigarette burning in the ashtray near her bed. "Last week I wondered what I would do if she set herself on fire," the well sister said to us. "Sometimes I can imagine just letting her go." But at another meeting the same woman spoke sadly about how she had come to allow her sister to move in. "She has no one but me," she said. "I was always the only one who cared about her."

I understood both sides of her response. I don't really know how Sally's own life has felt to her. I *can't* know that. But I think I sensed her anguish throughout my childhood and young adulthood. A great part of my own therapy was devoted to defending myself against identifying so strongly with the unhappiness that brought Sally to her knees again and again. In the group, we expressed a lot of anger, but our sorrow was boundless—almost beyond expression. If we didn't care so deeply for our ill brothers and sisters and parents, we would all have been better able to help them, better able to take the objective stance of a social worker or family friend—someone who didn't make the ill person's pain their own, someone who could go home at the end of each day without carrying the burden of wondering if our relative would make it through another night. There is a poem by W. S. Merwin that goes, "Your absence has gone through me / Like thread through a needle. / Everything I do is stitched with its color." I thought of it now and then when I was at meetings. The illness in our families had gone through us that way. Everything we did was stitched with its color.

What we were striving for was a degree of separation that would allow us to cut that binding thread, to live as freely *as possible*. That meant something different for each of us.

Most of us in the group were not taking daily care of our ill sibling or parent, but we all knew that supportive living arrangements were in criminally short supply, and we understood that any one of us might someday have to open our own door or see our sister, brother, father, or mother live on the street.

Sometimes the latter alternative looked like the only way to keep our own lives from being warped or destroyed. As

Gloria Steinem wrote in "Ruth's Song," a loving remembrance of her mentally ill mother, "Perhaps the worst thing about suffering is that it finally hardens the hearts of those around it. . . . Pity takes distance and a certainty of surviving." For those of us who had suffered from intense depression ourselves, such certainty was elusive at best.

We cried at our meetings, but we also laughed—sometimes ruefully, sometimes joyfully. One rainy Thursday evening I spent almost the whole two hours laughing. One group member, a woman in her forties whose ill sister remained in the family home and let it fall apart until the local health department forced her to evacuate, told us how she had learned to deal with her sister's off-the-wall plans. "I know it's useless to argue," she said, "and I've given up trying to make sense of what she's saying, so now whenever she says *anything*, I nod firmly and say, 'Now, *there's* a thought!' "

A twenty-four-year-old woman who left her home at sixteen talked about the oddities of growing up with a paranoid schizophrenic mother. "I thought *everybody* climbed in the back window to get into their houses," she said. "I thought *all* mothers were afraid to open the front door."

Every month, someone would voice a thought that rang a bell in me:

- "I feel very ripped off, because the family I got was not the family I wanted. It's a very aggressive family."
- "I never used to allow my business associates to know what was going on in my life, but now I'm more comfortable explaining my brother's illness to them. It's a measure of how far I've come, and how far society's come. All the books about alcoholism, incest, drug abuse—they've made it easier for me to talk about something that's worse in some ways but better in others. We all need help. That's the bottom line. Families with serious problems need help."

- "What's nice about the group is that people in it are functioning well. It gives you permission to do your best."
- "There were periods in my life when I was worried I might have psychotic tendencies, too, but I have lots of friends, I'm sociable, I like to talk, and I think this helps the awareness level."
- "The big thing in parents' groups is trying to disprove the notion of a 'dysfunctional family.' Well, I'm here to say that my family was *dysfunctional*."

I was learning from the group, however, that no dysfunctional pattern had to be permanent. Change usually began with one member who couldn't go on the way things were. A woman whose accounts of her alcoholic father and schizophrenic mother sounded hopeless told us one evening that she had decided to cut a deal with her father. She would have her mother committed for treatment if he would go to Alcoholics Anonymous (AA). The commitment was difficult, her mother moaning at one point, "How could you, my own daughter, do this to me?" But three months later the family was transformed. The mother was back home and taking medication faithfully, and her husband stayed on the wagon.

In her book, *Hidden Victims: An Eight-Stage Healing Process for Families and Friends of the Mentally Ill*, Johnson described two dysfunctional reactions to mental illness: that of the caretaker, who tries to do too much, and that of the escape artist, which I'd been most of my life. The goal, as she sees it, is to be a care *giver*, one who is able to give help freely by choice. The person who can balance his or her own needs with those of the ill person is the one who is ultimately blessed.

Johnson offers the "Eight-Stage Process," which is similar to the step programs used by AA and other groups, to achieve this equilibrium:

One: Awareness. I explore the ways in which the relationship has affected my life.

Two: Validation. I identify my feelings about this relationship and share those feelings with others.

Three: Acceptance. I accept that I cannot control any other person's behavior and that I am ultimately responsible only for my own emotional well-being.

Four: Challenge. I examine my expectations of myself and others and make a commitment to challenge any negative expectations.

Five: Releasing Guilt. I recognize mental illness as a disease for which no one is to blame.

Six: Forgiveness. I forgive myself for any mistakes I have made. I forgive and release those who have harmed me.

Seven: Self-Esteem. I return the focus of my life to myself by appreciating my own worth, despite what may be going on around me.

Eight: Growth. I reaffirm my accomplishments and set daily, monthly, and yearly goals.

The SAC Network meetings had successfully carried me through stages one and two, and I'd made inroads on several others—forgiveness, especially. But I still felt compelled to try to change Sally's behavior, and the thought of returning the focus of my life to myself at this point seemed laughable. I was dimly aware, however, that sooner or later I would be forced by circumstances to hoe the hard row Johnson had laid out before me.

I tried to think about my situation in terms of larger themes, such as the fact that blame belongs elsewhere—on a health care system that offers inadequate help to patients and their families; on an overburdened social services system that provides little appropriate residential care or rehabilitation; on a society that stigmatizes the mentally ill, making it doubly difficult for them to find a place to live or to get a job or even to make a friend.

And yet, no matter how many times I reminded myself that mental illness is a political and social issue, no matter how many times I repeated the numbers that told me how common it was—one in one hundred for schizophrenia, one in three hundred for serious manic-depression—I couldn't deny that for me, for most of my life, mental illness had been only personal. I had to be forced to find a new perspective, one that put mental illness in its place, as it were. I was helped by many people, but especially by the other members of FAMI and the SAC Network. Hearing their stories put me at ease to tell mine, and telling mine at last made it seem common, if not ordinary, rather than definitive.

I began to see that my lifelong dread had been a terrible waste of spirit, a wretched waste of time. When I had been paralyzed by anxiety, it was largely because I thought I knew how my future would go. I had been wrong. I was wrong about Sally, wrong about myself, and wrong about what life had to offer us both.

During the weeks when Sally was first sick, and then later, when she began moving around from shelter to shelter, I had made five or six calls a day to Virginia. I was trying to find out where she was, what she was doing, how she was feeling, and whether she was all right, or deteriorating. As time went by, I kept calling and calling. One day I finally told Rhonda I was exhausted, and she bluntly told me to stop.

"There's nothing you can do," she reminded me again. "If anything happens, I'll take care of it. That's what your mother intended, remember? Don't call me again until next week, Peggy. Really. I'll talk to you then."

I suddenly felt useless, as if I'd lost my *raison d'être*. I felt the way I always had when Mother told me after the fact about one of Sally's breakdowns. I was cut out of the family once more, exiled again. In fact, Rhonda had said, "Get back to your own life," before hanging up, and my automatic internal response was, "What life?"

I was sitting at my desk at work. Fred was editing copy, but he must have sensed a change in the weather from my corner. He turned and asked if something was wrong.

"Rhonda told me not to call for a week. There's nothing I can do," I repeated. "She told me to live my own life."

"Fabulous!" he said. "I'll order champagne."

"I feel like shit, for some reason," I said. I thought I was going to cry. "I can't seem to think about anything but Sally. I don't think I can concentrate on anything else."

Fred didn't look concerned. "So write about it," he said. "It's on your mind. Make it into something."

Fred's words struck a resonant chord. My new mission was instantly clear, and it looked much easier than the one from which Rhonda had just released me. In my excitement, I decided that what was needed was a book, telling what it was like to be a sibling of a person with mental illness and how it was likely to affect one's life. That night, after dinner, I sat down at my word processor and began making notes for a book on the siblings of the mentally ill: "guilt . . . responsibility . . . depression . . ." I wrote and wrote, and when I went to bed I couldn't sleep, for thinking of everything I wanted to say to others like myself. I wanted to tell my story the way we did at the meetings, and to describe how the stories of others had illuminated my situation for me. I wanted to talk about Rhonda and the Personal Support Network, and how they had made it possible for me to remain in New York. I wanted to talk about how difficult it was to live life day by day. You can't know what will happen next, I would say, so you have to learn to relinquish control and to respond as life dictates.

The next day I called a literary agent to ask if she would consider handling a proposal for such a book. I introduced myself, briefly told her what I wanted to do—and began to cough. I covered the receiver to muffle the sound, but couldn't stop hacking. I excused myself and coughed violently for a few seconds. I could hardly catch my breath. Finally, I had to hang up. I coughed uncontrollably for ten minutes. Mortified, I called her back, and we laughed about my "Freudian slip." "Maybe you should think about this a little longer," she said, "to be sure you really want to take it on." I had to agree. I didn't have a cold, I wasn't sick, and I hadn't coughed like that since I'd had a bad case of the flu, four years earlier. There was no explanation for it but that I was allergic to the thought of an extended project involving me, my sister, and mental illness. It apparently stuck in my throat.

It was a quiet day at the office, and Fred and I were chatting with a writer who had stopped by to deliver a manuscript. Paul was also a friend, who had called me many times after my mother died to ask how I was, and when I described my choking attack, he suggested that I "start small." "Query the *New York Times Sunday Magazine*," he suggested, "and do an article first."

I proposed an article about FAMI, the SAC Network, and my own story to the *Times*, and after it was accepted I went to work on the article. For background, I called the two national organizers for the SAC Network, Julie Johnson, who founded it, and Marylee Westbrook, the West Coast coordinator. It was then that I discovered Johnson had just finished her book, and I was grateful she had done the work, for after my reaction on the phone with the agent, I realized I wasn't qualified to write a self-help book for people like me. I was still in the throes of dissecting my own problems and not in any shape to shed the light of objectivity on the subject.

On the phone, Julie talked about groups she'd led, and about how it takes time for people to feel comfortable enough to explore the most difficult issues facing them. "Somebody will finally say, I wish my sibling would die, or were dead, and I say, 'Okay, has anyone else here ever had that feeling?' Very seldom will there be someone who hasn't at some time in their life felt that way. It only takes one person to admit it. But what eventually happens is you learn you hate the illness. You don't hate the person. You hate the disease, you hate what it's done to the family. You have a lot of anger and resentment toward the family and other people in the community. All the anger isn't really toward the ill person. Much of it is toward the parents, which is why it's harmful to have them at meetings, because we need to be able to express that anger freely."

When I talked to Rhonda about the article, I asked her if she had any words of wisdom to add. She said that she thought it was important to say that there are no answers that are right for every person. "How can you know what's right in any given situation? Your parents die, and all you've seen is how *they* did it. It's a struggle to figure out how to be a good sibling, and now you're having to make it up as you go along. And the problem is, there's another person involved—very inconvenient if you're trying to make decisions that affect both of you."

The most enlightening talk I had was with Marylee West-brook, whose energy and optimism suffused her conversation. She had two ill brothers, one of whom had been homeless for a long time. He lived on the beaches near her home in Venice, California, and occasionally came to her for money, or to take a shower, or rest. I told her I dreaded living that close to Sally, because I was sure I'd be overwhelmed by her needs. Marylee said a simple thing that I've carried with me since: "I believe it's important to pace myself," she said. She went on, "If I feel resentment toward either of my brothers, I know I'm doing more than I want to do—and more than they want me to do. You can't solve problems overnight. There are days you can't do anything at all. I know, now, that if I'm giving one of them some help, it's because *that day* I want to do it and have the resources."

The more I worked on the article, the more connected I felt to my own life, and to my past. I struggled to remember how it had felt to be my parents' daughter, and my sister's sister. Reading galleys of Julie's book, which raised every question I had ever asked myself, I thought of nothing else but how mental illness had affected Sally, my parents, and me. I cried when I read, in a chapter called "Disrupted Lives," "Families of the mentally ill are confronted with a lifetime of losses." She also wrote about "chronic grief," which "leads to feelings of hopelessness, regret, and failure." She wrote about families who grieve in silence, and how denial becomes the norm. "The family is disrupted as, more and more, family members follow separate paths as they deal with the illness." Johnson's years as a therapist, as well as her own experience as the sister of a schizophrenic brother, gave her the kind of perspective I could only strive for. When I was finished reading, I realized that there was a clear overall message: Know yourself and take care of your own needs. Only then will you be able to offer useful help to someone else.

Where all my life I had been a person with a secret, now I was surrounded by those whose lives were much like my own, and I began to sense that my new club—whose members were everyone in families touched by mental illness—was a large one. At a dinner party with Harvey and a group of his friends, someone asked casually what I was working on. When I described the article, a woman to my left said that she, too, was a member of FAMI. Her father was schizophrenic and had been refusing medication for years. Her brother had problems, too, and although they weren't so serious by comparison, she felt a responsibility to look out for him as well.

When I went for a haircut one day, my hairdresser asked me if I'd been under a lot of stress, because my hair looked *awful*. I told her what had been happening in my life, and she described her schizophrenic half-sister. "She really doesn't have anyone but me," she said. The week before, looking for a way to get a message to Julie Johnson, who was unlisted, I'd dialed Minneapolis information to ask if there was a number for the Alliance for the Mentally Ill. The operator gave me the number and then, instead of clicking off the line, paused for a moment. "Do they have information about mental illness?" she asked me. I told her about the New York chapter—its advocacy work and support groups—and said I thought the Minneapolis chapter was probably similar. She paused again, and I sensed she wanted to tell me something. At last, she said, "My son has manic-depression."

Every day, I would discover that another friend or acquaintance had a brother, sister, or parent with mental illness. Two of my fellow editors had siblings with serious problems. Then a writer who stopped by the office told me she'd heard about the piece I was doing and wondered if she could talk to me about her schizophrenic brother in Chicago.

Working on the article, I felt like a writer for the first time. In the eight years since I'd stopped painting, I'd written art reviews, profiles of artists, and news stories, but I never stopped thinking of myself as a failed artist. Writing was what I did, but it wasn't easy for me, and I'd had to learn how to do it in my thirties. I always felt that I wasn't a real writer—that I would be found out. I know now that such self-doubt is common among the siblings of the mentally ill, and that we often live as if we're waiting for our real life to begin. Now, I felt mine had begun. For the first time, I wrote without the lurching, halting difficulty that had always dogged me at the word processor.

I think I was especially fortunate to be able to do something concrete for myself that was related to what was happening in my life, but I believe that any action I'd taken at the time would have had a similarly salutary effect on me. I was doing what I could actually do—not trying to change the course of the events that were taking place around me. If I had done something else, such as advocate on behalf of the mentally ill, or start a support group, the action would probably have been as beneficial for me. I was learning to relinquish my fantasies of control while at the same time grappling with what at the moment was the most consuming fact of my life.

I asked Rhonda to tell Sally about the article, and when the editors of the magazine asked that Sally sign a release, she came through with a graceful note. "It is fine with me," she wrote in her shaky hand, "for my sister, Margaret Ann Moorman, to write as many articles as she wants to about me and our family."

When the article was edited, Sally was ricocheting among shelters, but my narrative nonetheless ended on a hopeful note. I said that I had faith in her inherent resilience, and that I was sure she would be all right eventually. In fact, I wasn't at all sure. I was extremely worried, and the slightly upbeat conclusion was my way of whistling in the dark.

AS PART OF my program of attending to my own life, I made plans to go away with Harvey for part of June and July. We were going to visit friends in Belgium and France, then make our way to Venice for the Biennale. After that, we would go to Florence and Sienna, ending up near Assisi, where some Swedish friends of ours had rented a large house.

As soon as we left, I began to feel sick about being an ocean away from Sally, and I developed a cold that stayed with me for more than half the trip. I couldn't stop wondering what was happening in Arlington, and even though I telephoned Rhonda each week, as before, I felt the miles separating us. I began to have the kind of premonitions that had haunted me when I lived in Seattle. One night as Harvey and I were leaving a restaurant in Florence, I told him I absolutely had to find a telephone. We went into a hotel, where the desk clerk helped me place a collect call to Rhonda. She said things were the same.

As we walked back to our hotel, I couldn't shake the impression that Rhonda was keeping something from me. The following week, I learned that she had taken Sally to a hospital that day, but the staff had not seen fit to commit her.

The next day, Tammy and Mike, coming through for Sally as I'd never imagined they could, had taken her back to the hospital, and this time a different doctor had admitted her on the spot.

Sally agreed to a voluntary commitment, thinking, she told me later, that the hospital wanted to study her supernatural powers. As Rhonda explained it to me, she was so far gone at this point that she was severely delusional. She was evaluated and given a strong sedative, and soon she was moved to the Northern Virginia Mental Health Institute, a public hospital in Fairfax, the county next to Arlington.

As soon as Harvey and I got back to New York, I called Sally in the hospital, and we had a quiet conversation. She sounded exhausted, as I might have expected, and her voice sounded flat, a side effect of her medication.

At the end of our talk, I told her I had missed her.

"I love you too, Peggy," she said.

Then I called the *Times*, which was holding my article, and told my editor I needed to rewrite the ending.

PART FIVE

HEALING

....

O n Rhonda's advice, I gave Sally a week to rest and recu-
perate, and then I went to see her. The Friday night I drove
down to Virginia, I ran into a bumper-to-bumper traffic jam
on the New Jersey Turnpike that went on for miles and hours.
It was late July and swelteringly hot, even after dark, and I
slowly passed dozens of cars pulled off the highway with their
hoods open and their radiators boiling over. It was past two-
thirty in the morning when I reached Lyn and Earl's, but I set
the alarm clock they left by my bed for eight, so I wouldn't be
late to pick up Sally. She had been given two day-passes for
Saturday and Sunday, and I knew she would be looking forward to getting out.

Lyn and Earl hadn't spoken to Sally recently, but Donald
and Betty had, and Betty reported that Sally had told her
Angela Davis and Charles Manson were in the hospital too. I
was unnerved by this, thinking that Sally might still be delusional. I'd had a reassuring conversation with her on the
phone, but this new information discouraged me.

When I left the house I noticed it was already hot. It must
have been in the high eighties, and it was only nine in the
morning. I got in the car and felt the smothering air envelope
me. The dashboard of my car was in the sun, radiating heat.

When I arrived at the hospital, a low building set among

neatly tended shrubs and lawns, I rang a bell and was let in by a volunteer who had me sign my name on a visitors' sheet. I thought Sally might be waiting for me in the patients' lounge, but she wasn't there. I asked for the number of her room at the nurses' station and was directed down a hall.

Sally was asleep when I walked in, but she woke up the second I spoke her name. The blinds were drawn and the room was dim, and my eyes took a while to adjust. Sally looked thin, but it wasn't until I opened the curtains that I saw how changed she was. Her face was drawn and gray. Her hair was clean, but it looked tangled. Wild and feathery, it seemed frayed, not cut. Her complexion looked rubbery and flaccid, as if someone had let the air out of her cheeks, and her eyes were withdrawn, with dark circles under them. When she spoke to me, her words were slurred and faint. She still did not have her upper plate, and her lips were sunken into her jaw.

In two-and-a-half months, Sally had lost more than ninety pounds. Although she was not thin, she somehow looked gaunt. I could see her collar bones, and her clothes hung on her frame.

Sally asked what we were going to do, and I told her we could do whatever she wanted. She slipped on a pair of rubber thongs next to her bed, and slowly rose to her feet. All the verve of her manic phase was gone. She was hardly able to move. It was as if the energy she'd been traveling on had burned a hole in her spirit.

As we were leaving the room, I reminded Sally to put on her glasses. "I don't have them any more," she said. She hadn't worn them for weeks. I'd noticed when I saw her Memorial Day weekend that she was wearing sunglasses, and I knew they weren't prescription ones. Apparently it was around that time that she'd lost her regular glasses. I said I would get Rhonda to see that she was fitted for a new pair.

I was suddenly overcome with sadness, to think that no one

had realized Sally's glasses were lost. She'd always worn them, but none of her workers had noticed when she stopped. Without her glasses, Sally's countenance had a vague cast. I didn't know how much of her inwardness to ascribe to the fact that she couldn't see well, and how much to the medicine she was given. When we were talking about what to do that day, I asked her if she would like to go to a movie, where we could keep cool. "I couldn't see it without my glasses," she said. I felt now, as I had when I was carefully sorting and packing her belongings, that no one would ever know Sally as well as I did. No one would love her as much. I felt sorry for her, thinking that I was the best she had, for I so often let her down.

Sally followed me out, stopping at the nurses' station to pick up her pills for the day. She seemed weak and exhausted. Whenever she spoke I had to ask her to repeat what she said. Her voice was so faint it sounded like a child's sleepy whisper. We decided to drive to Great Falls, where there was a park we both liked. On the way, we passed through old country neighborhoods that were gradually being developed, like all the areas around Washington. Although there were still long stretches of woods near the park, the sun bore down on us in the new clearings. I drove fast, hoping that the verdant woods along the Potomac would shelter us from it, and that the river might send up some breezes.

We parked and walked to the refreshment stand near the entrance. We were both parched. We bought sodas and sat on the benches for a few minutes while we drank. Sally seemed to need to stop frequently. Just the few hundred yards between the car and the benches was a long distance for her. After we rested, we went down a winding path to the picnic areas, and I spread out a blanket I'd brought. Sally stumbled as she lay down, almost as if she was falling. It was hideously hot. The temperature seemed to have climbed ten degrees in the last hour. We lay still for thirty minutes or so, not talking.

Sally couldn't get comfortable, and neither could I. Finally, she said she thought she should get back to the car. She struggled to her feet, and I folded the blanket. I felt weak too, by now, and Sally was lurching as if drunk. When we were almost to the parking lot, she stumbled and caught herself. "I feel faint, Peggy," she said.

I knew that Lyn and Earl were out for the day, so we went to their house, which was air-conditioned. I felt uneasy taking Sally there this time, for they had not specifically invited us to stop by, as they always had in the past. I knew they had been frightened by Sally's behavior when she was manic. When I realized that they hadn't called her in months, even after she was committed to the hospital, I wondered sadly if they had written her off.

I couldn't have made it through the previous year without Lyn and Earl. They always greeted me with open arms, urged me to stay with them, and made me feel completely at home when I did. "You're a daughter," they said to me, and I felt like one. Lyn cooked for me as if I were her child, and Earl regularly sent me congratulatory notes on articles I'd written. But now I couldn't help thinking, If I am your daughter, then who is Sally? Because she is my sister. We come as a pair.

Sally went to the basement and lay down on a bed, but I stayed upstairs. After an hour, Sally called to me from the basement to ask what time it was. I told her, and suggested we get some lunch. Then I heard a terrible crash.

I ran down the basement stairs to find Sally sprawled on the floor, the mattress she'd been lying on now lying on top of her. She was so weak she'd slid off the bed, and the mattress had flipped over on her. I grabbed an edge of it and pushed it back on the bed, then reached down to give Sally a hand. She could hardly get her feet under herself. I began to wonder if the sedative was making her sick.

Outside again, it was too hot to move. It was overcast, but not with rain clouds. The sky was a dull, heavy yellow-gray, like smog, and even though the thick film blocked the direct sun, it did nothing to cool the air. We drove to McDonald's and went inside.

We had barely spoken all day. Sally was quiet, and I didn't press her to talk. But as we lingered over our Cokes, I asked her as casually as I could about Charles Manson and Angela Davis. "I thought they were in California," I said.

"They're here now," she said. She kept sipping her Coke. This conversation didn't interest her in the least.

"I don't think it's possible, Sally," I said. "Could you be mistaken?"

"Well, that's who they *said* they were," she answered. I realized that two of the other patients had either been delusional themselves or, more likely, were playing with Sally. She had simply taken them at their word and repeated their claims as fact to Betty and Donald, as one would pass on a piece of news.

We couldn't spend the day at McDonald's, or at least not comfortably. Sally said she needed to lie down again, and she asked if I would take her back to the hospital. I hated to do it, because the rule was that if she returned early from her outing she had to remain there for the rest of the day. She wouldn't be allowed to take a nap and then go out again.

"I know the weather will break, Sally," I said. I didn't see how it could go on as it was.

"I can't hold on any longer," she answered. "I have to go back."

As we drove, she asked if I'd mind doing a little shopping for her at K mart. "I need two pairs of thongs," she said.

"Why two?"

"Oh, they're always wearing out or getting lost."

I said I'd be happy to get them. When we got back to the hospital, I walked her in and then left. There was no point in staying, for she was asleep as soon as her head hit the pillow.

I found the nurse on duty and told her that Sally was extremely dizzy, stumbling frequently and almost falling a couple of times. She made a note in Sally's chart, but she said it was probably the heat, not the medicine Sally was taking.

I needed to spend some time at Mike and Tammy's, where Sally's belongings were still in the basement. Sally told me she had unpacked some of the boxes again, so I wanted to see what needed repacking. I didn't know where Sally was going to go when she got out of the hospital, but I knew this time it wouldn't be there.

Sally remembered her promise to go into a group home, and she was prepared to keep it, but because rooms were scarce we couldn't be sure of a space for her. Rhonda called ACRI when Sally went into the hospital, they immediately put her back on their roster of clients, and one of their counselors, Jose Campos, began working hard to get Sally into a home that was expected to have a free bed within the month. There was someone else ahead of Sally on the waiting list, but admittance also hinged on interviews with the house's residents, who had a strong say in choosing new tenants. Rhonda told me not to hold my breath. "Never count on something like this," she said. "Be positive, but don't pin your hopes on it." I tried to put it out of my mind. I decided to get the basement in order again, and to leave it to Rhonda, Sally, Jose, ACRI, and the powers that be to decide if the boxes went to an apartment, a rented room, or a storage bin.

The basement was still in good shape. Sally had removed some phonograph records from one box, and had opened a few others, whose contents were spread nearby. These were easy to repack. I felt vague as I stepped around the boxes and furniture, as if I couldn't focus on the place any longer. I had mentally put the basement in our past. As I stood near the bed, I idly picked up a plastic ashtray on the bedside stand, and there was Sally's upper plate. I wrapped it in a tissue and put it in my purse.

I forced myself to take one last sweeping look. When I did,

I realized that there were new bags everywhere, which I some-how hadn't noticed. I dumped them out one by one on the bed. One contained a tape recorder and several celophane-wrapped packs of blank tapes, and the receipt was still in the bag. Another held a pile of new clothes, most of them with their price tags still dangling from their seams showing the name of the store where Sally had bounced a check. There were four or five exercise leotards in different sizes and some pairs of shorts, all too small for Sally even at her present weight. Another sack was filled with an array of sunglasses, some broken, some new. I stacked and folded everything into a loose pile and set it aside, in case some of the articles could be returned. It wasn't much of a haul for two-and-a-half months of mania.

When I opened the last bag, a paper sack from K mart, I found two pairs of rubber thongs. I put them in my purse and headed back to the hospital.

On the way, I went to McDonald's again and picked up some Big Macs, which Sally had asked for. When I got to the hospital, she was lying on her bed. I called her name and she sat up and said hello perfunctorily, rubbing the sleep from her eyes. I opened the bag of Big Macs and began to set out our dinner on her bed. Sally ate hers ravenously and then lay down again before I had a chance to put straws in our drinks. I waited a few seconds, thinking perhaps she was just resting, but then I asked if she wanted me to leave.

"I don't mind eating in the car," I lied.

"Maybe you'd better," she said. "I'm so tired, Peggy."

"Are you still dizzy?" I asked.

"No," she said. "I'm just tired."

The heat had drained me, and I assumed it had done the same to Sally. I packed up my half of the meal, and said good night. An aide walked me to the door, unlocked it, and held it open for me, but on my way out, I felt the heat hit me in the face like a blast of steam. I took a step back. "I think I'll stay a while," I told her. I carried my dinner to the lounge and ate there instead, watching the patients watching television. Four or five were gathered around the set, facing the screen, but none seemed to be watching the show. Their gazes all bore what a friend of mine called "the elsewhere look." I thought mine probably did too.

SUNDAY WAS just as hot as Saturday, but without the yellow-gray cloud cover to block the sun. As soon as I stepped outside, I began to perspire. By the time I was at the hospital I was drenched. I told Sally I didn't think it was a good idea to go out, but she wanted to go to a restaurant she liked, so we signed out and left.

Sally seemed much as she had the day before, but she talked a little as we drove. She said she had gone back to the basement to look for her records, and she'd been unable to find her old 45's from the fifties. She thought Mike and Tammy had probably stolen them, she said.

I'd heard this sort of thing many times. As she'd lost track of possessions over the years, she'd ascribed each loss to theft by someone who had betrayed her. Once, when Mother was moving her from one place to another, half a dozen boxes had been left behind accidentally. For years, Mother tried to crack Sally's conviction that someone had stolen the books that were packed in them, but Sally wouldn't hear of it. Now, with the story of the 45's, I found myself biting my tongue. When she moved back to the basement, she had given Mike and Tammy some of the furniture that the storage company had wrongly delivered to her, and had allowed them to use her table in their dining room. They had no reason to steal from Sally, who was happy to give or lend them whatever she had.

There were other components to Sally's paranoia this time, and talking about the records led her to mention one. "I think someone may have played tricks on me," she murmured. "I don't know, but I think some black man—a friend of Tammy's." As soon as she said this, though, she abruptly stopped speaking, as if she realized it sounded crazy. "I don't want to talk any more, Peggy," she said, and a second later she was staring out the window at a landscape she could barely see. Sally had learned what to keep to herself.

When we got to the restaurant, I found a place to park under a tree, hoping a little shade would keep the car from turning into an oven. It was sweltering, and I was perspiring furiously as we walked to the door.

Inside, a hostess took us to a table. She looked Sally up and down with obvious disdain, and even after we were seated she continued to stare at Sally from her spot near the front door. Her face was twisted into a sneer, and I fantasized getting up, walking over to her and popping her one in the mouth. Instead, I glared back at her, shooting what I hoped she would recognize as rays of hatred from my eyes. I knew it was the wrong thing to do, that I should have regarded her contempt as an opportunity for enlightenment, and tried to change her view instead of mirroring it, but I was too exhausted—too hot and irritable—to make the effort. At last, she turned her back.

Sally ordered crabcakes, and when they arrived she bolted them down in seconds, before I had taken more than a few bites of my lunch. She fidgeted nervously for a minute or two, and then she suddenly stood up.

"I need some air," she said abruptly. "Would it be all right if I took a walk?"

I reminded her how hot it was outside—in the upper nineties at least, and the humidity felt as if it must be near saturation point.

"I've got to get some air," she repeated.

I gave her the keys to the car and told her she could sit in it if she needed to. I watched her leave the restaurant, going past the ugly hostess, who recoiled as Sally swept by.

It didn't take me long to eat and pay the tab—ten minutes

at the most—and then I stepped out into the steaming afternoon to look for Sally, expecting her to be somewhere near the door. She wasn't there. I looked around the parking lot. I could see the car, but it was empty. I went back inside. She wasn't in the women's room or at the takeout counter.

"Have you seen my sister, by any chance?" I asked a waiter.

"She left," he said, pointing to the door.

The hostess spoke up. "She hasn't come back in," she said. Perhaps sensing my distress, she had dropped her condescending manner to try to help. I was grateful, and smiled at her. She smiled back. "I'll tell her to sit down and wait if I see her," she said.

Back outside, I walked to the street, a busy four-lane road, and looked down the sidewalk in both directions. No Sally. I walked around to the back of the restaurant, where trees from a neighboring yard overhung the baking hot macadam lot, making a spot of shade. When I still didn't see Sally, my heart began to race. I walked back to the front of the restaurant and wondered what to do. Sally had my car keys, so I couldn't drive around to look for her. It had been twenty, twenty-five minutes since she left. I was stuck, helpless. There was a telephone booth on the street, so I pulled a quarter from my purse and called Lyn and Earl to tell them what had happened.

Lyn heard the anxiety in my voice. "Stay where you are," she said. "We're on our way."

I hung up. I was dripping wet, sweating from panic as much as from the heat. Sally was faint and dizzy—what if she'd tripped and fallen? I had taken her out on a day pass, and I was responsible for her. I shouldn't have let her out of my sight.

As my thoughts spun, I automatically kept looking up and down the highway for her. Just when I was about to cry, I saw her walk around a corner. I called Lyn and Earl and caught them just as they were leaving the house.

"She's here," I said. "She's coming down the street."

Sally was making her way slowly toward the restaurant with her eyes down. I waited until she was near me, and called her name. When she looked up, I ran to meet her. "I thought you'd disappeared forever," I told her.

"I told you I was going to take a walk," she said.

"I know, but I thought it would just be a short one."

"Well, when you're cooped up in a hospital, it feels good to get out and move," she said.

Her words were so simple, so logical, I felt ridiculous for panicking. On the other hand, this was the first walk I'd known Sally to take without prodding. As I reminded myself to try to be more flexible in my expectations and reactions, an image of a baseball player popped into my mind—in the outfield, knees bent, glove raised slightly, ready to go in whatever direction the ball dictated. I needed to hang loose—hardly my forte.

SALLY AND I made a quick visit to see Donald and Betty, and then dropped by Lyn and Earl's house so I could pick up my overnight case. I wanted to drive back to New York directly from the hospital, instead of coming back into Arlington again. Lyn and Earl were as warm toward Sally as ever, and Lyn took me aside to ask if Sally was all right—she looked so terribly wan.

Back at the hospital it was cool and quiet. I walked Sally to her room.

"I'm going to have to take a rest, Peggy," she said.

"I think I'll be on my way, then."

"Thank you for coming."

"It's nice to see you."

"And thanks for the thongs."

We hadn't had much of a visit, I felt, but Sally didn't seem to mind. I told her I'd be back soon, and that the weather was sure to be better. I'd make certain Sally got new glasses, so at least she would be able to see.

The television in the patients' lounge was on, as ever. Passing by on my way to the door, I heard a newsbreak interrupt the regular program. Temperatures had climbed over a hundred for the second straight day, the newscaster reported. The elderly and those with health problems were advised to stay indoors. "It's hot out there, folks," I heard the broadcaster say as I left. "Dangerously hot."

In New York the next morning, as I was walking from the subway to my office, I heard a street vendor with a heavy accent somewhere nearby. I couldn't see him, but I heard him shouting, "*Hap*piness, yes, yes!" I was interested in that— very interested—and went to look for him. As I turned a corner onto Broadway, I spotted a man with a cart selling peanuts. *Hot* peanuts! Yes! Yes! I smiled and got out my money.

thirty-seven

....

The following week, Jose Campos took Sally for her interview at the group home. On the way, he told me, she sang "Ave Maria" to him. "She has a nice voice," he said. "And she's a very nice person." I could tell from his tone that he liked Sally, and I immediately liked him because of it. It made me hopeful. I knew he would push for her.

The interview went well, he thought. Sally stayed at the house for several hours, in spite of the fact that her first impression of it could not have been more daunting. As she and Jose walked up to the front door, one of the residents, sitting on the large verandalike porch to smoke, looked at Sally and pronounced, "I don't like you." If that had happened to me, I thought, I wouldn't have thought twice about withdrawing my application, but Sally was unfazed. Perhaps it was insignificant, considering what she had been through in her life. And, too, she was exceptionally tolerant of other people's quirks. I imagine she chalked it up to his illness—"It's the disease talking." Sally understood that instinctively, I'm sure.

A FEW DAYS after the interview, Sally was invited to move in, and two weeks later I went to visit her at her new place. The home was a surprise to me, a big bungalow-style house with a large front porch on a pretty, tree-lined street. Inside, it was completely renovated, spotless, and decorated with new, comfortable-looking gray-and-mauve overstuffed furniture. There was an air of peacefulness about it, and the counselors and other clients seemed relaxed and cheerful. I remembered a group home in which Sally had stayed a decade before, in a dreary neighborhood in Washington. It was dark, and looked depressingly impoverished inside and out. Seeing this new one, I thought of various articles I'd read in the *New York Times* about neighborhoods whose residents were fighting such residences, and I wished that every fearful homeowner could see what a well-run, well-maintained group home could be. Sally said her neighbors were "very friendly." She said it offhandedly, as if such kindness could be taken for granted. I mentally put the whole street on my private God-bless-you list.

Sally looked completely different than she had in the hospital. The greatest change was in her face, which looked happy, I thought to myself, savoring the word. Happiness, yes, yes. She had been seeing a different doctor at the mental health center ("Thank God," as Rhonda said), and she was on a new medication, a drug called Tegretol, which the counselors in the house dispensed daily. Her mood was even but buoyant, without the dragging torpor that characterized her years on lithium. For the first time, I saw how critical medicine was to her personality, and I thought, this is Sally, Sally is back. "You look *wonderful*," I told her.

She smiled and said, "Well, I like to look nice for my favorite sister."

She had new glasses, and the frames were stylish and flattering. I complimented her on her choice, and she told me she had bought two pairs, "in case I lose these."

I felt a vague impatience overcome me. "Why do you get several of everything?" I asked her, thinking of the exercise suits and sunglasses she'd bought when she was manic.

She thought for a minute, then shrugged and said, "I don't know. I guess because Mom did."

WE HAD A great day, shopping at K mart for shoes and Lane Bryant for turtlenecks and a fall coat. Sally picked out a beautiful cobalt blue wool jacket that went with her eyes and made her pale skin look luminous. We talked about how Mother had always insisted she buy tweeds because of her tendency to spill Cokes and cigarette ashes, and Sally promised to get this coat cleaned regularly, "whether it needs it or not." Sally bought what she liked, and it was obvious she knew what looked good on her. The only item we chose that wasn't a bright color was a black cardigan sweater. It looked classy with the red, green, and yellow pullovers.

"And it's slimming," Sally said. She had gained back some weight in the hospital, and her skin had lost its slack, unhealthy look.

"You look just right, Sally," I told her, and I meant it.

We talked as we drove around from mall to mall, not so much about the past few months as about Sally's new home and her plans for the future. She loved the home, but I expected that, for she always loved new situations at first. The proof would be in how she handled the inevitable dissatisfactions with her new "family." She had already made a friend of the man on the porch. She described the others, tenants and counselors, in detail. She was animated and yet there was a reassuring calm underlying her enthusiasm.

We talked about the upcoming presidential election between Michael Dukakis and George Bush, and I asked Sally if she planned to vote. She had never lost the normal rights of an adult, such as the right to vote, which are denied to those mentally ill persons who have been declared incompetent in court. I remembered Mother taking Sally to her polling place every election. "How does she know who to vote for?" I had asked. "She doesn't read the papers."

Mother had answered vehemently. "She votes for who I tell her to, that's who!"

Sally said she had already made up her mind to vote for Dukakis, and I smiled, thinking that Mother would be pleased. I asked her what had led to her decision.

"I read his message on a coffee mug," she said. "It was all about sharing with others, and I'm for that." She had also examined a Republican mug, but, she said, "Their message wasn't so good."

THE NEXT morning, I met the movers at the basement, and showed them what to pack. We were taking everything to storage. Mike helped retrieve a pile of garbage bags, filled mostly with yarn, that had been stuffed in a crawl space under the stairs ever since Sally moved in. One was lumpy, and I opened it out of curiosity. There were Sally's old 45's, in their twenty-five-year old record boxes. I felt triumphant when I found them, not only because it would be an argument against her suspicions that people regularly stole from her, but also because I knew how happy she would be when I told her. I was elated, imagining her pleasure.

I had arranged to rent a large bin that I thought could hold everything, but after it was filled the moving truck was only half empty. I rented another across a hall from the first and we shoved in as much as possible, but there was still a mountain of bags left over. I called Sally and told her there was no way to store everything she owned, and I thought maybe this was the perfect time to give up the yarn.

"I want to keep it," she said, her voice so urgent I had to push myself to argue with her.

"But you've had it for years and years and you've never used it," I said weakly.

"That's because I never had a place of my own where I could spread it out."

I knew that wasn't quite the case. She could have spread it out in her old room at Mother's house, where she lived for almost two years, or she could have taken it to her own apartment when she had it. But I didn't remind her of these opportunities. I now realized that the bales of yarn represented hope to her—for a place of her own, for time and inclination to work, for success. I dropped the subject and managed to stuff the bags into the bins. This was one argument we wouldn't have again.

PEOPLE WHO didn't know better kept saying to me, "You must feel good, now that everything is settled." Nothing is ever settled. Sally and I were both in good shape, but it wasn't clear how much we had learned in the last year. I thought I was above irrational rage, for instance, but I soon discovered I wasn't. Not long after Sally had been in the group home, she decided to bring her piano from Mother's house. Rhonda, telling me about it on the phone, said she advised Sally to wait a month, to make sure she liked it there.

I blew up. "She'd *better* like it there," I said. "I'm not moving her again!"

"You're being unreasonable, Peggy," Rhonda said calmly. "You don't have to agree to move her again, but Sally is free to decide for herself where she wants to live, and you can't force her to stay in the group home if she doesn't want to. If Sally decides to leave, she'll leave, and there's nothing you can do about it."

The thought depressed me. "I just don't want to have to think about Sally for a while," I said, with more than a touch of my old escapism.

"Not possible," Rhonda reminded me in a matter-of-fact tone. "You're in this for the long haul."

Sally wasn't a new person either. About a year after her illness, we were talking about her breakdowns, and she once again discussed her idea for a halfway house. I managed not to get upset, though, and as I listened, I realized that this was a real dream of Sally's, whether she was sick or well. When she was manic, it was just easier for her to try to make it come true.

THE *TIMES* published my piece at the beginning of October. A week later, Harvey took to calling it my "woodwork article," as in people coming out of the. . . . I heard from practically everyone I'd ever known, and it turned out that most of them had their own stories to tell me. An artist we knew well revealed that she had a schizophrenic sister who had been institutionalized for years. An old boyfriend of mine from college called to tell me his little sister had had numerous breakdowns in the twenty years since I'd known his family. An art dealer took me aside when I went into her gallery one day to tell me she had cried when she read the article, thinking of her schizophrenic brother. The husband of one of Harvey's ex-sisters-in-law asked if I could give him a phone number for the Boston area SAC Network.

The office of the Friends and Advocates of the Mentally Ill in New York received several hundred calls from people asking for information on meetings, and at the next sibling support group, we had to move to a larger room at the church. Where there were usually twenty-five or thirty of us, now there were more than a hundred. People thanked me again and again, and for the first time in my life, I felt I had done something valuable.

I had tried to write the article with sensitivity to Sally's feelings, leaving out details that I thought would embarrass her, but it was impossible to be honest and not reveal traits of mine and of hers in a harsh light. Rhonda suggested that she

be the one to show it to Sally, so she wouldn't be alone when she read it.

When I went to Virginia at the end of October for Sally's birthday, I asked her what she thought.

She looked serious for a moment. "Well, when I *first* read it I could have *killed* you for telling people all those things about me," she said, frowning.

I held my breath for a second. "And then?"

Sally laughed. "But I guess I'm famous coast-to-coast now, right?"

"Right," I said. "And thank you, Sally, for letting me do it."

"Aw, that's okay, Sis," she said. "Actually, I feel pretty lucky to have you for a sister. At least you never swept me under the rug."

··

thirty-eight

It is two and a half years since all that now, and Sally is still living in a group home. She stayed at the first one until just a few months ago, when she moved to one that allows—and expects—more independence in its clients. I think she has been satisfied for the most part, although she still wants to have her own apartment some day. On Tegretol, she functions at a much higher level than she did during all the years she was on lithium. She isn't depressed, although she still likes to lie around and "rest" as much as she can.

I don't blame Sally for that awful year. It was a trial by fire for the two of us, learning to live without Mother, learning to take on new responsibilities. And I think that Rhonda's tactic of allowing Sally all the freedom she needed to direct her own life was brilliant. Even though Sally became very sick before being hospitalized, I know she appreciated Rhonda's respect for her autonomy, and I think the trust between them is solid because of it. I don't know how our future will go, of course, but I feel confident that we can weather it, no matter what happens.

Sally is stronger without Mother around to lean on. She has to be. She really is finally in charge of her own destiny, and she is, as many people used to say, more capable than we knew.

Last year, Sally even began working again—a decade after going on disability. She held down a job as a checkout person at K mart, and she also worked at Sears for several months. She had difficulty standing on her feet for long hours, for she had gained back some of the weight she lost when she was manic, and eventually left both stores, but as Rhonda pointed out, it was a triumph nonetheless. She is now enrolled in a computer-programming class at the local community college.

ACRI has proved an invaluable resource. Their counselors have constantly relieved the tensions inherent in Sallys group-home life, talking with her whenever she grows restless and, perhaps most important, listening to her with sympathy and respect. When I think back on their response to Sally's emerging mania, I realize that they were reluctant to see her mood as pathological because they, like all her other workers, were glad she was feeling positive and energetic. Because they cared for her, it was impossible for them not to derive plea-sure from her happiness.

PSN is going strong, and Rhonda is still its director. It has expanded to hire other counselors, and Sally has twice been invited to participate in interviewing candidates. Rhonda told me she is excellent at it. I asked Sally about her technique.

"Oh," she said, "I ask them things like, 'If I suddenly de-cided I was leaving the group home, what would you do?' "

"What would be a good answer?" I asked.

"It would be a good answer if they said they would sit down with me and try to find out the reasons why I wanted to do it," she said.

I feel secure, knowing Sally will have the Personal Support Network's ongoing care. A nonprofit organization, PSN is dependent on grants and donations (including the valuable time of several first-rate volunteers) as well as fees, but it is so good at what it does, I feel confident it will continue to pros-per. Sally sees her counselor there once a week, and occasion-ally makes use of telephone consultations. Whenever I feel my old crankiness or pessimism overtake me, I know that someone at PSN will calm me down before I say anything hurtful or discouraging to Sally.

Our relationship continues to be somewhat distant. We telephone a couple of times a month, and Sally visits Harvey and me Upstate in the summer. We've spent Christmases in Pittsburgh with Trenie and in New York. When Sally came to New York, her train arrived in a snowstorm that had begun that morning in Washington. She was wearing no socks and carrying only a light jacket. After listening to me ask her repeatedly if I couldn't take her to a store and buy her socks and a sweater, Sally finally said with mock impatience, "Oh, Peggy, stop trying to mother-hen me." I always hope visits will be smooth, and usually they are, but not always.

In the spring of 1989, one year after her breakdown, I was down in Arlington for Easter. Sally knew I was going to write this book, and she said she would be willing to talk to me to try to help with it. We drove to a park near Mother's house and sat at a picnic table.

We weren't having a good time. We'd started to fight the day before, when Sally complained that Mother never loved her. I was tired of what seemed to me to be her endless rage. I still missed Mother, and I hated hearing her maligned, especially when I knew she had done her best with the most difficult job of her life. I thought about Mother's planning and saving for Sally, and of her constant vigilance during the last years of her life. If that wasn't love, what was it? A sense of duty? Compassion? Guilt? It didn't matter to me: Her love for her firstborn showed in countless concrete ways.

I couldn't stand listening to Sally's age-old complaints, and I told her as much. She said that Mother wouldn't let her move home, that she wouldn't let her live her own life, that she meddled. She fumed and raged about the involuntary psychiatric commitment Mother had arranged ten years before, when Sally was manic. I argued with Sally about her past, defending Mother at every turn.

I was surprised at my reaction. I thought I had learned to nod benignly at Sally's tirades, treating them as broken records of blame. Perhaps Sally needed to deny her illness to the extent that it made optimism possible, and perhaps scapegoating Mother was an easy way to do it. It didn't do any good to fight, and it only made us both feel worse. But this time, I was completely unable to tolerate her anger at Mother because I was about to become a mother myself.

At forty, I had become pregnant a week after a meeting of the SAC Network at which we had a guest speaker, a researcher in the genetics of schizophrenia. During the question period after the doctor's talk, someone had asked, "What are a well sibling's chances of having a mentally ill child?"

"Oh, about the same as the general public," said the doctor. "Maybe a little closer to two percent than one."

Later, I told Harvey about my reaction. "I could feel every pore in my body open up," I said. "I felt as if I were Jacob, after a long, long fight, finally blessed by the angel." I could have found out the information by myself, but I had never had the courage to try. And in my general unconsciousness, I hadn't really known I was concerned about it, until I was old enough to tell myself it was too late, anyway.

When I talked to Sally, the old fears hit me again. The thought of having a child who in her late forties would continue to blame me for my distant mistakes chilled me. I loved being with Harvey, and my Mother's sad words—"Bob and I were so happy before we had children"—echoed in my memory. Whenever I heard Sally complain, my back went up, as if I'd been attacked personally. By defending Mother, I was defending all mothers, including, primarily, myself.

All during my pregnancy, I was possessed by a deep sense of well-being, and I often heard myself laughing as I talked with my friends. I had never been so happy, so optimistic, and yet, every so often, I would be felled by the fear that my pleasure would turn to pain, that I would respond to motherhood as my own mother had, or that I would have a baby who, like Sally, cried and cried until I began to doubt my ability to mother. And because I had suffered terrible depressions throughout my life, I steeled myself to expect a severe postpartum attack.

After Emma's birth, I waited for the blues to eat away at what I can only describe as my postpartum elation. It never happened. Emma was what is called an easy baby, crying when she was hungry or tired, but otherwise beatifically content. She was plump and strong, fun to pass around to friends, who would remark, "I thought newborns were more fragile than this." She seemed to like everyone, but she made it clear that she liked her relatives best, snuggling comfortably whenever she was held by Harvey, Sally, or Harvey's first daughter, Rebecca. Emma gave us a smooth start as a new family, and erased my worries about repeating the past.

When the three of us went to Arlington to spend the following Easter together, Emma smiled at her Aunt Sally as if they were old friends. We spent Saturday strolling around the gardens at Dumbarton Oaks and going out to dinner. The next morning, after Easter services at our old neighborhood church, where I showed Emma off to many of Mother's friends, Sally suggested we take a drive to the cemetery where Mother and Daddy were buried. It was a warm, sunny day, and the trees were filled with birds, chattering and singing. I sat down on the grass to feed Emma, while Sally stood over the graves.

In a minute, Harvey came over to me and took the bottle out of my hand. "I'll do this," he said. "I think Sally needs you more."

Sally was crying softly as she looked at the headstone. I put my arm around her shoulders, but I wasn't sure if I was comforting her or intruding on a private moment. We stood there together for a while, and then Sally said the words I'd always hoped to hear from her: "I can't help thinking how much Mom did for us."

I think this was the moment when I realized that resolution was possible, after all. It was true that Sally and I had grown up amid family conflict, secrecy, and sadness, but here we were to tell the tale—both of us strong, both of us going forward in our lives, both of us more whole than we had ever been. We had come through a lot, together and separately, and we were no longer controlled by the past. I've always felt that the relationships that are most difficult to resolve are those in which we continue to long for something—approval, respect, recognition—that will never be ours, at least not just the way we want it. When Sally spoke of Mother with sympathy, she was, in effect, forgiving her for all the disappointment she'd felt at not being able to elicit the kind of love she wanted. And I had at least begun to accept Sally as she was, without so much of the resentment that marked my years of denial.

The weekend was over too soon. As we left Arlington, I was sincerely sorry not to have more time to spend with Sally.

Five weeks later, I got a message on my answering machine. "Hi, Sis. It's me. Just calling to wish you the happiest Mother's Day anybody ever had."

RESOURCES

•••

SIBLING AND ADULT CHILDREN'S NETWORK DIRECTORY

If you are interested in starting a group in your area or wish to be listed as a contact person, please write the NAMI/SAC Network, 2101 Wilson Boulevard, Suite 302, Arlington, VA 22201 (703) 524–7600. Group facilitator guides are available.

ALABAMA

Kay Phillips
3424 Clairmont Avenue,
  #13
Birmingham, AL 35222
(205) 323–0180

Susan Baty-Pierce
3348 Montcrest Drive
Birmingham, AL 35210
(205) 833–6536
(205) 956–2084

Al Garrett
P.O. Box 31
Demopolis, AL 36732
(205) 289–3564

Marcus Allen
123 Mitchell Street
Florence, AL 35630
(205) 766–3915

Annie Saylor
7813 Michael Lane
Huntsville, AL 35802
(205) 881–1779

Carol Singley
3661 Airport Boulevard, #273
Mobile, AL 36608
(205) 342–2521

Jill Rawlings
4132 Carmichael Lane, #437
Montgomery, AL 36106
(205) 277–9460

ALASKA

Yvonne Jacobson
Alaska AMI
Suite 103
4050 Lake Otis Parkway
Anchorage, AK 99508
(907) 561–3127

Joy Albin
954 Woodway
Fairbanks, AK 99709
(907) 474–9512

Frances Cater
Kodiak AMI
P.O. Box 1472
Kodiak, AK 99615
(907) 486–5604

ARIZONA

Jeanette Hauser
P.O. Box C-12009-514
Scottsdale, AZ 85253
(602) 443–3331

Brenda D. Gibson
Pam Little
Andy Mosko
AMI of South Arizona
738 North Fifth Avenue
  #100
Tucson, AZ 85705
(602) 622–5582

ARKANSAS

Janice Norris
AAMI—North Arkansas
  Chapter
2422 Murray Lane
Heber Springs, AR 72543
(501) 362–7793
(800) 844–0381

CALIFORNIA

Gale Brown
325 West Third Avenue
Chico, CA 95926
(916) 342–6118

Wendy Kelly
26135 Flintlock Lane
Laguna Hills, CA 92653
(714) 831–7410

Joel Drucker
3239 Kempton, #9
Oakland, CA 94611
(415) 434–3540
(415) 836–4696

Jo Ann Wobensmith
1296 Glenwood Drive
Petaluma, CA 94954
(707) 763–3906

Cheryl Stewart
San Diego AMI
450 Olive Street
San Diego, CA 92103
(800) 523–5933
(619) 543–1434

Mary Gullekson
2192 Green
San Francisco, CA 94123
(415) 474–7010

Karen Dillon
1186 Camino Palomera
Santa Barbara, CA 93111
(805) 967–7494

Jody Hansen
c/o AMI—Santa Cruz
P.O. Box 1516
Santa Cruz, CA 95061
(408) 427–2160

South Bay Group
Marylee Westbrook
meets in Torrance, CA
(213) 396–0135

Marylee Westbrook
444 Lincoln Boulevard,
　#328
Venice, CA 90291
(213) 396–0135

Van Nuys Group
Marylee Westbrook
meets in Van Nuys, CA
(213) 396–0135

Ventura County AMI
Suite 140-A
1068 East Main Street
Ventura, CA 93001
(805) 643–4364

COLORADO

Ruth Lane-Wierzba
15806 East Saratoga Place
Aurora, CO 80015
(303) 699–8616
(303) 721–7686

Kathy Dewey
2840 Dover Drive
Boulder, CO 80303
(303) 494–8624

Rita Nichols
437 Thirty-second and
　One-eighth Road
Clifton, CO 81520
(303) 434–4535

Lynn Cooper
700 South Vine Street
Denver, CO 80209
(303) 778–8001

Mary Ann Arling
3919 San Isabel
Pueblo, CO 81008
(719) 544–2347

Lorie Schiffer
Spanish Peaks Mental Health
　Center
440 Yucca
Pueblo, CO 81005
(719) 545–2746

CONNECTICUT

DELAWARE

FLORIDA

Ann Purcell
828 Tuscarora Trail
Maitland, FL 32751
(407) 647–4846

GEORGIA

Cherry Finn
Georgia—AMI
Suite 412-S
1256 Briarcliff Road NE
Atlanta, GA 30306
(404) 894–8860

Carole Galanty
1484 Wessyngton
    Road NE
Atlanta, GA 30306
(404) 872–3373

Pearl McLean
555 Morton Avenue
Athens, GA 30605
(404) 549–7321

Leslie Coy
1733 Granger Court
Chamblee, GA 30341
(404) 454–7832

Jim Reiser
283 Oak Hammock Drive
Kennesaw, GA 30144
(404) 427–3312
(404) 875–3205

Stephanie Mayes
231 Allenwood Drive
Statesboro, GA 30458
(912) 764–7878
(912) 764–9868

Lei Stidham
Apartment B-1
1302 Pearl Street
Vidalia, GA 30474
(912) 537–1401
(912) 537–9316

HAWAII

IDAHO

Bob King
Idaho State AMI
6500 Park Drive
Hayden Lake, ID 83835
(208) 772–4633

ILLINOIS

Carl Hays
25150 North Iroquois Court
Barrington, IL 60010
(708) 655–0550

Donna McCormick
Phyllis Jydstrup
Portage Cragin Counseling Ctr
4840 W. Byron St
Chicago, IL 60641
(312) 282–7800

Peter Illing
Thresholds
2770 North Lakeview Avenue
Chicago, IL 60614
(312) 281–3800

Shirley Woyt
AMI of Greater Chicago
833 North Orleans
Chicago, IL 60610
(312) 642–3338
(312) 642–8457

Mary O'Neill Siebel
3040 Harrison Street
Evanston, IL 60201
(708) 328–0328

Norm Zuefle
918 Crain Street
Evanston, IL 60202
(708) 328–0244

AMI of Greater Joliet
Room 308
1000 South State Street
Lockport, IL 60441
(815) 838–5721

Christine Gosenpud
8438 Linder Court
Skokie, IL 60077
(708) 470–1562

INDIANA

Leanne Lafuze
742 Lockefield Court,
  #B
Indianapolis, IN 46202
(317) 637–4154

Roberta Simmons
2620 North Washington Street,
  #95
Kokomo, IN 46901
(317) 452–7567

Dorothy Lordi
St. Joseph County AMI
P.O. Box 866
Notre Dame, IN 46556
(219) 272–7180

IOWA

Mary Spear
1216 Twenty-sixth Street
Ames, IA 50016
(515) 233–1419

Judy Meyers
209 Hill Court
Cedar Falls, IA 50613
(319) 277–2387

Vickie Sylvara
M.H. Advocates of Linn
  County
Suite 10
221 Fourth Avenue SE
Cedar Rapids, IA 52401
(319) 364–6305

Karen Cordes
1919 Fortieth Place
Des Moines, IA 50310
(515) 277–6932

Rose Marie Friedrich
2911 Eastwood Drive
Iowa City, IA 52245
(319) 338–1629
(319) 335–7065

Deb Capaldo
Building 8, #151
1800 Grand
West Des Moines, IA 50265
(515) 224–6052

KANSAS

Carol Ann Kladuson
6000 West Fifty-seventh Street
Mission, KS 66202
(913) 432–8240

Terry Larson
Kansas AMI
P.O. Box 675
Topeka, KS 66601
(913) 233–0755

KENTUCKY

LOUISIANA

Maizie and John Thibeaux
FFAMI
178 Ronald Boulevard
Lafayette, LA 70503
(318) 232–1808

MAINE

Leslie
AMI of Maine
Box 222
Augusta, ME 04332
(207) 622–5767

Caroline Roux
3 Rogers Point Drive
Eliot, ME 03903
(207) 439–0323

Roger G. Ralph
AMI of Greater Portland
P.O. Box 15115
Portland, ME 04101
(207) 772–1248

MARYLAND

Marilyn Kresly-Wolff
AMI of Metro Baltimore, Inc.
2114 North Charles Street
Baltimore, MD 21218
(301) 539–0525

Elizabeth Emerick
Apartment 1
3728 Manor Road
Chevy Chase, MD 20815
(301) 656–1708

Eve Annick
5737 Stanbrook Lane
Laytonsville, MD 20882
(301) 977–8592

MASSACHUSETTS

Neil Kutzen
42 Middlesex Street
Cambridge, MA 02140
(617) 868–0963

Estella MacFarlane
496 Marrett Road
Lexington, MA 02173
(617) 862–4989

Claire Cunningham
11 Rockwood Lane
Lincoln, MA 01773
(617) 259–8291

Rita Powers
80 Seventh Avenue
Lowell, MA 01854
(508) 454–4628

Suzanne Pike
4 Keith Street
Middleboro, MA 02346
(508) 946–0294

Barbara Teich
255 Pond Street
So Weymouth, MA 02190
(617) 335–5406
(siblings only)

Mary Alice McQuade
370 C Montague Road
Sunderland, MA 01375
(413) 665–8638

MICHIGAN

Rose Dilloway
AMI-Wayne County
24920 Hickory
Dearborn, MI 48124
(313) 562–8316

Myron Zerger
AMI-Dearborn Area
Box 5339
Dearborn, MI 48128
(313) 278–1041

Lucille Bigham
AMI-Downtown Detroit
8710 West Davison
Detroit, MI 48238
(313) 834–7412

Maureen Fabiano-Guzman
Kenneth Gray
407 West Greenlawn
Lansing, MI 48910
(517) 374–8000
(spouses included)

MINNESOTA

Diane Fay Fossum
403 Van Buren Street
Anoka, MN 55303
(612) 421–7019

Barbara Koropchak
AMRTC
3300 Fourth Avenue N
Anoka, MN 55303
(612) 422–4150

Joyce Schut
5110 West River Road
Rochester, MN 55901
(507) 282–6676

Mary Jane Steinhagen
Catholic Charities
215 Old Sixth Street
St. Paul, MN 55102
(612) 222–3001

MISSISSIPPI

MISSOURI

Robert W. Berrey IV
R.R. 1, Box 72
Carrollton, MO 64633
(816) 484–3551

Tina Hacker
Apartment D
472 West 104th Street
Kansas City, MO 64114
(816) 274–3542

Shelia Justice
2323 Grand Avenue
Kansas City, MO 64108
(816) 474–2497
(816) 531–0807

Leslie Norman
Swope Parkway Mental Health
   Centre
4900 Swope Parkway
Kansas City, MO 64118
(816) 923–5800 x361
(group for minor children)

Carol Bowes
74 Kelly Leaf Drive
St. Charles, MO 63303
(314) 441–6059

Rosemary Garagnani
4507-A South Grand
St. Louis, MO 63111
(314) 352–2978

Allin Walker
St Louis AMI
Suite 8
131 West Monroe
St Louis, MO 63122
(314) 966–4670

MONTANA

AMI of Helena
Box 1021
Helena, MT 59624
(406) 443–7871

NEBRASKA

Ann Pierce
Greater Omaha AMI
6146 Charles Street
Omaha, NE 68132
(402) 551–7163

NEVADA

NEW HAMPSHIRE

Christine Hoppe
P.O. Box 375

Rollinsford, NH 03869
(603) 742–3350

NEW JERSEY

Marilyn Auffret
West Bergen Mental Health
  Center
120 Chestnut Street
Ridgewood, NJ 07450
(201) 444–3550

NEW MEXICO

Pat Thalhammer
Albuquerque AMI
617 Truman NE
Albuquerque, NM 87110
(505) 262–1601
(505) 298–8521

Laura Van Dilla
2820 Arizona
Los Alamos, NM 87544
(505) 662–6346

NEW YORK

Janet Skrivanek
451 Chenango Street
Binghanton, NY 13901
(607) 773–8584

Leslie Fischer
1865 Ocean Avenue
Brooklyn, NY 11230
(718) 377–5619

Rosalie Weiner, CSW
AMI/PATH
Hillside Hospital
Suite G110
2001 Marcus Avenue
Lake Success, Queens, NY 11042
(718) 347–7284
(718) 357–4940

Margaret Moorman
119 West Seventy-first Street,
  #5A
New York, NY 10023
(212) 874–5414

Gene Marie Sinclair
12 East Ninety-seventh Street
New York, NY 10029
(212) 289–8469

Richard Raskin
Community Missions
Fourth Floor
41 Park Row
New York, NY 10038
(212) 346–1523

Hilary Ryglewicz
Building F
Dr. R. L. Yeager Health Center
Pomona, NY 10970
(914) 354–0200 x2366

Joan H. Welch
Families and Friends of the M.I.
111 North Chestnut Street
Rochester, NY 14604
(716) 423–1593

Rena Finklestein
FAMILYA
P.O. Box 208
Spring Valley, NY 10977
(914) 356–2358

Brenda Lopez
Staten Island AMI
147 Ada Drive
Staten Island, NY 10314
(718) 761–4710

Phyllis Caldwell
William Cross
116 Concord Place
Syracuse, NY 13210
(315) 472–6497

Shelia Legacy
Promise, Inc.
423 West Onondaga Street
Syracuse, NY 13202
(315) 478–4151

NORTH CAROLINA

Jacki Jones
3216 Coachman's Way
Durham, NC 27705
(919) 489–7329

Gary Stephenson
1118 Fourteenth Street
Greensboro, NC 27405
(919) 375–4362

Sue Barefoot
1807 Bickett Boulevard
Raleigh, NC 27608
(919) 876–1515
(919) 828–6743

NORTH DAKOTA

Marge Christensen
ND—AMI
Box 637
Kenmare, ND 58746
(800) 338–6646
(701) 852–5324

OHIO

Helena V. Peters
924 Rowe Street
Akron, OH 44306
(216) 724–1438

Anne Hendricks
Winifred Beam Kessler
2014 Eleanor Place
Cincinnati, OH 45219
(513) 421–1998

Brent A. Williams
Union County ADAMHS
    Board
131 North Main Street
Marysville, OH 43040
(513) 642–1212
(513) 644–2235

Paddy Kutz
MHA of Licking County
65 Messimer Drive
Newark, OH 43055
(614) 522–1341

Gail G. Johnson
Neighboring for Mental Health
1657 Mentor Avenue
Painesville, OH 44077
(216) 354–9924

Joni Glotfelter
AMI—Solo of Clark County
1101 East High Street
Springfield, OH 45505
(513) 328–5319

Judith A. Remele
26678 Luckey Road
Walbridge, OH 43465
(419) 837–6003

OKLAHOMA

Valentine Joy Smith
AMI Caring Folks of Edmond
P.O. Box 153
Edmond, OK 73083
(405) 341–5551

Jon R. Wallace
Family Mental Health Center,
   Inc.
2725 East Skelly Drive

Suite 200
2600 Center Building
Tulsa, OK 74105
(918) 749–3030

OREGON

Anita Crawford
16649 Southwest Alvord Lane
Beaverton, OR 97007
(503) 642–5033

Curry County AMI
15889 Sunset Strip, #1
Brookings, OR 97415
(503) 469–7828

AMI of Lane County
Suite E
59 Coburg Road
Eugene, OR 97401
(503) 343–7688

Liz O'Brien
2223 Donovan
Eugene, OR 97401
(503) 485–5270

PENNSYLVANIA

Lillian Meyers
2624 Bethel Crest Drive
Bethel Park, PA 15102
(412) 833–0374

Patricia Suchniak
105 Griffin Pond Road
Clarks Summit, PA 18411
(717) 586–2845

Betty English
504 Prospect Street
Dalton, PA 18414
(717) 563–2469

Elaine Itle
Road #1, Box 570
Ebensburg, PA 15931
(814) 472–6955

Gaye Sheehan
Road #1, Box 23 B
Loretta, PA 15940
(814) 866–2661

Loretta Ferry, Jr
5823 North Seventh Street
Philadelphia, PA 19120
(215) 424–8451

Marie Mayer
1726 Fox Chase Road
Philadelphia, PA 19152
(215) 725–7001

Michael Polgar
Box 121
3909 Spruce Street
Philadelphia, PA 19104
(215) 898–8625

Ruth Dreschler
United Mental Health, Inc
1945 Fifth Avenue
Pittsburgh, PA 15219
(412) 391–3820

Christian Bohlen
419 Ridgewood Road
Shippenville, PA 16254
(814) 226–7580

Judy Flanigan
1622 Red Mill Drive
Upper St. Clair, PA 15241
(412) 831–3956

Marianne Bunch
809 Washington Avenue
Wallingford, PA 19086
(215) 566–7711

Berta Rains
Chester County AMI
P.O. Box 102
Westtown, PA 19395
(215) 444–6042

RHODE ISLAND

William Emmet
AMI of Rhode Island
P.O. Box 28411
Providence, RI 02908
(401) 464–3060

Elizabeth Herbert
107 Medway Street
Providence, RI 02906
(401) 274–0996
(also spouses group)

SOUTH CAROLINA

Mary Tichenor
South Carolina AMI
P.O. Box 2538
Columbia, SC 29202
(803) 779–7849

SOUTH DAKOTA

TENNESSEE

Julia Magee
Clarksville AMI
408 East Coy Circle
Clarksville, TN 37043
(615) 647–2543

Kimberly Renee Rains
Route #1, Box 3912
Jacksboro, TN 37757
(615) 562–6222

Melissa Eskridge
Tennessee AMI
Suite 511
1900 North Winston Road
Knoxville, TN 37919
(615) 691–3707

Carolyn Key Raney
AMI of Memphis
499 Patterson
Memphis, TN 38111
(901) 323–5928

Linda Steen
FIND
3102 Belle Grove Road
Memphis, TN 38115
(901) 363–2583
(for minors)

TEXAS

Pam Johnston
1705 Kerr Street
Austin, TX 78704
(512) 448–4094

Terri Stelly
Apartment 17
1145 Oregon
Beaumont, TX 77705
(409) 832–0034

Harriet Saunders
KAMI
P.O. Box 533
Center Point, TX 78010
(512) 634–7116

Nancy Bracey
1715 West Pleasant Run Road
DeSoto, TX 75115
(214) 223–3236

Cliff Reuschlein
El Paso AMI
Director's Office
600 Satelite Drive
El Paso, TX 79912
(915) 581–8457

Candace Schaper
2105 Hibiscus
McAllen, TX 78501
(512) 687–2397

Lynne Burke
Apartment 204
4110 Wellington
San Angelo, TX 76904
(915) 949–8469

UTAH

VERMONT

Cathy Aines
AMI-Vermont
67 Main Street
Poultney, VT 05764
(802) 287–5566

VIRGINIA

NAMI (National Contact)
Lynn Saunders
Suite 302
2101 Wilson Boulevard
Arlington, VA 22201
(703) 524–7600

Lindsay Glover
Piedmont Psychiatric
  Professionals
Suite 103
1139 East High Street
Charlottesville, VA 22901
(804) 296–9740

Tammy Trestrial
c/o Henrico Mental Health
  Center
10299 Woodman Road
Glen Allen, VA 23060
(804) 266–4991

John Schmelzer
Patti Schneider
AMI—North Virginia
P.O. Box 651
McLean, VA 22101
(703) 525–0686

Tommi Cubine
c/o Beach House
3143 Magic Hollow Boulevard
Virginia Beach, VA 23456
(804) 430–0368
(804) 481–6964

Eugenia Ferrell
Schizophrenia
  Foundation—AMI
414 Pembroke One
Virginia Beach, VA 23462
(804) 499–2041

WASHINGTON

Well Mind Association
4649 Sunnyside N
Seattle, WA 98103
(206) 547–6167

Mary Hodson
East 12410 Boone
Spokane, WA 99204
(509) 534–7494

Roxanne Manly
3525 West Government Way
Spokane, WA 99204
(509) 624–1967
(also group for minors)

Shirley Pederson
East 2102 Eighteenth Avenue
Spokane, WA 99203
(509) 535–8130
(509) 328–4220 x3140

WASHINGTON, D.C.

WEST VIRGINIA

WISCONSIN

AMI of Dane County
Suite 173
1245 East Washington Avenue
Madison, WI 53703
(608) 255–1695
(also has spouses group)

Mary Gemlo
Northeast Spouses and Sibling
  Group
5237 North Kent Avenue
Milwaukee, WI 53217
(414) 964–8549

Barbara Corgiat
North Central Health Care
1100 Lakeview Drive
Wausau, WI 54401
(715) 848–4538

Edith Peterson
3504 North Tenth Street
Wausau, WI 54401
(715) 845–9183

Pamela Erickson
2459 North Sixty-ninth Street
Wauwatosa, WI 53213
(414) 771–7190

WYOMING

Dennis Fransted
WYAMI
1949 East A Street
Casper, WY 82601
(307) 244–0440
(800) 244–7199 in WY

CANADA

Sharol Caswell
95 Alepin
La Salle, Que.
H8P 2C9 Canada
(514) 367–1210

Francoise Beauregard
190 Desrochers Street
Mt. Ste. Hilare, Que.
J3H 3C8, Canada
(514) 467–2146

Diane Beattie
Families of Manic-Depressives
3746 Seaton Street
Victoria, B.C.
(604) 479–1391

Friends of Schizophrenia
941 Kings
Victoria, B.C.
(604) 384–4225

VIRGIN ISLANDS

Jeannette Joseph
P.O. Box 11523
St. Thomas, U.S.V.I. 00801
(809) 776–2442

Branca Marsh
P.O. Box 10644
St. Thomas, U.S.V.I. 00801
(809) 775–3177

The National Alliance for the Mentally Ill [2101 Wilson Boulevard, Suite 302, Arlington, VA 22201 (703) 524–7600] offers many parent and family support groups around the country and publishes a monthly newsletter, *The Advocate*, for its members. NAMI has also compiled an extensive reading list for families of the mentally ill. Two books that have been of great help to me are Dr. E. Fuller Torrey's *Surviving Schizophrenia: A Family Manual* (New York: Harper & Row, 1983) and Julie Tallard Johnson's *Hidden Victims: An Eight-Stage Healing Process for Families and Friends of the Mentally Ill* (New York: Doubleday, 1988). Both contain lists of recommended reading.